SOMETIMES I FORGOT TO LAUGH

PETER
ROEBUCK

SOMETIMES I FORGOT TO LAUGH

ALLEN&UNWIN

First published in 2004

Allen & Unwin
83 Alexander Street
Crows Nest NSW 2065
Australia
Phone: (61 2) 8425 0100
Fax: (61 2) 9906 2218
Email: info@allenandunwin.com
Web: www.allenandunwin.com

National Library of Australia
Cataloguing-in-Publication entry:

Roebuck, Peter.
   Sometimes I forgot to laugh.

   Includes index.
   ISBN 1 74114 389 6.

   1. Roebuck, Peter—Autobiography. 2. Cricket players—England.
   3. Cricket—players—Australia. 4. Cricket—Anecdotes. I. Title.

796.3580924

Typeset in 12/16 pt Galliard by Midland Typesetters
Printed by Griffin Press, Adelaide, South Australia

10 9 8 7 6 5 4 3 2 1

CONTENTS

To all my friends, and especially

*The Pattersons, Remonds, Egans, Escourts, Caplices,
Pandits, Ulms, Heals, Vlachos, Cowans, Nothlings,
Maxwells. O'Keeffes, Halls, Martin, Mike, Patrick,
Laurie, Mungo and Toby in Australia*

*Chris, Adrienne, Joy, Andrew, Lorika, Ant and Moira,
the Volsteedts, Parfitts, Boeta and the rest in South Africa*

*Sharda, Rohit, Harsha, Dileep, Rahul and all my friends
and respected colleagues in Indian cricket writing*

*Ana, Sidath, Kushil, Skanda, Lal, Charlie and
all my friends in Sri Lankan cricket*

*Blisters, Crocks, Riggers, Jon, Justin, Shome, Ant, Carlo,
Bruno, Heinrich, Aaron, Ian, Kevin, Alok, Siya, Michael,
Garreth, Ed and Omari, constant students*

*The Evanses, Roger, Jack, Donners, Farmer, Folly,
Gapers, Olly and the boys at Devon*

Norm, Proccy, Daws, Rob and my pals at Budleigh

*Captain Psychology, Immigration, Integrity and
Pride in Harare*

Malabika, of course, and Charles in London

And last, but not least, my long-suffering family

FOREWORD

Peter Roebuck is the most stimulating telephone cricket conversationalist in the country . . . we have known each other for over twenty years and must have had close to one thousand phone 'chats' during our friendship . . . my wife reckons she knows immediately when I've been on the 'blower' to 'Robey' because I look enlightened and tend to speak with an English twang. Telephone gems aside, it is his prose via newspaper articles which has so entertained and informed fellow Australians in recent years. And now, of course, he has written *Sometimes I Forgot to Laugh* . . . and too often he jolly well did!! Quite simply, in this country, he is possibly the most polished writer of the modern era . . . and a mate.

He is many other things, too. A loner, for starters. If on tour with ABC Radio cricket and the call went out one evening to find his whereabouts, my strongest advice would be to scour the darkest corners of 'one-star' Indian restaurants and there, reading anonymously by candlelight on a table set for one, would be P.M. Roebuck. It is not a judgement . . . it is his way. And he, by and large, has mostly lived his life this way. Former Somerset team mate Viv Richards is quoted as saying this author is like 'a country house with fierce dogs outside'. That may have applied during his playing days . . . suffice to say, his personality is now a 'lived in' federation in trendy Bondi and those hounds have become more Cocker Spaniel than German Shepherd. Throughout his mellowing, he has lost none of his perception . . . despite constant admissions of ignorance, Peter is quietly as well-informed as an Australian cricket writer. On hearing media area cricket gossip, he will often express no prior knowledge and add 'nobody talks to me about those sort of things'. Possibly, because, deep down they feel he is already across it. Heh! The blessed fellow has the clothes sense of a blind man . . . and shoe laces that appear twenty years older than the footwear itself. His eccentricity and his perspicacity work in perfect symbiosis whenever he puts pen to paper. In this book, he reflects honestly on being 'trapped in cricket's tangled web' and that 'becoming an Australian citizen counts as among the happiest days of my life'. I, too, have been consumed by the game and can relate to his mental battles with on-field success and particularly, failure.

'Aussie Pete' Roebuck, still however, has a certain hollowness when you consider his Cambridge accent and correctness . . . but, be assured, he has a respect and a love of this country that so many 'born and bred's' could well copy. His deep affection for Australians bounces off the pages of this book. When I decided to write a collection of my memoirs, Peter was the first person I contacted for advice. We met for coffee on a damp autumn morning in Sydney's eastern suburbs. His strong recommendation was to take the book 'beyond cricket . . . to be honest and straight-forward . . . and to, above all, tell your story'. That is what Peter Roebuck has done in his book. If you feel you need further enlightenment, telephone him!!

Kerry O'Keeffe

INTRODUCTION

Peter Roebuck was born to write about cricket in the manner Sachin Tendulkar was born to play it. The right grammar, style, substance and the occasional rasping statement that takes your breath away. Peter wraps cricket in fine clothing, he lends the weight of words to the deeds that a Tendulkar performs.

Indeed, I have long felt that the writer needs to look upon himself as a performer in much the way the sportsman does. Peter does that. He will be the first to admit though, that his barely legible scrawl did the words it is meant to shape no credit at all! They deserved better and when the impersonal typeface finally replaced the medieval shapes he created, it came almost as a relief.

Peter once told me of the twin loves in his life—cricket and the English language. In his hands they forge a fine partnership, the equivalent of Greenidge and Haynes, Hayden and Langer, Dravid and Laxman. The relative timelessness of Test cricket, the sub-plots within the larger story, the personalities who seem to have enough time to pose for a writer, all create a game that demands the beauty of words and a writer to produce them. And yet the game suffers in its obsession with the post day 'quote', a collection of words that have no feelings, coming from men who are far better at putting bat to ball. Peter bucks that trend and does so with a combination of defiance and beauty. He gives you a reason to read the newspaper even if you have watched the day's play.

I met Peter for the first time in a commentary box though his forthright, rasping style took some time getting used to. I hope he doesn't remember much of that first session of commentary in

Brisbane in November 1991 for, unable to pick his accent immediately, I could offer only a slightly stupid grin to most things he was saying. As that summer wore on, and many more after that, I looked forward to the experience because Peter always challenged you with his views. He made you think and you worried about a sentence you might have let gone lightly.

Peter the commentator is little known outside Australia. Sometimes one skill can overpower another—how many remember what an extraordinary fielder Viv Richards was, but he brings a very different air to broadcasting. Where Peter's writing in the newspaper shows the love the English have for language, in the commentary box he is so Australian: direct, unafraid to be blunt and perfectly capable of saying in 10 words what his column the next day will take 100 words to dwell over. I like both facets to his personality but there is a greater permanency to writing, the spoken word is like an arrow that permanently departs its quiver.

I can see now why Peter is more Australian than English now. Australians are rather more feisty, game for a difference of opinion, holders of strong, often intractable, views and yet perfectly capable of laughing over a drink at the end. I suspect they secretly admire people with a contrary point of view. The English on the other hand, a bit like the Indian brahmans, tend to pronounce judgement rather than debate it; occasionally the conversation will grow cold. With his strong views on the game, and his willingness to listen to others, Peter took to Australia like the great white did its coastal waters.

I can't imagine Peter in a jacket and tie amidst the establishment at Lords. If I had to paint him, it would be in a loose shirt, slightly dreamy eyes beneath the glasses and his straw hat looking like it was nicked from a lampshade. He would be sitting in a corner of a press box, an occasional darting comment ('Why isn't that Harbhajan going round the wicket?') interrupting the words settling around his thoughts.

But there is more to Peter than the mere magic of words; and that by itself is not to be trifled with. He understands the subcontinent better than most, has strong views on Zimbabwe and South Africa, and has an acute sense of history. You can see that in the metaphors that abound, the awareness of politics, the grasp of history.

I don't remember when I first heard his name or indeed sampled his works. It might have been the lone season Sunil Gavaskar played for Somerset when suddenly I heard names like Denning, Rose, Roebuck and Slocombe. And by the time I went to Australia in 1991, Roebuck was already the king of the written word in my eyes. Like good home cooking, the precise moment of discovery is lost in a world of pleasure.

By then I had decided I wanted to write like Peter; the keen observation mingling with the precise metaphor and then, that throwaway line delivered like an actor who knows he has the audience in his grip. I gave up pretty quickly—I might have been condemned to an unfulfilled life otherwise.

Long ago, in a book sale in Mumbai, I picked up a copy of his *Great Innings*, the kind of subject to appeal to a journalist in the off-season. I found some gems in it, like this description of Javed Miandad:

> Only those who have driven through the streets of Karachi can hope properly to understand Javed Miandad. Imagine a baking sun, smoke and noise, picture a scene like bedlam and place in it a boy with flashing eyes threading his battered and croaking rickshaw through non-existent gaps, darting on to pavements, cheerfully shouting abuse at pedestrians so that they might grant him a thoroughfare.

An autobiography is a different genre of writing from say, an expression of joy at another Gilchrist swashbuckler. Peter manages it with equal élan and his grandmother emerges as much a heroine as some of the stars he writes about. Luckily for Peter he too has a long innings ahead of him; maybe he will want to laugh a lot more. After all, he has even learned to use a laptop!

Harsha Bhogle

1

ANTECEDENTS

Grandfather Roebuck came from the North. He was born early in the 1890s, attended Wood Street Missionary School in Salford, known locally as 'the ragged school', and left school at fourteen, as would Father when his time came. He saw active service as a Lewis gunner in Egypt, Mesopotamia and Gallipoli. Small and pale-faced, he had not yet discovered he was a pacifist and despite the protests of his wife and belonging to a reserved occupation, he joined the Lancashire Fusiliers and went off to war. He fought at Ypres and Passchendaele. After five years of soldiering he was appointed lance corporal, a rank my father surpassed in the second conflagration by a single stripe. Along the way he was gassed, narrowly survived drowning in a shell hole and returned weighing less than eight stone. In his own way he was a remarkable man and he was in his eighties when he quietly passed away. He never mentioned the war or his fallen comrades and did not return to religion till near the end. He could not equate a loving God with the sights he had seen, and never forgave God for allowing the carnage to go on for over four years.

The eldest of a large family, his first job was in the publishing department of W.H. Smith and he eventually became a branch manager in Halifax. Not wanting to work away from home, he resigned and returned to Manchester to join the *Daily Mail*. By the outbreak of the war, he had become an ardent socialist. He was a dedicated trades unionist, a shop steward and an admirer of the mighty A.J. Cook. He thought that poverty and degradation could and should be avoided. To the horror of Grandmother Roebuck, he also believed in votes for women.

Gambling appalled him for he saw it as the curse of the working classes. Once caught, it led to penury or prison. Cards were not allowed in his house. Any pack smuggled in was torn to shreds and thrown on the fire. Not that David Roebuck was a dour man, for he enjoyed the comic ditties and sentimental ballads of the music hall and attended performances every Saturday night, joining in the choruses. He did not frequent theatres, preferring the more stirring sound of the brass bands that played in the parks on Sunday afternoons. These bands played waltzes, polkas and marches, noisily and cheerfully. Nonetheless the churches were the most important source of music in those grimy industrial days. Blessed with a pleasant voice, which has not been handed down, Grandfather sang in the church choir and enjoyed the Negro spirituals of the low church, militant Wesleyan hymns, sung high mass and monastic chants. After the war, this part of his music died. He stopped going to church and the music hall and, strangely, listened only to regimental marches and army songs like 'It's a Long Way to Tipperary' and 'Pack Up Your Troubles'. He enjoyed the bagpipes and loved marching alongside surviving comrades wearing a bowler hat and his ribbons. He was proud of the Fusiliers and often said 'Seventeen Victoria crosses before breakfast and don't ever forget it', a feat apparently achieved by his regiment at Gallipoli.

Grandmother Roebuck never forgave her husband for going away to war and leaving her with two small children to raise on a soldier's allowance. She was the daughter of a cultured Irish

Catholic father and a somewhat ignorant English Protestant mother. Her father died when she was only seven, and her mother soon remarried. Her stepfather was a drunken brute who made her life intolerable. Refusing to hide her contempt for him and unable to attend school regularly, she eventually obtained a post as a live-in maid with a Jewish family who taught her to read and write and to appreciate music. She felt herself to be refined and assumed superior attitudes and accordingly was ridiculed as the 'Duchess of Hulme'. She liked opera, Gilbert & Sullivan and the theatre, and scrimped together enough money to sit upstairs and watch musical comedies. Often she cheered and clapped when her favourite tunes were played on the radio. The music hall was not for her.

Somehow this superior nineteen-year-old Catholic girl with conservative views met a simple 23-year-old man imbued with Wesley and socialism. He stood for the collective improvement of the working class through the trades union movement. She advocated improvement of the self through hard work. They married in 1912.

During the war Grandmother Roebuck was obliged to take a job in a flour mill and to pay her neighbours to look after her children. What Grandfather regarded as his duty, she saw as a desertion of their family. Over the years the differences between them deepened.

These differences sharpened in 1926 when, as shop steward, David felt bound to lead his men out in support of the General Strike. The action collapsed and his company became non-union. Grandfather refused to tear up his card and was thrown out of work. By then the couple had four children to feed, their eldest son having died in the 'flu epidemic that followed the war. They lived near the docks. Grandmother began to offer board and lodging. Keeping a boarding house for thirteen people was hard work; meanwhile her husband was looking for a job. Not for the first or last time she accused him of playing the hero. Enormously houseproud, she used to dust the coal and not a speck of dirt could be found on her settees. Towards the end she stayed in our flat in Bath and seemed formidable, even domineering. But then, she'd had a hard time of it and knew the world to be a rough place.

The relationship further deteriorated when two of their surviving children passed away, Winifred (two) of diphtheria and Veronica (twelve) of tuberculosis on Armistice Night of 1928. That left Gerald and Jim, my father. Advised to leave the family home with its memories, my grandparents moved to a semi-detached house near Old Trafford Cricket Ground. No one in the family was interested in cricket but the boys could hear the cheers of the crowd and sometimes father would sit in the stands alongside men with their flasks, the crowd growing as word spread that Washbrook was in. He can recall Roses matches between Yorkshire and Lancashire in which no shots were played, or expected, before lunch. It was immensely serious and the players were folk heroes of a sort. Father knew nothing about the game, but could appreciate its strange beauty. He never played cricket except upon the beach, but he saw the great men of the age and remembers them fondly.

My grandparents could afford this house because David had been appointed to the staff of the *Daily Express* where he quickly rose to be night publisher, a promotion that cost him his circle of socialist friends. Since his principles did not allow him to join the Masons, a prerequisite for further promotion, he was not trusted by his superiors either and remained in the same position till shortly before his retirement in 1965, around the time I saw my first county match at the Recreation Ground in Bath, where Derek Morgan of Derbyshire bowled medium-pacers to Bill Alley, the bellicose all-rounder from Australia.

Grandmother's determination to improve the lot of her children never wavered and, by the mid-1930s, the family was living in a respectable suburb. Uncle Gerald would stay in that house for the next 50 years and I'd visit him whenever Somerset arrived in Manchester. My grandparents' marriage lasted until death did them part but it could not be called happy. Survival was itself a triumph.

My father had arrived in 1919, when the family lived in a soot-blackened terraced house without gas or electricity. The tiny backyard contained a water closet. Manchester was an industrial town, crowded and dirty, in which large families huddled together without prospects amidst the throbbing factories and narrow, defeated streets that housed men looking for jobs that did not exist. Washing lines hung across the street and children entertained themselves as best they could. As my father wrote:

> They lived in sunken cells
> From the sun
> And suffered through the clutches
> Of each day
> Who were not asked.

My grandmother could not imagine her remaining sons reaching beyond an apprenticeship with a craftsman and accordingly instructed them to learn a trade. Grandfather just wanted to make sure they joined the appropriate trade union. Nor was their pessimism unreasonable, for the brothers were bogged down in the bottom streams of indifferent schools, defying the pallid efforts of insipid teachers to instil knowledge. It was a long way from here to Oxford and Cambridge, but both father and I made it and some pride can be taken from that.

Grandmother Morrison, on the other hand, was the oldest of four children born to a dispensing chemist in Bradford. Her parents retired to the waters of Scarborough where, much later, we all lived for a while and where the bowlers must take wickets with the new ball or they are in for a hard slog. She attended Birmingham University where she pursued literature and botany, a combination that also appeals to her grandson. She found work as a teacher in Wigan where she also found the time to knit, cycle, swim and play tennis, in which activity she served underhand for she was a most decorous creation. She was a capable woman who involved herself in many charitable works and had the intelligence needed to keep her husband's flame alive without allowing it to burn those nearest at hand.

Grandfather Morrison was another case entirely. He was the eldest of thirteen children of a poor Irish farmer who owned a few struggling acres in Galway. A tall, intelligent man blessed with enormous energy and considerable humour, he swiftly realised that the farm could not provide for all the children so he applied for and won a scholarship to Galway Grammar School where his light shone in every direction. Unfortunately he could not afford to go to university and instead took the examination for the British Civil Service, with the intention of joining the tax department. He was duly appointed as a clerk and dispatched to Wigan, where Grandma unknowingly waited. He was well enough pleased.

Soon the irrepressible Irishman with flaming red hair met the quiet English teacher and the pair courted till war broke out whereupon Grandfather, unwilling to miss a scrap, joined the Royal Artillery, whose duty it was to lay down barrages. He spent his time at Ypres trying to stop the Germans breaking through or to help the Allies break out of the Salient. He fought at the hell-holes of the Somme and Passchendaele. After the war the couple married and Grandfather was promoted to a senior position in Surrey, not a bad effort for an Irishman with twelve siblings and without a university education.

Mother was born in Penge, where her parents had bought a house. By then her mother had given up teaching to concentrate on building a proper middle-class life. Grandfather bought a car and played tennis with speed and flair. By all accounts his serve was singular, a low toss and lots of power and spin. He rushed around the court, a red bomb of a man, and was a feared opponent in club tournaments, many of which he won. His wife was his doubles partner but was seldom allowed to hit the ball. Cricket was played in the summer holidays, and he would arrange the teams and arrive in a striped blazer and a straw boater. Of course he was cunning. Beach matches are won and lost upon the turning of the tide. Cards were played to a code enforced by his better half.

It took the Second World War to interrupt family life. Grandfather joined the Home Guard and his two daughters were evacuated. Towards the end of the war Grandfather fell ill and had to resign from the Inland Revenue and take a less stressful job in a munitions factory. He died before the end of the year, still in the prime of his life. Mother lost a parent of colour and vitality. The house was sold and the family moved to Scarborough to take care of an ailing relative. It was left to my mother to sustain the sense of fun and enthusiasm for games of all sorts instilled by her father, a task she accomplished with élan. Fortunately the loss of her beloved father did not break her spirit. Not even the premature death of her second son could do that.

My father's early days were different and a good deal less fortunate than mine. After attending various junior schools named after various saints he was admitted to an institution bearing the inscription 'St Joseph's Roman Catholic Reformatory School', though it had since changed its patron and broadened its clientele. It was a soot-covered building situated within a concrete quadrangle, located beside an old printing works. Every day around 450 boys walked to this establishment, most of them unwillingly. Doubtless the teachers wore their own cloaks of doom. Father remained in the doldrums of the 'C' stream throughout his schooling and was considerably relieved that he was not required to pass a leaving exam. He was not entered for a great deal but managed to fail the lot, including the 11+ and the Post Office entrance exam for boy messengers. Accordingly he left school as soon as the law permitted and joined the workforce. He had been a quiet schoolboy, hiding his emotions, trying not to draw attention to himself, feeling that he was useless.

However Father did nourish two overwhelming enthusiasms: soccer and reading. Besides playing football for the school he trained with the Manchester United youth team, and made several appearances for its 'A' side before the war curtailed his career. The significance of his devotion to books was not grasped till much later, when his brain began to escape from its confinement.

At fourteen, Father left school. Football seemed the only area in which he might make a mark. Such dreams were dashed when his parents insisted he spend the next seven years apprenticed to a master printer. It took his employer a full fortnight to realise that his charge was not interested in the project. Later attempts to bind Father to a compositor were thwarted when he refused to attend the interview. Sundry trials at a counting house proved unproductive, but eventually a job was found as a warehouseman. During these otherwise wasted years Father continued to train two nights a week with Manchester United and also attended night school to learn shorthand and book-keeping, neither of which later illuminated his life. Despite the poor wages and his reluctance to apply himself, he stuck to the warehouse job till the outbreak of the Second World War whereupon, without any particular conviction, Father signed up to fight for King and Country. Reflecting on these times, he wrote:

In those far off days
When the world was young
When not to work
Was not to eat
And many starved
When tramways ran through busy streets
And people walked

War was not for him a romance nor even a means of escape, merely a change. He completed the appropriate forms during the evacuation from Dunkirk and took part in the D-day landings in Normandy. Apart from preserving his life, his main concern was that the war should not affect him as it had his own father. Accordingly he had as quiet a time as circumstances allowed, kept his own counsel about the absurdities of military routine and command, and managed to survive.

After four years of service Father rose to the rank of corporal. Apart from that, the only noteworthy feat he could claim was failing the British Army intelligence test in the middle of a world war. It did not seem likely that he would attend one of the great universities or produce six offspring, all of whom ended up with degrees.

Of course the war did change him. Thereafter he was determined never again to live in a polluted city, so he sought work in a town or village in the south of the country. His task was considerable for he was 27 years of age, had not passed any exams and had no skills. Demobbed in June 1946, he reluctantly returned to his former occupation. Within a month he had given his notice, whereupon he found a better paid job as a night publisher with the company for which his brother Gerald worked till retirement came upon him.

By now he had won and lost his first wife and fathered two children. When in Belgium, he had met and married Rosa, the daughter of the owners of a sweet shop. James was born in 1948. Unfortunately, complications followed the birth of their daughter, Rosalie, and Rosa passed away on 18 October 1950. Unable to cope with the demands of two infants and a full-time job, Father sent James to live with his parents, while Rosalie ended up with a nurse from the hospital, Father sending money to help with her upkeep. It was a sad episode and was never mentioned in our family.

Father continued to search for a way of avoiding his apparent fate. He discovered that his trade union awarded an annual scholarship to Ruskin College in Oxford. He pursued a correspondence course offered by the union, studied grammar and much else, applied for the award and won a place at Oxford University.

His reaction upon seeing the city of dreaming spires for the first time can scarcely be imagined. It was as if dozens of medieval cathedrals had been placed side by side. Most of the students at Ruskin were much younger than him and much more committed to the cause. Besides school-leavers and activists there was a group of dreamers who would have made St Thomas Aquinas appear energetic. Miners and dockers were few and far between.

Father set about studying with the intensity often detected in the desperate. He made friends with a young miner from Durham, a car worker from Birmingham and an American Negress, a group whose worldliness he respected. He was awarded a grant to continue his studies for a second year. By way of passing the time he attended a lacrosse match and was presently surrounded by a bunch of marauding female students, one of whom also kept wicket for the University ladies team.

Mother's cheerful, bright simplicity contrasted with her prospective husband's tortured sense of failure. Her cheerfulness sat uncomfortably beside his morbid pessimism. In her teaching days she wrote umpteen maths books, many of them still in use, but also danced in a school production of 'Swan Lake' and performed as a punk. Not for the first time in this story it seems odd that two such different characters should form, let alone sustain, a relationship.

Mother's individuality had revealed itself at an early age. At school she was outstanding at study and games. Nevertheless at the age of thirteen she decided that religion was not a proper academic subject and refused to be examined in it. At seventeen she was awarded a scholarship to Girton College in Cambridge to read mathematics. To the astonishment of the college and the dismay of many she declined the award on the grounds that she had no intention of becoming a blue-stockinged academic. Instead she accepted an offer from the Bedford School of Physical Education, from which institution she qualified with distinction three years later.

By now Mother was flourishing upon the sports fields, representing England at lacrosse and also playing regularly for the Yorkshire ladies' cricket team. She had taken up cricket in her final year at school and took a liking to guarding the stumps, a task she carried out sufficiently well to earn an Oxford Blue.

For three years after leaving Bedford Mother studied the art of literature and aspects of British culture since 1870. She studied the social circumstances of women in Victorian England at Hull University and presented a thesis on 'The Role of Women in Britain from 1870 to 1940', upon which matter she had forthright opinions. She also became interested in modern dance and was able to include it in her timetable when she taught physical education. Encouraged by the success of her work, she applied for and secured a scholarship to the Department of Social Studies in Oxford University. This time she took her place and it was during a lacrosse match between the University Ladies' and Gentlemen's teams that my parents met. Within a year they were married.

Mother resigned her scholarship, embraced her partner's Catholic faith and otherwise carried on in her own indomitable way.

Meanwhile Father had been awarded one of three dozen Mature State scholarships made available by the *Education Act* of 1944. He gained admission to Christ Church College to read PPE and felt that he had arrived. A cottage was found in a village outside Oxford and the family moved in. My birth was not far away.

Oddington was a tiny settlement, whose eight houses lined a curved street with a church at one end and the rectory at the other. Silage and manure wafted through the air, and wild ducks flew around. Voices travelled considerable distances, bells chimed and the inhabitants led simple lives and talked darkly about the dangers to be found on the nearby moors.

Our fellow Oddingtonians lived in thatched and almost derelict houses without luxuries or decorations of any kind. Now and then local authorities tried to persuade the ageing citizenry to move into old people's homes only to be met with defensive bats. Passing strangers brought the hamlet to a standstill, with all and sundry watching their progress through the street with hardly less interest than that paid to Gary Cooper in 'High Noon'. It was quite a contrast to Manchester, and a step in the right direction.

The family settled easily into rural life. Too poor to contemplate a holiday, they made the most of the surrounding countryside. Sundays meant a fast from midnight and a long journey to the nearest Catholic church, undertaken on bicycles unlikely to be entered for the Tour de France. Mother was proud of her machine, calling it Gertrude. Father could ride with his arms folded, which raised him in his children's estimation far more than his studies at university. On sunny mornings it was a beautiful ride through pretty lanes. On wintry days it was a hard slog through fog and rain. None of the bicycles provided much in the way of comfort or speed so the journey towards salvation was often gruelling.

Mostly life went along quietly, as a collection of contrasting characters crammed into a small cottage, trying to find room to breathe. James and Rosalie were sent to the local Catholic school. In November 1954, my sister Margaret was born. As always Mother tried to make the best of things.

Meanwhile Father had started his course at Christ Church College. Somewhere along the way his accent lost its Mancunian edge and became sophisticated. Perhaps it was just part of fitting in. My voice has also adapted to its surroundings and, somewhat to the irritation of English observers, has been affected by 25 years spent mixing with Australians.

Every weekday Father caught the early bus to Oxford, whereupon he'd go to the Bodleian Library within whose precincts he'd remain till 5.30 p.m., searching for that combination of information and wisdom that the university promises. Upon returning home he'd continue studying into the night, trying to decipher squiggles that had made sense at the time of their composition. He completed the course and passed the exams, not a bad effort for a lad from the bottom set of a run-down school located in the poorest parts of a northern industrial city who had left school at fourteen, had fought in a war, had lost his first wife, had been left with young children and had had no way of supporting them or himself except by taking a humdrum job in a warehouse.

Unfortunately Father now developed a serious illness and, unable to take his place in the workforce proper, accepted a position as a research assistant to Mr P. Andrews, who was writing a work entitled *The Economic History of the Electrical and Musical Industries Company*.

After a couple of years of rural life Mother fell pregnant again. Your author was on his way. Expected on St Patrick's Day 1956, the fourth child of the family arrived eleven days earlier, an appearance that caused considerable consternation within the household.

Father met me that evening. It is probably unwise for a son to write about his father; it is such a difficult relationship. As a rule boys cannot grow until, in some form or other, they have rejected their male progenitor. Many years later I would tell James Packer that sooner or later he would have to fight Kerry or forever live in his shadow. During my childhood I knew Father only as the crumpled, emotional, bad-tempered figure who sat in the sitting-room watching 'Match of the Day' and scribbling poetry with a pencil. I did not know his story. He taught me cricket, a task he went about with an intensity that did not suit a sturdy but private youngster who, though determined to succeed, did not relish the pressure he felt under, as if he had to carry the weight of the family. In adolescence I kept away from his sometimes tortured assistance. He'd sit in his room, waiting to be asked for help, frustrated by this rejection. Reluctant to tolerate any more of those struggles towards perfection that were the hallmark of Father's long practices, I'd persuade my younger brother to throw balls to me. Meanwhile Mother tried to keep the peace.

Oddington remained our home until 1958. By then I was two-and-a-half years old and the neighbouring farmer's right-hand man. Apparently he regarded me as a 'game 'un'. Just like him I carried a stick everywhere. My main job was to collect the cows for milking. Like the farmer, I'd shout at them and whack them across the rump with the stick. Whether anything has changed over the intervening years others must decide! Chasing poultry, though not geese, also appealed to me. Apparently I was alert but unusually quiet. But, then, wine had not yet entered my realm and no blithering idiot of a fieldsman had let one through his legs off my bowling.

Presently the news arrived from Scarborough that Grandmother Morrison had been taken ill, forcing her mother to go into a nursing home. Mother rushed northwards, a flight of mercy that had as its only drawback the fact that the cooking was now entrusted to the male of the species. Fortunately I was still sucking gobstoppers. Cooking has never been my strong point. Advised to boil an egg by putting it into a pan and turning on the gas for three minutes, a fellow did exactly as he was told. A fellow can only follow orders. No one ever said anything about water.

No sooner had Mother returned than a policeman knocked on the door and said that Gran had passed away. Of course the sorrow was felt only by the older members of the household. Not for another 30 years did death enter my life, when Ivan, a colleague in Sydney, died in a car crash on his honeymoon. Ivan was a fiery Irishman with a fondness for gambling (this may be tautological). His system was simple: back the favourites and keep doubling the bet till a winner emerges. Visitors to his room often found him suffering dreadfully, listening on the radio to an evening dog race in a remote part of the antipodes. At its conclusion he'd say, 'Oh, thank God, my last shirt was on that one. Never again. Let's go for a drink.' We never thought he'd get around to marrying.

Mother returned to Scarborough, from which vantage point she summoned the rest of the family because her grandmother hated the Home in which she was spending the last few overs of her long innings. It was no small matter to transport a family so far without money or car. Trains seldom stopped at our local station in Islip, which did not prevent the station master putting on a grand show, with uniform, dignity, walrus moustache and the courtesies of a bygone era. The approach of the train had a galvanising effect upon him for he ran around blowing his whistle, waving his flag and shouting, 'Islip, Islip, this is Islip! Those going to Scarborough change at Banbury and Leeds!' thereby imparting the required information to his only clients.

His style brings to mind the old Australian joke about the pompous president of a football club who demands more butter at the annual dinner. Refused, he berates the waiter saying, 'Do you know who I am?', whereupon he outlines his impressive curriculum vitae. When he has finished, the waiter asks, 'Do you know who I am?' Answered in the negative, he adds, 'I'm the bloke who gives out the butter.'

Some of us had never seen a train. Some of us had never seen the sea either, which is not to say we had never been to Weston-Super-Mare. Our journey began in a contraption that coughed and spluttered like an ageing bloodhound. It was a slow journey, with our train politely slowing down to allow others to pass, a recourse that did not seem necessary. Nor did it neglect to stop at every station along the way. Chugging through the countryside, enduring the grim suburbs of Leeds, it eventually reached its destination. Indian trains are more fun, leaving at dawn, puffing through sprawling places where men empty their bladders yet retaining a certain style as tea, papers and refreshments are brought by various *wallahs* so that time passes easily before the pink city of Jaipur is reached, where one can see an elephant pulling a cart being overtaken by a camel dragging something similar.

At this point the youngest member of the family was regarded as rather a solemn chap, possibly destined for the church, the first of numerous mistaken characterisations.

Royal Avenue in Scarborough proved to be a steep, tree-lined avenue that stretched down towards the sea. It was an area full of rich spinsters and drawn curtains, a prim and proper place and quite a contrast to Oddington. Our house was large, red-brick and semi-detached. In better days it had been the home of two genteel old ladies. Now the family had plenty of room inside and not much outside, except a tiny back garden in which a man could not have swung a bat. Moreover there was a need to behave with more decorum as the furniture and fittings resembled senior officers taking the salute. Sculleries and so forth could be found downstairs, and the second floor offered lots of bedrooms. Exploration of the city was undertaken between meals that were never rushed and quite formal. Scarborough had its compensations, however, not least the sound of seagulls (later discovered to be not worth the trouble) and nearby Catholic churches. We were a striving family with a mother of astounding energy and intellect and a father with a strong sense of justice and many frustrations that sometimes brought him to the edge of hysteria.

With its beaches and castle, Scarborough looked beautiful that late summer of 1958. Three piers reached out into the sometimes tempestuous sea, like a child's fingers into a pie, and along the shore were stalls selling lobster and shrimp. Further along the cliff there were churches and fishermen's cottages, and the old town seemed full of hustle and bustle. It was on the beach that a strange activity was encountered, a game played by entire families and discussed with the intensity seen in Greek cafes when the topics of politics or *Panathinaikos* crop up. It seemed to dominate every living moment of these red-bodied holiday-makers. Nor was the general citizenry any less interested in this apparently simple pursuit. We were in Yorkshire and the game was called cricket.

Without fridge, car or telephone it was not easy to settle into life in a northern outpost overrun by tourists every summer. Scarborough's remoteness had bred an independence reinforced by the medieval walls that had protected its inhabitants from invasion. In its time the castle was regarded as among the strongest fortresses in the kingdom. It had endured six sieges, the longest and most important being that of 1645 which lasted for twelve months after the local aristocrat had declared for the King. Stubborn resistance was put up in the Yorkshire way before the loyalists were overwhelmed by the forces of Parliament. Since then the civil wars have been cricketing affairs, most of them confrontations between supporters of headstrong players and officials of doubtful merit. Not in Yorkshire alone, either.

Father needed to earn a large enough wage to feed his family. Too old to seek further qualifications, he decided to try his luck in education and secured an appointment to teach economics at Scarborough College, a public school of some 280 boys situated on the highest point on the South Cliff. Strong in games and with a sturdy military tradition, it was not the most obvious place for him to begin his white collar life. Apart from his own soccer, he had avoided sport and searched instead for development of the mind.

Owing to unforeseen circumstances, Father's role changed before his first term began. Having prepared himself for high-level economics, he found himself instead teaching low-level mathematics. Worse, he was asked to take a rugby team and appointed as master in charge of IVB, a position that was not hotly contested. Only seven weeks earlier the dreaded IVB had been the no less feared IIIB and its promotion was due more to the passing of time than to any intellectual accomplishment.

Public school life came as a surprise to the boy from the soot-covered former reformatory. Whenever the staff strode into assembly in their gowns an unearthly silence came over the hall, whereupon he felt like launching into a rousing chorus of 'Oh, When the Saints Go Marching In'. He was impressed by the awesome majesty of the acting headmaster whose glare alone was enough to shrivel the most mischievous pupil, though the tactic of sending recalcitrants to wait for him outside his study also proved effective.

Class IVB had lots of fun with its new man. He tried to take a list of their names in alphabetical order, an enterprise that did not go entirely according to plan. The subject of mathematics had not, they thought, previously been raised in their company and history was a closed book.

Mother's miscarriage was the saddest part of the family's stay in Yorkshire. Rushed to hospital after feeling poorly, she gave birth to a baby boy three months prematurely. Our parish priest arrived in time to baptise him John William. Mother was devastated and blamed herself for the loss of the child. Her strength slowly returned but the mental scars took far longer to heal. If a shadow thereafter hung over her life it was hidden from her remaining children. Upon the surface she remained her old sunny self, never mentioning the loss so that it was not until many decades had passed that the younger members of the family realised anything untoward had occurred.

Scarborough was bound forever to be associated with the loss, however, and the decision was made to move. Apart from anything else, our house was owned by relations, one of whom wanted to return. Also Father had been indulging in numerous confrontations with a zealous new headmaster, besides which appropriate Catholic schools had to be found for the five of us, for Beatrice, a cheerful soul, had joined us. James, the oldest, was approaching the age for taking the Common Entrance exam and entering senior school.

It was time to go south and, for the first time, to visit the West Country. Again this was easier said than done without money, a car or anyone able to drive. Jobs and schools had to be found and accommodation for a large family without money to spare. Somerset's future opening batsman was now a robust child of six years.

2

TO BATH

By now Greatgran had died at a ripe old age, and in her will bestowed 500 pounds upon our otherwise struggling family. Since Father's annual salary was only twice as much (but still higher than the 15 pounds a week young Somerset professionals were paid in 1974) the legacy was as substantial as it was timely. A car was needed, and some driving lessons. Mother flew through her test like a horse jumping over a feeble obstacle. Father was much less calm and coordinated and his lessons were dreaded by teacher and pupil alike.

Our parents bought a second-hand Bedford van, one of those solid, plug-ugly constructions with a tiny bonnet that looked like a sly pig. Still, the family was catching up with the times. Television came next.

After several months spent scrutinising the teaching vacancies advertised in the local newspapers, Father found a possible position as Head of Mathematics at a Catholic school in Bath. Not daring to take the car so far so early in their fraught relationship, he decided to partake of the services offered by British Rail. Happily the main interviewer for the position in Bath had been a young and popular teacher at Father's school in Manchester, and he remembered him as a promising footballer. Impressed that Father had managed to overcome his background and its supposed limitations to take a degree at Oxford University, the panel invited him to accept the post.

Mother also decided to find work to help pay the bills and also to engage her mind and restore her spirits. Spotting an advertisement seeking a teacher of physical education sufficiently versatile to give instruction in maths, she applied and after an interview with a cheerful Reverend Mother she was duly appointed. Moreover the girls were invited to attend the school. Now it was merely a matter of finding somewhere to live.

Bath Council had nothing to offer by way of accommodation except a flat which was pretty run-down as it had not been occupied for many years. Number 9, Broad Street proved to be a large, three-storey building with a shop on the ground floor, storage on the second and a dishevelled, appallingly-decorated abode previously used as Corporation offices on the top floor. Take it or leave it, said the council officer. Mother wanted to take it and her view prevailed. A place was found for James at Downside School, a cold-cloistered Catholic boarding school about 15 miles away, for whose holiday cricket team such luminaries as Siegfried Sassoon, Jack Fingleton and Dennis Silk sometimes played. Catholic schools attached to our parish church were found for the rest of the brood.

Determined to leave Scarborough on a cheerful note, my parents took the family to the local theatre to see The Black and White Minstrels, Thora Hird and other local delights. Father caught up with an old friend from Manchester, Joe Gladwin, a comedian destined to play Norah Batty's husband in the long-running television series, 'The Last of the Summer Wine'.

Education and cricket entered my life in Bath. In 1962 the family had been given its first television set, black and white and with a 12-inch screen. Apart from 'Dixon of Dock Green' and

'Maigret', sport dominated our set viewing hours. After school and in the holidays I'd watch the Test matches and saw Colin Cowdrey, his arm in plaster, walk out to bat against the 1963 West Indian team. I decided to become a cricketer and 40 years later am still trapped in the game's tangled web. Despite the setbacks the decision was the right one. A man must follow his spirit for otherwise something dies within.

As far as schooling goes and insofar as any interest is held in all those David Copperfield things, I was dispatched first to a Catholic junior school that had its rough side and at which I once found it necessary to spend an entire break running around the concrete playground, trying to avoid a gang bent on vengeance. Stopping now and then to discourage one of the pursuers recommended itself as a tactic, an early and, as it emerged misleading, indication of acumen. These disputes seldom last long in the world of juveniles and by the lunch break the matter had been forgotten. Otherwise the school has slipped from memory.

Park School followed, a small, private establishment a few miles outside the city that had its own sports field. Although the school had its fierce side, personified in the gentlemen appointed to teach French and English, it was an amiable environment. Games and academics fought an unequal struggle for the attention of the student body. Ball-games were my strong point, a statement easily confirmed by witnesses to my unavailing attempts to jump and sprint.

There were brighter boys in the class. Jacobsen was the best performer, a little bespectacled lad who sat at the front of the class, rarely smiled and was not nearly as bad as he sounds. Stollmeyer was the cleverest boy, a wiry fellow whose dad was rumoured to be an American ambassador. Concentration was his weak point for he chattered a lot and was inclined to wrap his legs around his head. Among the rest Steer was in trouble most often while Pitt Senior had a hole in his heart, or so his fellow boarders maintained. Conkers and a rough sort of basketball were played at every break in our supposed studies, all the usual boy things.

But these clever chaps were not my closest friends, a privilege reserved for Stephen Driscoll, an Irishman at whose house we'd sometimes play football. He had a garden and we thought he must have lots of money. Moreover his mother gave us cakes. He was a gentle, vague youngster and twenty years later he re-emerged as a policeman in Derby. Michael Charlton was another skinny fellow who enjoyed football, while Matthew Guillaume, son of the headmaster, was a splendidly mild chap and deaf in one ear. His dad was an eccentric and a pianist who used to brighten up Latin lessons with tales of heroism. None of them was ever invited back to our flat, for it was too tense and exposing. Rather I preferred to lead a double life, gregarious among school chums, withdrawn at home. It is a common enough resolution to the embarrassment of family.

Park School was a bus trip away and the fare was fourpence. By walking to the next stop a penny could be saved and by the end of the week a fellow was well placed to buy a Mars Bar on the way to watch Bath play rugby at the Recreation Ground or else soccer over at Twerton Park.

Even in those days Bath had a strong rugby team, a fact that seemed to escape its critics who were forever singing the praises of bigger clubs like Bristol and Gloucester, not to mention well-favoured competitors from further afield. Bath had a rugged pack that included the Parfitts, brothers built along the lines then regarded as compulsory among those hoping to be taken seriously as front row forwards. David Gay played at number 8, and once—or maybe twice—represented his country. Ian Duckworth was a particular hero, a dashing winger whose tackling was regarded even by his staunchest supporters as being slightly suspect. In those days rugby players' positions could be deduced from their frames. Tries were few and far between. Certainly they were not regarded as a vital part of the afternoon's entertainment. Beating Bristol and Llanelli in the rag doll match was the important thing, and no objection was raised if the score was 6–3. It always seemed muddy and there was an awful lot of kicking. Of course it is a much better game nowadays, but those fellows belonged to us.

Bath was not as strong at soccer. Indeed the team did not play in the main League. A noisy fellow called Malcolm Allison was in charge. A quiet chap called Tony Book was the right back. Not until they fulfilled the same roles at Manchester City were they accorded the respect they presumably deserved even then. Roger Gough played at right half, a chunky, busy player who rose to the heights of Swindon Town. Neither player commanded the attention of the youngsters in the stands, a privilege reserved for Fleming, a bald, fierce, flying Scotsman who played at centre-forward and would have scored lots of goals if only the posts were a couple of yards higher. Repeatedly his shining dome appeared above the crowd in the penalty box and hopes rose only to be dashed as the ball flashed over the bar. Fleming could shoot as well, thunderous strikes that sent the heavy leather ball into the massed ranks of his cheering supporters. Compromise was not in his vocabulary. Hitting the target was not his main concern—he played soccer with passion, fire and elbows.

Appearing before adolescent scepticism and television took their holds, these men were, and remain, my only sporting heroes. Soccer was my winter game, and I joined a team run by a splendid old man who later wrote kind letters in a time of crisis. We travelled to matches in his minibus and a trial with Bath City juniors followed. Father came along once and I ran around for the entire match without touching the ball. It was a protest against paternal influence.

Very soon cricket claimed its place in my life. Like many children I created and occupied a world of my own. An entire island was imagined. Combining Ted Dexter and John Kennedy, I captained the distinguished team representing this fantastic place and also served as President and sole arbiter of taste. Add Lord Wilberforce and Charles Dickens and a picture begins to form of the stature of this character. Davies was my cricketing name and I batted at first wicket down and led many courageous fightbacks. My squad contained fourteen distinct characters, batted forcefully and collapsed occasionally. We fielded an attack containing erratic spinners and fast bowlers who, in hindsight, bore a marked resemblance to Lindwall and Miller. Sometimes our matches were played with ''owzat' dice, though they were unsatisfactory since a West Indian tail ender, say Wes Hall, might score as many runs as a fine batsman, say myself. Every ball was recorded in a scorebook. Decades later the cricketing world found itself following a 'computer' Test supposedly played between the greatest players from England and Australia. Meanwhile an actual Test was taking place in Sydney. Normally intelligent people kept ringing the press box to ask for the score, not in the actual contest but in the imaginary match which was entirely random in its organisation, apart from Don Bradman being given a life in both innings in an attempt to add realism to the amusement and to help the Australians win. Nonplussed to be told that Larwood was not actually bowling to Neil Harvey on some field of dreams the inquisitors invariably replied, 'Yes, but what's the score? Is Bradman out?'

Larwood retained his sanity. Upon being told by a reporter that he had been carted around in the second innings he said, 'Aye, well, I'm 82 tha' knows.' Alongside Bill O'Reilly, he was the greatest former cricketer I have met. Upon arriving in Australia he applied for jobs not as a celebrity but as a new Australian, eventually finding work in a factory. Neither his accent nor his manner ever changed and to the end he called Douglas Jardine 'Sir'. Of course Jardine was the greatest captain his country has produced.

Jardine achieved the seemingly impossible, and Larwood was his unrelenting strike force.

More active matches were played on the landing below our flat as a plastic ball with holes in it was thrown at a wall, and the rebound hit or missed. These events were described with a running commentary of the type heard from Australia while huddling under a mattress on a cold English morning. Usually I'd slide down the banister and once came a considerable cropper and never whispered a word about it. Big boys don't cry. Actually, I did cry during my first hiding, but resolved never to repeat the mistake. Next to this indoor arena was a strange little room in which some odd people gathered every so often. Wary, haggard celebrants filtered into this back room to commence their laying on of hands. Gradually it became clear that cricket and spiritualist meetings were not happy bedfellows. They'd hear this 'thud, thud' and, alerted, would try to unravel its meaning. Just as the message was being translated they'd hear this piping voice saying 'and Basil Butcher is beaten by that one'. Apparently the spirits were being scared away by the noise and the player was asked to occupy himself differently during these meetings.

Eventually a maniac with a grudge against spiritualists tried to burn down the building and almost succeeded in destroying the entire family, because parents, several children, Uncle Gerald and his wife Mairead were in residence when the blaze took hold. Since the flat did not have a fire escape, the firemen had to raise a ladder to the third floor and help the occupants through the windows and down the steps. By all accounts, they arrived just in the nick of time. On the way back from school I bought the *Evening Chronicle*, across whose front page could be found the account of a rescue from a top floor flat of a family of thirteen. Of course, it went unread. Immersed in the cricket reports, I did not notice the smoke until halfway up the stairs, when a policeman put his hand on my shoulder.

After the family's narrow escape from the conflagration a fire escape was installed. As far as this young cricketer was concerned, this was a breakthrough because it meant we could climb from the back window, over a roof and into the yard of the garage next door. Throughout summer cricket occupied every waking moment of my life and it was a matter of persuading James that he had nothing better to do at weekends than to play with an irritating younger brother who might, in hindsight, have allowed him to bat longer. Before cricket I had been quiet, playing contentedly in my room. Now the same watchful child was goading his older siblings into hours of bowling on a concrete surface smelling of petrol and carburettors. Eventually the whole family took up the game, except for Father who contented himself with putting his middle son (my younger brother Paul was born during our stay in Bath and was to become a much better cricketer in everything except achievement) through his paces. Cricket forced me into family life, and turned a reticent child into a leader.

No longer able to ignore this growing enthusiasm for a strange game, my parents decided to send me to the indoor cricket school recently opened by Peter Wight, the former Somerset batsman. Peter was a slim, gentle soul born and raised in the Indian community in Guyana. He had a squeaky voice and a mild manner and no harsher words ever crossed his lips than 'Oh my sainted aunt!' and the observation that it was 'perishing cold'. Fast bowling had not been his cup of tea but he was a lovely stroke player and could turn the ball a yard in either direction.

My parents' willingness to take their cricketing son to a coach must not be mistaken for encouragement. In those days cricket was a run-down game with poor wages, paltry crowds and few prospects. It did not seem much of a life for a bright young fellow. Father later admitted that he assumed I'd be put off the game forever after being hit by the hard ball a few times. In this respect his approach was correct. Better find out immediately whether the lad had the stomach for a fight, otherwise a lot of time and money could be wasted. Not until I had been put in hospital by a nasty blow to the unprotected unmentionables from a fast and short ball sent down by James was my resolve properly tested. Probably it was neither especially short nor fast (having seen my brother bowl in years of more reliable judgement, it seems extremely unlikely), but an operation was required. My request was played on the hospital radio, an undemanding ditty called 'Bits and Pieces' by Dave Clarke and his five. Immediately upon leaving hospital I resumed playing, whereupon Father realised that this boy was not for turning.

Mother was already an ally. She persuaded Peter Wight to take a look at her eight-year-old son after church one Sunday morning. She went to Woolworth's and bought a bat for 3/6d. For the time being pads and gloves were beyond the family budget. No one had ever shown me where to stand at the crease, or how to hold the bat. Peter uncrossed my hands, stopped me knocking the stumps over and somehow detected a modicum of talent. He continued to show the utmost patience as his student learnt the strokes and started to bowl leg-breaks and googlies. Indeed he was so pleased with my progress that he invited me to join other practices by way of learning from my elders and betters.

Every Saturday morning I'd report to Peter with my 2/6d and practise from 10.00 till 12.30. Individual lessons took place on Sunday mornings and cost 13/-. David Turner, later of Hampshire, turned up now and then as did a laughing black man called Hallam Moseley who had been sent over by Garfield Sobers in an attempt to secure a county contract. Hallam would eventually become a team-mate at Somerset. He was a genial man who, cricket apart, wanted to work in an abattoir.

Joining a club was the next step and I began with Bath Under-12s, which was run by an old gentleman called Mr Ruddick. On Saturday afternoons I'd serve both as scorer and scoreboardman for the club's First XI, a combination that proved hazardous in close finishes. For some reason Bath proved unsatisfactory and I moved to their rivals, Lansdown. A red cap appeared on my head, a sign not of allegiance to the teachings of Mr Mao Tse-tung but of membership of a club. It was also a sign of defiance. Not once in the ensuing 40 years of batting and bowling have I appeared bare-headed upon the field. A few years later I took to wearing hats around the house, partly as a means of keeping the world at bay, partly as protection against the usual adolescent afflictions.

By now Father was immersed in my career and took upon himself the roles of coach and driving force. Knowing nothing of the game, he studied it scientifically, realised it was a game of straight lines and set about instilling the techniques required till they became second nature. This was the beginning of a strained relationship between father and son from which the son gradually withdrew, so that by the end he would scarcely utter a word at home, in marked contrast to his ebullient nature at school.

Modern thinking always condemns the father in these situations. Hardly an article is written about a female tennis player that does not conclude that success had come at a terrible cost and despite the interventions of the male parent. Boys always succeed despite hardships endured at school, never because of them. And so the liberal world imposes its judgement. Certainly it is not fashionable to say that the relationship between parent and child is often diffi-cult or that the obsessive personality of the gifted youngster plays a part in those problems or that adult life is immeasurably enriched by achievements for which the aggressive parent deserves some credit. Suffice it to say, then, that I had nothing to complain about. I can look back on 35 enjoyable and eventful years in cricket and upon a life that has taken me around the world and produced many close friends and three fine houses and households in three differ-ent continents. It has been rich and rewarding. If someone is to blame, might not they also deserve some credit?

Nor should the well-being of the child be judged entirely from the tension that surrounded his cricketing endeavours. It was about this time that I started performing plays at home for the entertainment of a household that managed to grit its teeth and appear amused. After transforming my small room into a theatre with stage and curtain, I'd play the parts to the utmost, as a usually watchful child suddenly became excited. Titles included 'The Life of Catharine Parr' and 'Bombers Over Berlin' and, one gathers, the productions went along at a pace that somewhat assuaged the sufferings of an audience that laughed often and sometimes in the right places. Perhaps this child could have led a normal life but I doubt it. Many years later Geoffrey Boycott, himself driven by so many forces, talked about his brothers and the lives they had led as family men and miners. Sadness entered his voice, the sadness of the isolated. Much moved, I observed, 'You'd like to swap places with them, wouldn't you? But it's not possible, is it?' He looked across wistfully and said, 'It wasn't possible.'

Father erected a line of string in one room from which hung a plastic ball. Every day we'd practise for an hour or so, repeating every stroke till he was happy with it. Usually the practice session began at his instigation. It was not that the pupil was unwilling or that his help was not appreciated. My reluctance was caused by the excitement evident in Father's manner when things did not go well. Throughout I remained silent, trying to give satisfaction, always feeling under enormous pressure to perform and to improve the family fortunes. A part of my spirit rebelled against these intrusions, wanted to be left alone. Ever since there has been a certain conflict in my life, between the absolute commitment to succeed and the desire to step back from the world and to lead a more relaxed life in a harmonious household.

By now I had passed my 11+ examination and the opportunity arose to attend St Brendon's, a robust Catholic school near Bristol with a high reputation. If their rugby was anything to go by,

St Brendon's was a hard and committed place and might have suited this young all-rounder. However, it was decided that I should follow my older brother and become a boarder at Downside School. It was just a matter of passing the Common Entrance. Money was still tight, and though the fees were not exorbitant my parents were ready to consider other possibilities. Peter Wight suggested approaching R.J.O. Meyer at Millfield School to enquire about a sports scholarship. Meyer replied that the school only awarded academic scholarships, a strategic move aimed at silencing criticisms of the school put forward at the Headmasters' Conference. Of course an application for an academic scholarship would be considered on its merits. Patently my studies were sound rather than inspired, but there was something encouraging in the tone of the letter and at the appointed time we climbed into the van and went off to see the headmaster of a school about which I knew nothing and my parents very little.

3

MILLFIELD

Millfield was defined and directed by its headmaster. 'Boss' Meyer was an extraordinary man. By the time my family came under his supervision he was coming towards the end of a rich and varied professional life. Whether sitting in a study packed with piles of papers, empty bottles of tonic water, bowls of soup, history books and the intellectual magazines required to satisfy an endlessly curious mind or striding around his school, he was a compelling figure. Long, lean and tireless, he was a gifted sportsman capable of beating the best the school could offer in any of the numerous codes available, as he sometimes proved on the tennis courts or on the tiny nine-hole golf course located outside the study in which he lived and slept. Creature comforts were of no concern to him. Boss had a brilliant and original mind and was something of a maverick. Of course he was not a saint for the twinkle seldom left his eye. Blessed with principles rather than scruples, he tried to extract the last ounce of talent possessed by his pupils. Doubtless he failed for the aim was high and his school imperfect, but he had started from scratch and in a handful of years built an unorthodox and challenging place of learning. Boys and girls, rich and poor, gentile and Jew, black and white, gifted poor and wealthy dullards, all had their parts to play in his scheme of things. Not that Meyer should be mistaken for a misty-eyed theorist. He was liberal and tough, a combination with enormous appeal. Children were free to choose their goals but were then expected to pursue them with vigour.

Born into a religious family, Meyer had to fight his way into the world. He began by scoring the century he needed to persuade a reluctant and impoverished father to send him to Haileybury where he was regularly beaten till he started to apply himself to his sport and studies. Oxford followed and then there was a long stint in India, where he hoped to make his fortune in cotton. Unfortunately his timing was poor as the Great Depression brought only financial ruin. On his journey home he bumped into Duleepsinhji, who arranged some teaching and coaching for him by way of assisting a cricketer in distress. Boss recalled trying to give lessons to a man so lazy that his servants had to carry him from bed to bath.

Before going to India he had made his mark as a hard-hitting batsman and as a bowler capable of using his long fingers to cut the ball sharply. Had not an urgent need to make money arisen, he might have played for his country. In some respects he regretted the decision and decades later advised this aspiring youngster to try his luck in the game. Not that professional cricket could have contained Boss. Playing against Bradman once, he put all his men on the leg-side boundary and sent down a shoulder-high full toss which the maestro hit on the ground between fieldsmen, whereupon Boss turned around and called out, 'Orthodox field please.' Another time he bowled underarm for MCC against a school whose captain wrote to *The Times* to complain, for which protest he was promptly punished, against the bowler's wishes. Within a couple of summers either Meyer or his comrades would have gone mad. As it was he played for The Gentlemen against The Players and, after the war, and then again when in his dotage, he stepped into the breach to captain Somerset. After surviving that 1948 season, thanks to the aspirin tablets he took to placate a complaining back, Boss returned to the school he had opened on an army camp near Glastonbury in deepest Somerset. Twenty years later my first lessons were in Nissen huts and old wooden buildings called chicken runs. Nowadays the school looks and thinks like a university campus.

Eventually Meyer was ousted from his school. It was not a pleasant time. He was not bothered about money, but he was a gambler and did not always distinguish between the school funds and his own. For 40 years they had been intertwined. Sometimes he'd work all day and then drive to the gambling houses in London before returning to resume his duties next morning. Meyer maintained that he met many of his finest parents at the casinos and the school benefited from these excursions. Probably he was stretching a point, though the school did seem to attract a wide variety of characters. Fees were a moveable feast arranged by the headmaster. A dull child born into money was charged double so that free scholarships could be given to gifted children without a pound to spare. Accordingly places could be given to promising lads from obscure schools in Bath. Men like Boss cannot be sub-divided. They must be taken as a whole.

Unaware of this colourful past and hoping only to secure a free place at this expensive school for their middle son, my family arrived at the headmaster's study at the appointed hour and waited upon events. Meyer's beleaguered secretary opened the door whereupon an orange came flying in my direction. Certain pace bowlers will be surprised to hear that the object was caught. From behind a bundle of papers came the call, 'Well done, throw it back!' With us in his wake, Meyer strode off to the tennis courts and gave me a racket. He then invited my sisters to bowl, a task they accomplished with aplomb. Having caught the bug, they would continue playing and represent various women's cricket teams. Meyer posed several lateral thinking puzzles which defied disentanglement by a brain altogether too prosaic for these purposes. Unable to detect any sign of life in the thinking department, Boss dispatched me to the schools' intelligence tester and received a report confounding his first impressions. Out of the blue Boss announced he was prepared not merely to find a place for this boy but wanted the entire family to come, the children as scholars and the parents as teachers. The idea of my boarding at Downside or St Brendon's was abandoned, and a house was found in Street into which the entire family moved in the summer of 1968.

Senior school life began that September. Every morning the Bedford van would deposit its passengers, whereupon we'd go our separate ways. James and Rosalie were at university while Beatrice, the bounciest of the siblings, attended the junior school where she was followed by Paul. Margaret, my middle sister, and I worked our way through the senior school.

Millfield was a considerable undertaking for an independent child thrown into a hurly-burly full of confident and comfortable people, or so it seemed to me. Senior school started under the auspices of a fierce man called Smith whose moustache bristled and who spluttered as he issued orders. I was dispatched to study Latin, attend mathematics classes in an old army hut, read books under the guidance of a beautiful young lady later encountered in Greece, and to try to find out what all the ties meant for my new boy's test. Lessons were given on Saturday mornings and sport was played on Wednesday and Saturday afternoons. Teams travelled to the fields miles away and returned to shower and change before walking home. Any hesitation about showering was ended when a head of house, who took after the splendid Flashman, was overheard asking if he was allowed to cane boys who did not have showers.

Prefects were massive figures permitted to walk down the drive, which they did with a swagger absent in the teachers, most of whom had frayed cuffs. Boarders lived in houses dotted around the countryside and run in various styles. Survival was a matter of keeping a lowish profile and waiting for the better days that, rumour insisted, lay ahead. Not that Millfield was ever intimidating. Rather it was large and a fellow had to work hard to find his niche. Convention was not followed slavishly. Ties and jackets had to be worn but otherwise pupils had a free hand. My mate Joe habitually wore a long, dirty army coat, tinted glasses and greasy hair. Then one morning a man with his surname absconded to New Zealand, having fleeced the stock market of thirteen million pounds in a deal which, while not criminal, was widely condemned. The next morning I mentioned this coincidence to Joe, who replied that his dad had indeed 'buggered off to Dunedin and taken the lot with him'. He did not seem put out so we continued studying and clogging opponents on the football field.

Not having suffered a winter in any country for 25 years, I now find it hard to recapture those struggles to get out of bed, the time spent scraping frost from the car windows, and the night that arrived to spread its gloom in mid-afternoon and stayed till breakfast had been consumed. Although Millfield was not exactly Spartan, it was no picnic either. Cross-countries could hardly be avoided, though a fellow did try. 'Cadets' was compulsory until a friend refused to hold a rifle on principle. Guns contained leather and he was a strict vegetarian. He was an odd fellow and I afterwards heard that he was living in a grotto in Cambridge, writing poetry. His obstinacy and effrontery forced the authorities to change their system. My response to military requirements was more discreet and involved joining the RAF because a cricketing chum took the roll call, so Friday afternoons could be spent puffing cigarettes in the cricket pavilion and hoping to hell no fool asked me to fly an aeroplane.

At Millfield I discovered rugby, and secured a place in the junior Colts team as a hard-tackling centre. No one ever showed me how to kick or pass, deficiencies that created unnecessary limitations. I played soccer in the second term, as a sweeper in a presentable side. Studies started slowly as a year had been missed. Not until after I had taken 'O' levels did my academic side begin to assert itself.

Cricket was my game and to the dismay of some observers and the delight of my father promotion to the Ist XI came in that first year. Wickets had been tumbling to my flighted leg-spinners and the only other spinner in the school was a giraffe of a left-armer called David Graveney, one of the quieter members of a team that included dreamers unable to pass 30, smokers, drinkers, military types, Derek Shackleton's son (later to torment all and sundry with Dorset), a jovial Welsh rugby player called Dudley-Jones and a chap called Le Breton, who seemed wise beyond his years and would eventually become somebody important behind the scenes in the Liberal Party, or whatever it is called these days. Le Breton advised me to listen to one coach, and one only. Alongside Close's condemnation of the lazy mind and Tom Cartwright's technical point about dropping the bat down and through the ball, thereby engaging the leading shoulder in the drive, this was the most important tip received in many decades in the game. David Budge was our captain and wicket-keeper, a soldierly type who could not control the rougher element or read my googly. Accordingly, I was instructed to brush back my hair to indicate its imminent appearance.

My first match was against Marlborough, who were considered a bunch of toffs by our democratically minded lynch mob. Taking three lowly wickets for five runs helped to placate those concerned about my rapid elevation.

The summer holidays found me playing for Street alongside Gilbert Wall, who emptied the dustbins and took me under his wing, and Johnnie Wilmott, a round man and a fine exponent of the leg-break. Father kept a scrapbook and it must be around somewhere, but these experiences have not faded. Playing with adults at such a tender age was an advantage and the club took good care of its youngster.

Meanwhile my performances with bat and ball had attracted the attention of the county. Selection for the county Under-15 team followed, alongside Colin Dredge, Phillip Slocombe, Keith Jennings and a bright-faced lad from Yeovil who said he could hit sixes and bowl these fellows out. Only rarely would Ian Botham change his tune in the following seventeen years.

Since I was taking wickets, Bill Andrews decided his Under-19 side also needed a leg-spinner. Bill was a complex man with a cheerful manner. My first encounter with him was at the trial match when he walked onto the pitch during the tea interval, lay down and fell asleep, a turn of events that surprised some parents. 'It's just Bill,' the locals said, and so it was. Organisation was not his metier and weeks might pass between matches and then he'd realise that three had been arranged for the same day. Arriving in Cornwall once, we discovered that only two rooms had been booked for the whole team. No one complained. A youngster could have fallen into safer hands, but none better.

After I had played a few matches with the Under-19s, Bill announced that he wanted his thirteen-year-old spinner to play for the County Second XI against Devon in the last match of the season. Of course it was ridiculous but what was I to do? Bill said to meet someone or other at some pub or other to get a lift to Bideford. By Bill's standards this was precise. Experience revealed that his directions generally involved public houses. Unfortunately I had not been listening, a fault that reappeared most memorably when Vic Marks and I were almost arrested in Derby for three times asking the same policeman for directions to the hotel.

My puzzled parents drove around Taunton until we bumped, quite by chance, into Bob Clapp as he emerged from the Crown and Sceptre. As it turned out, Bob had not been planning to leave until closing time anyhow. He was a tall, humorous and not particularly accurate paceman, who opened the bowling with Dusty Hare, who was somewhat less precise and had a lot more hair. Bob was a delightful chap and eventually became the housemaster of Liam Botham, a likeable young man.

The following summer my cricketing skills improved enough to secure selection to represent the Public Schools Under-16s in the annual match against the State Schools, whose team was chosen from trials. Vic Marks and I travelled to Norwich to fulfil the engagement. Vic was not yet at the peak of his powers and did not greatly inconvenience opponents or scorers. He is not the most analytical of intelligent men. His game did not change much over the years, defiantly retaining its rustic look. Asked years later what went through his mind when he was out he replied, 'Cor, bugger, I'm out!' Nor does he relish confrontation. His farming father wanted to take him shooting. Vic did not want to hurt anything. Nor did he care to give offence. The solution was simple. He shot to miss. Playing under my captaincy the Public Schools secured victory by a handful of runs.

A year passed and the teams met again, this time in Liverpool. Much to our relief, State Schools did not choose the aforementioned all-rounder from Yeovil. By now we had realised that Botham was not, after all, a cowboy, a mistake made by even the wisest. His roughness concealed skill and intuition. Botham had been at his most irrepressible during the trials and the selectors had been unable to detect rhyme or reason in his performance. He was furious. Throughout his life he has feared rejection by the supposed establishment. Always he has hated to feel anyone is looking down upon him. Accordingly he detests being described as ignorant or oafish. Isolation is his other great fear. Botham is far more vulnerable than he pretends. That's why he must always take the masses with him.

Assisted by the blindness of the opposing selectors, Public Schools recorded an easy victory after the follow-on had been enforced.

By now the patterns for the next few years had been set, both at school and at home. Tea was at six o'clock every evening for the working-class habits endured. The recently purchased television remained on throughout, allowing those devouring fish fingers, toad-in-the-hole and other English delicacies to watch the last few minutes of 'The Magic Roundabout' and then the news. No one had heard of pasta. After that we'd go to our rooms, Mother to her course and Father to his sitting-room, which had its own television and into which his children rarely ventured. He remained a tormented man, lost somewhere between frustration and fury. Mother remained energetic and patient. After years of teaching maths without an appropriate degree, she started studying at the Open University and passed her exams with flying colours, whereupon she began writing textbooks in partnership with her head of department. 'Monty Python' was the main attraction on television before nature's sweet nurse was embraced once again. The first two episodes were missed, as the idea of watching a circus at 10.00 p.m. did not appeal. Once I grasped the true nature of the programme, it became compulsory viewing and the leading topic of conversation the next day.

After I had scraped a few 'O' levels together it was clear the time had come for some serious study. At last bewildering subjects could be set aside. Biology seemed to consist of disembowelling locusts, not an attractive way to pass a Monday morning. Chemistry was an absurd story of unlikely cause and impossible effect reduced to a series of incomprehensible letters. Physics and French had in common only the fact that they proved impenetrable. History was a matter of writing down notes monotonously dictated by our teacher. I had no ability in art or music. There wasn't an awful lot left. I was not at all brilliant, a fact I knew well enough.

Not until the last couple of years at school did the first signs of academic ability appear. I attempted maths under an eccentric called 'Flash' Fletcher. In his time he'd been a hot debater at Oxford and a guest on 'Brain of Britain', on which quiz show he produced answers that, though authoritative and profound, were rarely accurate. Previously he had taught a group called Les Misérables, the dyslexic lot regarded elsewhere as lost causes in the field of academe. From his first class of desperadoes he had produced a bank manager, a top civil servant, a racehorse owner and several criminals. It was, he maintained, the only entirely successful group he had taught.

As a teacher of mathematics, Flash cut an unusual figure. A delightful fellow, he habitually wore a long, grubby raincoat containing large pockets into which could be stuffed whatever valuable objects emerged from his searches of the school bins. He'd approach a dustbin, peer around like a spy making a drop, quietly lift the lid and pounce upon any item that seemed useful. These included old copies of the *Radio Times* and numerous other rejected goods. Then he'd wander off as innocent as can be. Needless to say he was observed but no one took any notice or thought any the worse of him. If Flash wanted to stuff his pockets with curiosities or go into the staff room to pinch as many sticky buns as possible, it was a matter for him. He cycled to school on a battered old bike, and skied when snow had settled. He was a gentleman. Unfortunately a more rigorous approach was required because no one in my class was nearly as clever as its teacher.

Better progress was made in economics and English. Both subjects captured my imagination: economics with its analytical penetrations, English with its endless joys. Long essays came easily to me, and some of them reached beyond the syllabus. D.H. Lawrence and T.S. Eliot provoked particular interest and I wrote theses as long as booklets about both writers, arguing that their clearest voices could be heard variously in *Sons and Lovers* and

The Hollow Men. Not before time regular study became a habit, with the desk occupied from 6.30 till 9.30 every night. Not that it was all grim, let alone pure. At 6.30 the temptation to listen to the half-hour of entertainment provided by Radio 4 was seldom resisted and 'The Navy Lark', 'Just a Minute' and 'Round the Horne' often gave the innings a lively start. I read an enormous amount in the holidays, including the novels of Conrad and Forster. *Ulysses* was devoured at two sittings and the plays of Shakespeare were read in turn.

Cricket practices had been put in the hands of my younger brother. Improvements owed more to experience than to realised ability. The prodigal feats of my youth had been with the ball. As I grew, added inches made it harder to toss the ball into the air and the bowling gradually fell back, to be revived twenty years later in the last few seasons of professional cricket and then as a leading light in the amateur game. Although my batting was promising, it was neither inspired nor unusually productive.

My last two years at school were more notable for academic advances than cricketing progress. In 1972 I was appointed captain, which resulted in mixed fortunes as a young team struggled to maintain previous standards. A tendency to overreact emerged, an inability to wait until things turned around. Neither inevitable failure nor cynicism had much appeal. Better to make or break. My periods as captain were either disastrous or inspired, never dull. Players were left to develop their games under the genial supervision of Gerry Wilson, formerly of the Lord's ground staff. Selection for representative teams came in my final year but not even scoring 69 and 85 out of 142 in the second innings against India could secure selection for the national Under-19 team. As ever, Father felt the slight more than a son concentrating upon building a career with his county.

Millfield was not the right school for this determined, independent and sometimes prickly boy. Not until the final few terms did student and school reach an understanding, but by then university was beckoning. As usual I avoided the sporting crowd and chose friends from the general populace. Most were fellow day boys. Ashley's farmer dad used to leave the lights on between his bed and the cider vat as he could not survive the night without a pint of scrumpy amidships. Once we wagged school and went racing, won a few bob and had a few port and lemons on the way home. Tim was from Yorkshire and intended to be a doctor. David was a local and wanted to be an inventor except, alas, everything had already been invented. Another chap is a spy, so they say. Among boarders, Norman Ho and Mark Cleverly were particular pals. Not being a sentimental fellow, I lost touch with all of them upon leaving Millfield.

Oxford was approached first but the interview went frostily and my parents lost interest. A master at school suggested Emmanuel in Cambridge and a letter was written on my behalf. English was my preference. Inspired by an excellent teacher called Len Smith, I had explored the world of literature and sampled its numerous attractions. Concerned about my prospects after university, Father suggested law. An interview was arranged. When the college was finally found it proved to be relaxed, welcoming and blessed with a fine, perceptive young senior tutor called D.G.T. Williams, an expert in constitutional and criminal law. Oxford had not been interested in my cricketing abilities but D.G.T. wanted the entire man. A place was offered to me, contingent upon proper 'A' level results. In the event, maths let the side down but Emmanuel said to come anyhow.

Having secured a place at Cambridge, I decided to spend another term at Millfield anyhow, the Oxbridge term as it was called. The idea was to make up for all those hours spent studying when others were cavorting or playing cards. Suffice it to say that I did my best to square the account.

At the end of that term the dreadful thought occurred to me that it was time to find a job. Somerset had offered a contract for the summer of 1974 so there were only a few months to fill. A stint testing shoes in a local factory ended when the three-day week began as the government and miners locked horns. Our household sided with the strikers and did not think much of the conservatives or the royals. Quite rightly, the company kept its regulars and sacked the Johnny-come-latelies. Next came a job testing peat in the laboratory of a factory located on the Somerset Moors. Of course I had not the slightest idea what was meant by the phrases 'pH content correct?' or 'potash right?', but following instructions was easy enough and it was better than working in a factory full of dust and coughing. Of course the boss had the best job, driving around in his sports car and playing golf.

After I had spent a few curiously enjoyable months wearing a white coat the time had come to embark upon a career as a professional cricketer.

4

PROFESSIONAL DEBUT

Six young cricketers reported to Taunton for training at the start of the 1974 season. Although short of money, Somerset had decided to invest in youth. Not that these novices cost all that much. Apart from an obscure overseas player from an unheralded island in the Caribbean, none of them was paid more than 20 pounds a week and some were not so generously rewarded. No one played professional cricket for money in those days. Although one-day cricket had taken its grip, the game remained impoverished till cheques started arriving from commercial television.

These youngsters, among whom only the West Indian was no longer a teenager, were simply taking the next step in their pursuit of the game that touched them. It was a diverse and gifted group with an individual and collective determination to succeed, and a commitment to helping their rural county raise its lowly reputation. Somerset was everyone's second favourite county because it had lots of characters, a rich history, plenty of spirit and in a hundred years of trying had not won anything. It was never going to be enough to satisfy the young men whose careers began on that April Fool's Day 30 years ago. Some of them would stay together for a long time and the breach, when it came, was bitter.

John Hook was a tall, gentle and slightly deaf off-spinner, with whom it was impossible for captains to lose their temper. They might bellow across the field or roar accusations of incompetence, but he'd simply cup his ear and politely ask for the message to be repeated. John tried terribly hard. After dropping a catch once, and desperate to redeem himself, he dived full-length after something much more difficult and watched from a prostrate position as the ball bounced over him and went to the boundary. After an appropriate period of mourning, even the bowler laughed. Alas, his services were terminated at the end of this first season because he was not quite good enough. He disappeared into club cricket and conventional employment, and did not return.

Phillip Slocombe was a young batsman raised on a housing estate in Weston-Super-Mare who completed his schooling at Millfield, where he gathered more airs and graces than was wise for those seeking acceptance among professional sportsmen. Slocombe was a neat, quick-footed batsman born a decade too early or a decade too late. Unfortunately the competition was red hot. As it was he played for the MCC at Lord's, where his technique was lavishly praised. Few men survive glowing references arising prematurely. Setbacks followed and he had to fight for the last batting position with your author, who prevailed. It was dog eat dog.

Frustrated by his inability to secure a regular place in the one-day team in Somerset's glory years, Phillip tried to change his game, went beyond its boundaries and paid the penalty. Without being exactly enemies, there was no love lost between the rivals. Insecurity concentrates the mind. Everyone had seen youngsters shattered by the news that a fresh contract was not to be offered. No one wanted to be next on the list and the only way to avoid this calamity was to score lots of runs or take lots of wickets. Staffs were small and there was no room for error. Nor were there the props enjoyed by modern players: the back-room boys, coaches, trainers, dietitians, psychologists and so forth presumably required to keep the show on the road. It was all wickets and runs, facts and figures and then a committee meeting in August to determine our fate. Inevitably players were inclined to build their positions against a rainy day. Desperate to succeed and fearful of failure, I put my head down and kept it down till the task had been completed. Modern batsmen are much more attacking because they were raised in a more confident era. Slocombe survived for nearly a decade, played in a Cup Final and then withdrew to America to help his wife further her interest in antiques. Our paths have not crossed since he left the county ground for the last time.

Vic Marks came from farming stock and was destined for Oxford University where he was due to study classics, a challenge met with such *sang-froid* that his books were still uncut in the summer term of his first year. Vic had been a boarder at Blundells in Devon and on his brighter mornings was known to take his guitar and burst into song. More often he was watchful in that canny rural way, twisting his hair with a finger whenever stress levels rose.

Although not much of a stylist, he was a terrific cricketer and a fine competitor. He bowled his off-breaks off the back foot, dropped them on a length and kept his nerve and temper through numerous poundings. As a batsman he relied entirely upon intuition. To mark his retirement we tried to find a picture of him letting a ball pass but none could be located. Instead we gave him a rocking chair. Vic scored quickly and mostly square of the wicket and was altogether a good man to have in the side. In his time he captained Oxford and Somerset, and scored runs and took wickets for England and Western Australia. His England career ended on a high note with three successive 50s against Abdul Qadir and never mind that he could not read his googly. Vic never worried about things like that. He could not read anyone's wrong'un. He was a resourceful fellow and a cussedly effective all-rounder, one of the best his county has produced.

Isaac Vivian Alexander Richards had been approached and signed by a bookmaker who also served on the Somerset committee. Hearing of his reputation as a brilliant but tempestuous cricketer, the bookie had taken a gamble and Somerset signed the unknown on his recommendation. He had already been banned on his home island for reacting furiously and publicly to an umpire's decision in a crucial match. Viv had been born and raised in Antigua by a fierce father who worked in the prison near the island's main cricket ground. Many West Indians are raised by their mothers and the difference showed in this man with an intelligent look and a high-pitched laugh.

Viv had appeared in a trial match towards the end of the previous summer and we had batted together for the first time. In those days he was a skinny young man with broad shoulders and a zest for life that did not involve dropping his guard. Also he had sweet timing and an eye for the ball. Viv was a simple batsman, erect and blessed with brutal and incisive power. He looked like a champion. Repeatedly he stepped out to drive the ball thunderously past the bowler or else he moved back and drove through point in a manner bringing to mind descriptions of the batting of Everton Weekes. His bat hardly seemed to move as the ball was flicked or cracked away. He made it all seem ridiculously easy and his bespectacled partner was inspired to produce some stylish shots of his own. Unfortunately our partnership was cut short when Vivian responded to one of my more speculative calls, a mistake he did not repeat. While we youngsters were enormously impressed with the force and range of the newcomer's shots and the power of his personality, the older players were not quite so sure, arguing that he played across the line and might struggle against medium-pacers wobbling the ball around on a damp English morning. Of course the same thing was said about Bradman.

Ian Botham was likewise supported by the junior players at the county. His maverick spirit and boisterous sense of humour were appreciated and his contemporaries were confident that he'd confound those convinced he was merely a wild boy from the provinces. Already he had played a couple of matches for Somerset after drawing attention to himself in his time on the Lord's ground staff. In those days he was slender but strong and intent upon plunder. He was also generous and permanently broke, for he was not inclined to live within his means and had usually spent the next month's wages before they had been earned. Of course his aggression had its darker side, but that was not our concern.

We changed, in that first season, in a brick shed behind a pavilion itself so decrepit that visiting captains considered themselves to be under a severe handicap, their rooms being hidden somewhere in the damp inner workings of decay. Viv alone was permitted entry into the senior room with its communal bath into which the team would plunge at the end of the day. Nowadays the youngsters' shed is used for storing bottles of soft drinks. There were just enough pegs for our clothes and a single shower that sometimes worked.

Tom Cartwright was the county coach and also my lift in the mornings as his journey from Wells took him through Street. Tom was a master-craftsman, a medium-pacer of supreme accuracy and with numerous variations upon his theme. He was a fine technician and Botham had the sense to listen to him. Tom and I had much in common, not least leftist sympathies and a detestation of apartheid. In these younger days the idea of making a name in cricket and then fighting against apartheid had much appeal. Later thoughts turned to survival and batting averages, a combination closely connected. Actually political matters remained in the forefront of my mind and in later years I would assist black African players, sponsor several orphans in Harare and make regular unpaid visits to schools in South Africa and Zimbabwe.

Professional cricket did not come as a surprise, and for all its ups and downs my eighteen years within its precincts were satisfying. Certainly its bloody-mindedness did not dismay me, for I had long since come to terms with that quality. Long before joining the staff I had become used to the ways of paid players and the working man which, in 1974, were much the same thing. My first appearance had been followed by numerous other opportunities, usually as an opening batsman. The Second XI always included a few professionals unable to command a place in the first team and players raised from the ranks of the amateur game whose numbers included Ray Windsor, a bearded smiter from the heart of the county and a convivial fellow whose technique was not sufficiently robust to survive closer scrutiny, and Commander Moylan-Jones, a naval man. Once, standing at the bowler's end on a damp pitch, the Commander saw first the ball and then a piece of turf rise past his partner's ear, whereupon he called out, 'Up periscope!' Later he reappeared, doubtless after all manner of heroics, as chairman of Devon CCC and as a strong and loyal supporter in hard times.

Contact with professional cricketers had not so much shattered, as rendered irrelevant, any remaining illusions. No farmer appreciated the onset of rain more than the struggling professional cricketer. Some could spot a dark cloud far away and seemed almost to beg it to turn its attentions upon their cricket match. Rain brought respite from worries about mortgages and meant they could be paid for sitting around playing cards, an activity with widespread appeal. Also it allowed players to immerse themselves in the black humour of the dressing-room, an attraction for most cricketers. Repeatedly, retired players say they miss the banter more than the game itself. It becomes the reason for staying in the game.

Steve 'Aggro' Wilkinson was my particular friend among the small group of battling pros. Aggro was a spindly Cockney, somewhat accident-prone and decidedly more interested in horses than cricket. Brian Close liked to discuss the racing prospects with him, which may have prolonged his career. In Second XI matches Aggro used to get to 50 and then throw away his wicket because his name was now in the paper, the committee would see it and anything further was a waste of good *Sporting Life* reading time. On the field he'd stand at slip, seldom catching much and never chasing anything. Twice he missed catches off the first ball of a game, twice the ball struck him on the knees, whereupon he'd howl and limp from the field. He could bat, though; correctly but without much power.

Altogether he was an amusing fellow. We went to the races once. On the way he met some bookie friends and was given a tip for the fifth race. Aggro kindly gave me the winners of the first four races, none of which featured in the finishes, though I gathered this was the fault of the jockeys, who did seem to be having a bad day. 'At least,' I pointed out, 'we can recover our losses on the fifth.' Aggro replied that we did not want to back that thing as it was the favourite whereas his fancy was quoted at 8/1. Our nag was not mentioned and the tip romped home. When Aggro was sacked he took up life as a bookmaker.

Not even these salutary experiences quite prepared the youngsters for their first day as Somerset professionals. For the entire morning the older sweats discussed the expenses offered by the committee. Various opinions were broached, though the suggestion that Somerset had been unduly generous was not among them. Money was tight on both sides and every pound did count. Mervyn Kitchen, a forceful left-hand batsman inclined to walk like a duck, observed that he was getting the same allowance for his 90-mile trek from Bristol as another fellow was for cycling in from a nearby village—which did seem a bit rough. Apparently the official response was that he could live wherever he liked. Mileage allowances, meal money for away matches and so forth were debated for hours before the thought occurred to change into whites. This custom lasted until the working players from the 1960s were replaced by better qualified and rewarded men from a different age.

Training was left in the hands of the individuals. Most of the staff had played soccer and, though not athletic by modern standards, were in reasonable shape. Not until Brian Rose's appointment as captain in 1978 did Somerset focus upon stretching and fitness, running around the ground an hour before play, loosening limbs and turning a group of individuals into a fighting force. Mind you, the main reason for these endeavours was to ensure the leading players arrived on time. Accordingly astonishment was felt when other counties started copying these preparations.

After all the meetings about expenses, pre-season training did eventually begin. Far from being the cruellest month, April was the most enjoyable because serious matches did not start till the end of the month so everyone was relaxed and the rooms full of humour. About the only incident in our little shed occurred when Slocombe accused Botham of being ignorant, whereupon he was grabbed and held against a wall. A nerve had been touched. It had been a foolish remark and our sympathies were with our gregarious companion.

Already Botham was leading an energetic life, staying in a small flat attached to the ground with Dennis Breakwell as his room-mate. Breakwell was a left-arm spinner of nervous disposition signed from Northampton. At once unselfish, immature and amusing, Breakwell remains Botham's closest friend in Taunton. Nowadays he coaches at a school in town and relies more upon enthusiasm than rigour as he prepares his charges for the greater world. Our temperaments are poles apart. To my mind he has made little of the talent at his disposal. One youngster arrived from a junior school in Africa with the discipline and technique routinely instilled in those establishments. After a couple of years my opinion was asked and I pointed out that the boy had lots of potential but could not field or run between wickets so some hard physical training was required. We might as well have been talking different languages. His coaches replied that they wanted him to enjoy his cricket and could not contemplate such a programme. Despite manifestly being the best young batsman seen in the county since Trescothick, the boy did not make it. Nor did his supposed advisers take any of the blame. More players have been ruined by indulgence than intemperance.

Viv soon confirmed his stature with some thunderous contributions and only a habit of losing patience in the 30s and 40s held him back. Our paths crossed on several occasions. It was customary for a youngster to accompany the First XI as twelfth man. As far as young players were concerned it was a prime posting, not so much for the opportunity to mix with the experienced men but for the five pound daily allowance which was bestowed upon uncapped players in the senior squad.

Taken to Northampton, I found myself rooming with the Antiguan. Every morning he'd rise to complete a series of strenuous exercises, press-ups and sit-ups piling upon each other. His majestic appearance was no mere accident. On Sunday mornings he'd take advantage of the afternoon start to run round and round the ground at a pace a good deal faster than our captain had managed in April. Brian Close used to trot around the greyhound racetrack at the county ground like a heavyweight boxer preparing for a bout. Now in his forties, Close hardly seemed to be moving but, then, he fielded at short leg so it did not matter. Perhaps he was thinking about batting. More likely his thoughts were turning to the next dog or horse race and the tip he had received from the mysterious 'Jackie lad'. Most of the players gambled on the horses. Close also attended the dog meetings whereby Somerset boosted its income. He once dispatched me with instructions to put a fiver on number 3 and his disgruntlement with the news that I had mistakenly placed three pounds on number 5 did not ease when my greyhound flew home to win by a length.

Viv and I went out for supper in Northampton. Heads turned in the restaurant as a furious argument began about black power. Viv maintained that his people's time had come and an imbalance had to be redressed. I replied that both black and white power were as bad as each other. Neither man gave an inch. Over the years we spent more time together than our backgrounds might have suggested. Respect was mutual, fondness was discernible. Viv produced the nickname of 'Professor' and we talked a lot and listened to his Marley or my Dylan. He'd walk around singing 'Emancipate yourself from mental slavery, none but ourselves can free our minds'. Like many great sportsmen, Richards and Botham married young and took around with them a confidant capable of keeping the world at bay when required. Viv's batman was a round, cheerful, footballing Scot, Peter McCombe, who enjoyed fry-ups and lager and never mind the angina.

Viv was a remarkable young man, explosive and delightful, intolerant of weakness and falseness. Also he had a rich sense of humour and used it to make his points. We tended to like and trust the same people. Of course there were also numerous differences. At the end of each day Viv spent hours rubbing creams on himself and dressing immaculately before eventually making his appearance downstairs. As he was king on the field so he was comfortable in the rooms. Sometimes he'd lie on a couch in the dressing-room, half dozing, half listening. When a wicket fell he'd rouse himself, put in some eye drops, pick up his blade and walk magnificently to the crease, delaying his entrance till the stage was empty.

My only other away trip that season was to Brighton where, notoriously, there was only enough hot water in the geyser for one of the big baths, a fact revealed at the end of the first day when the players trooped wearily from the field to discover that while their opponents were bathing in luxury, they were condemned to shivering. It did not go down well. Next day, determined to atone, I opened the taps twenty minutes before stumps. Unfortunately the thought did not occur to turn them off till the players were leaving the field, whereupon I rushed into the rooms, found the bath overflowing, jumped in whites and all, pulled the plug, grabbed a bucket and worked to save the situation in the five minutes available. Now wrapped in a towel I greeted the players, congratulating them on a splendid effort. Once more the bath was lukewarm but so was our hosts'. The plumbing was blamed.

In August the chance arose to play for my county. Warwickshire were the opponents and Weston-Super-Mare the venue. Derek Taylor, a seasoned campaigner from London who was superb over the stumps to medium-pacers and batted as sensibly as he lived, was my opening partner. Nervous as a ninny, I would have settled for ten runs. After scoring five I was caught at short-leg but my legs refused to leave the field. The umpire shook his head. Thereafter things improved and runs flowed, with several hits over the top. Warwickshire had a curious attack, with David Brown leading the way with his height and pumping elbows and A.C. Smith abandoning the gloves to bowl in-swingers in a cravat. Upon reaching 46 I drove across a full-length ball from Eddie Hemmings and departed. Without quite remembering my name, for he was inclined to call all and sundry 'doo-dah', Close said a hundred had been there for the taking and he was right.

Thereafter my fortunes sank so swiftly that two ducks and several dropped catches followed as this first opportunity was squandered. Never having been dropped from any side before, I felt these failures and this rejection keenly. Most rising players endure struggles of this sort but the dashing style remained intact, hooking anything short, hitting strongly to leg and damning the consequences. A thick skin is needed to play in that vein, and soon the analytical mind demanded the elimination of risk.

Somerset managed without me for the rest of the summer. Still, I'd made a mark and in October was expected at Cambridge University, so things were not going too badly.

5

MORE BLUES

Never having met a lawyer, the prospect of studying the subject among the brightest and best of my generation was intimidating. Never having heard of torts, I dutifully read the recommended preparatory material provided by the college and arrived in Cambridge with some slight idea about legal process. Under the impression that brilliant minds swarmed around the colleges, and eager not to be left behind, it seemed that a pattern of regular study was needed, especially as the summer term would be dedicated to cricket. Throughout, the need to impress has been a strong motivation, the feeling of commanding a measure of respect at least within the profession. Others were not so delicately framed. Few fellow Millfieldians were studying at the university but a Kenyan Asian economics classmate called Halim was around. Visiting him once at noon, I teased him for being still abed and he roused himself sufficiently to boom, 'Peter, I feel no need for justification.'

Imagining myself to be a grafter, perhaps even a plodder, I decided to attend lectures and study books in my room or in the library for eight hours every weekday and six hours at weekends and to let the third term of the year take care of itself. It was a self-denying program that was maintained throughout and meant that neither university nor its inhabitants were given much time to make an impression. Not that student ways appealed to an eighteen-year-old uncertain of his abilities and already embarked upon a career. Young sportsmen reach the critical time of their lives early and, accordingly, do not enjoy the licence available to most students. In any case, it was quite fun leafing through ancient tomes or going to the criminology department to read the arguments for and against ducking and so forth. During the holidays I worked almost as hard, staying in the attic whose creaky and winding stairs were a considerable deterrent to anyone thinking of disturbing the peace. Everything was condensed onto cards which were hung upon the bedroom wall. I admired Lord Denning, especially for his willingness to cut through the rich language of the law to find the justice in the case. He seemed to be generous towards ill-protected parties like old ladies and married women yet retained common sense and simplicity of expression. Our lecturers did not like his unpredictability and suspected that the bluff rural manner concealed a cunning brain which, of course, it did.

These lecturers were a mixed lot. One kept saying 'in fact' when a lesser man might have drawn breath. Inevitably his 'in facts' were counted and his best effort, 132 in 50 minutes, won a round of applause that perplexed the performer. Another fellow meticulously subdivided every topic into point A, sub-point 1, sub-point (1) and so forth. Besides ten lectures a week we were subjected to fortnightly cross-examinations in our various subjects. D.G.T. Williams took us for criminal law and a veritable hawk took us for Roman law. David Fleming wore jeans and leather jackets as he posed questions about contracts and five years later wrote a kind letter about my first book, adding that he had marked my finals paper in jurisdiction, in which I had done surprisingly well.

And the funny thing was I had not the slightest intention of becoming a lawyer. Too stuffy, too inhibiting, too formal, too enclosed, too many collars and ties, not enough sunshine, fresh air and laughter. In truth I wanted and needed to get out of England. Moreover, cricket was calling. By hook or crook I was going to survive in that often unkind game. Beyond that there was not a thought in my head, apart from an enduring but less prominent detestation of racism. Away from cricket my life has followed a predictable and simple course. Playing cricket was a requirement of my character. Everything else followed and most of it was more enjoyable but not as necessary. Beyond a common desire to be noticed, I am almost entirely without ambition. Accordingly I have always been more relaxed away from the professional part of the game, and probably a better and more likeable person. But a man blessed with a certain ability cannot leave it alone even if it eats into him. Always as a coach I have advised youngsters to try their luck, for otherwise life is safe and dull and not properly lived. Once I was established as a professional my worries eased and the more extrovert part of my character began to emerge, a part best known by readers of newspapers, colleagues at Devon CCC, students at schools in Africa and the numerous members of my various households. My personality was at its worst in the Somerset years. Perhaps, though, my character was at its strongest in that selfsame period for determination and guts were needed to overcome the obstacles that presented themselves. Everything settled down once the cricket career had taken hold. For twenty years I've led more or less the same life, seen the same friends, worked for the same newspapers by and large, and thoroughly enjoyed the experience.

For a year I held other students in awe. They might appear limited but razor sharp intellects must lurk beneath those mundane exteriors. Those not appearing to work must be studying secretly while everyone else slept. The thought that some fellows really did not give a damn or were sufficiently sure of themselves to bide their time did not occur to me. Apparently there had been a lawyer who spent his entire three years in pubs except for an hour from 3.00 p.m. every afternoon when he'd lock his door and ignore all distractions. He had become a High Court judge, so they said. Of course the female of the species was diligent and one lecturer was apt to say 'Good morning,' and then 'Got that down, girls?' Always there were myths with which to contend. County bowlers could land the ball on a threepenny bit. Cambridge students had incisive brains.

My rooms were on the top floor of an old building behind the pond around which ducks walked importantly. Another first-year lawyer lived opposite, Robert Alexander, who seemed to have lots of theatrical friends. Otherwise the floor was populated by fellows studying computers, who did not seem to lead exciting lives. Downstairs was Carl, a Welsh lawyer with sudden enthusiasms. One month he'd start buying the *Financial Times*, the next he'd dedicate his life to yoga and yoghurt. Gradually realisation dawned that Cambridge was not full of great minds discussing Tacitus, but of ordinary folk who filled in football coupons and stood in line for their cafeteria meal every lunchtime.

As usual I chose a small group of friends and stayed with them till the course had been completed. My particular chums were Rory McGrath, who helped to write an amusing pantomime and later became a comedian; Robin Spencer, a gentle, dutiful soul who wore denims, played the guitar, had a steady girlfriend and became a prosecutor; and Charles Bott, who was from Hull and resembled Ted Hughes.

Charles was a Jew who had worked on a kibbutz and a Yorkshireman who had watched Geoffrey Boycott bat. Still barely eighteen he was bright, impatient and blessed with a shock of black hair which he'd sweep back in times of agitation. He had read Dickens, worked in a fish-finger processing factory, a provision he thereafter refused to contemplate, and was a member of the Labour Party. He read classics, moved around with the

Footlights people, even Griff Rhys-Jones, and ended up as a tough defence lawyer. We were friends long before my cricketing background was revealed.

In three years I did not once attend formal dinner at 7.30. Wearing gowns was not my cup of tea and I even ignored the degree ceremony. Tea, toast, hot chocolate, games of squash, Joni Mitchell, cheap meals in town and movies sustained this private character through those first terms. Muhammad Ali's victory over George Foreman also brought cheer, for alongside Martin Luther King he was a particular hero and had been since he started dancing, teasing and saying things others left alone.

At last summer came around. I had already met most of the University cricketers, since most of them were members of Emmanuel College. Bill Snowdon, our senior man, was a gruff northerner with a dry sense of humour, a stunning girlfriend who could cook but could not speak English (incredibly, some observers thought it could not last) and a solid defensive stroke. I encountered him on my first morning in residence. Not having bought any Shreddies, I arrived for breakfast and saw Bill sitting alone, hidden beneath a great coat, hinting at a contempt for students, suggesting an unapproachable majesty. With tray in hand, I approached this great man and asked to join him as if seeking an audience with Charlemagne. He muttered something about hoping I'd settled in well and apart from elliptical comments calculated to prick my enthusiasm for Emmanuel, Law, breakfast, conversation, friendship and life, that was about it. Patently Bill was a mighty figure. Only later did I discover that all his meals were free because the lady responsible for stamping our tickets only pretended to stamp his. He returned for supper at 6.00 p.m., sitting at his private table, not a whit more impressed. At 10.00 p.m he'd go off with his splendid girlfriend for another meal, ground he tried to recover with a game of squash next morning. Bill was an observer of people, a quick, ruthless assessor of their characters. He issued warnings about Steven Coverdale (nicknamed 'Brian'), saying he was the most sensible person he had met. It took me a month to understand the withering implications of this remark. Snowdon brought a peculiarly indestructible quality to his cricket and his life. An amusing companion, he left at the end of the year and went to the West Indies and then Harrow.

Steve Coverdale was an earnest Yorkshireman inclined to say sound things and then blow through his teeth. None of the other players took him seriously but this did not seem to bother him. He was regarded as disconcertingly sensible and his words did tend to dull the senses. Once he told me not to worry about not rising early to study, a thought that had not occurred. Steve mentioned that he rose at dawn but investigation revealed that most of the time was spent reading the *Telegraph* cricket reports. Sometimes he'd stare at a page of text for a considerable period but no one ever saw him turn it. Nowadays he is a cricket administrator. Tim Murrills was a steady chap who became a solicitor and Richard Smyth was a cheerful type from the northern regions, the opposite of his dour opening partner. Smyth played forward to every ball, drove an eccentric vehicle and became a headmaster.

Playing cricket for Cambridge was not easy for an inexperienced but highly competitive young man. More than necessary, I took losing and failing to heart. Inevitably the team was constantly in trouble and I lacked the ability possessed by another newcomer, Alastair Hignell, who looked and batted like Henry VIII, to ignore circumstances and have a go. Nor was there any elder around to offer advice. In any case I was too tense to listen. Years later Viv Richards described me as a country house with fierce dogs outside. Doubtless, too, the books were a distraction for, disdaining the sporting crowd, especially the rowers, I returned to them every evening.

Accordingly I played poorly until asked to open the batting in a run chase against the MCC, whose batsmen had encountered difficulties against my presentable off-breaks. About 70 runs were needed in eight overs and my promotion was an excellent move because it meant throwing the bat. A swift 20 or 30 helped to restore confidence. At last came a 50 against Essex, whose Scottish pace bowler responded to any boundary with a beamer.

Next, Cambridge went on the road to prepare for the big match against our ancient rivals at Lord's. Already it had been a trying season and we were not so much a team as a mob. Chris Aworth was captain, one of those fellows able to charm people into thinking he was neither ruthless nor selfish. I did not like him, and nor did Bill, though it was not a battle either of us expected to win. Just before the varsity match we had a ferocious argument across the floor of a restaurant. Doubtless the tension of the approaching contest had something to do with it, as well as the fact that this freshman could be a pain in the backside. Aworth scored a duck in the first innings of the varsity match and was offered no words of comfort as we crossed. Later he played for Surrey for a while, but complained that they did not laugh enough and withdrew to some more compatible walk of life.

Majid Khan led Glamorgan against Cambridge in the last match before Lord's. Normally senior players rest when their county plays against the students but Majid remembered his university days fondly and turned out against his successors. Alongside Ken Barrington and Harold Larwood, the grave Pakistani was my favourite cricketer. These men had in common commitment to the cause, defiance and a refusal to lower themselves. Majid spoke in a deep voice, batted in yellowing pads and a floppy hat and was entirely incorruptible. He was also a brilliant batsman, a patriot and a Muslim whose puritanical ways caused him to frown upon his nephew, the mighty warrior Imran, who was due to lead Oxford University's attack at Lord's.

Our match against Glamorgan was played at Swansea and proved something of a turning point. After lamely chipping a catch to short mid-wicket in the first innings, I went for a walk around the Mumbles and did some thinking. After several gloomy hours I decided to stop fiddling around and to start hitting the ball. The next day I scored my first 100 in 'first-class' cricket. The quotation marks indicate a hesitation about the legitimacy of so describing this contest, but the standard was not bad and it just about crossed the line. Half the trouble with English cricket is that the classification 'first-class' is not given the respect it deserves and needs.

After saving this match and with one batsman belatedly in form, Cambridge arrived at Lord's in good heart if not exactly as a unified force. Oxford batted first and lost early wickets to Ed Jackson, an amiable left-arm swing bowler from Winchester, inclined to turn up in clothes ordinarily associated with motor-bikes, before Dave Fursdon saved his side with a fighting century. Jackson had opened the season with a few double-bouncers to John Edrich, who remarked that he had not seen much of that sort of thing from Lillee or Thompson the previous winter. Fursdon counted a young lawyer named Tony Blair among his closest friends at Oxford.

In reply Cambridge sank to 20/3, whereupon I produced the innings of my life. Missed at 20, I punished a strong attack that included Vic Marks and Imran, who bowled in-swingers in those days. About the only stroke of the innings that I recall is a hook off Imran that landed in the pavilion. Otherwise it was full of strong strokes to leg, many of them leg-clips off the bowling of the Reverend Wingfield-Digby, whose worthy Christianity did not appeal. Rightly the innings was praised. For a fortnight hereabouts I looked and even played like M.J.K. Smith. Thankfully no one said that the next Peter May had appeared, a fate suffered at the start of the next season.

Cambridge led by 50 or so but could not dismiss Oxford a second time and though we had a stab at a token target, the match petered out. Afterwards the players chose Tim Murrils as their next captain, though some preferred me. Probably it was the right choice because intolerance and impatience are not the ideal qualities for a captain of a university team. But it did condemn Cambridge to defeat at the next meeting of the sides. Tim was a lovely man and a good friend but not entirely comfortable as a leader.

Thereafter university life followed an easier course. After securing a high second in the first and second year exams, I continued to work methodically towards my finals. If law was to be rejected it must be from a position of strength. In that second year I remained in college, close by a well-bred Conservative with a double-barrelled name (which escapes me) who passed his time either with a charming girlfriend or listening to Pink Floyd. My time was spent studying and warming cans of macaroni cheese. About the only highlight of this year of battling with the law of property was a knock on the door one morning at 1.00 a.m. Ian Botham appeared, said he had a friend in Cambridge, was going to get married and here was the invitation. As ever he was impossibly full of life. A month later he joined Kath in holy matrimony.

In the drought-stricken summer of 1976 I faced Andy Roberts for the first time. It was a disconcerting experience. Roberts bowled a routine bumper and, in a pickle, I ducked into it and was struck a fierce blow on the side of the head, whereupon I crumpled to the ground, not much hurt but aware that my spectacles were broken and that there was a certain spinning in the world. At hospital the nurse said it was just as well the ball had not hit a couple of inches to the left. Sitting in hospital, clutching a sore head and with a bump closing one eye, it did not seem that things could be much worse. She repeated that a little to the left and I'd have been a goner.

After an hour lying in my room listening to music, I returned to the ground to find our team striving to avoid the follow-on. Returning to the crease at the fall of the ninth wicket, looking not unlike a mummy, I survived until Roberts was recalled. He produced a bumper that whipped off my cap which landed at gully's feet. Facing him with both eyes working was not much fun. Facing him with one closed was beyond my capabilities. Helmets had not yet been contemplated so batsmen relied entirely upon their wits.

The near miss preyed on my mind. 'A couple of inches to the left,' she'd said. With the varsity match approaching, Cambridge encouraged me to return as soon as my body was ready. We played against Clive Rice on a fast, cracked pitch in Nottingham and made the mistake of removing him for a duck. Determined to sort out these presumptuous fellows, he responded by peppering us. Every ball looked like a bouncer and I was shaken by the experience. For years afterwards these opponents thought I was scared of fast bowling. My confidence took a beating and, despite dry pitches and parched outfields, the season was a disaster. Eventually I looked around, realised that others were not braver or sharper than I was and promptly set about the slow process of restoring my confidence by practising against tennis balls and training the mind to duck, weave and hook. Cricket balls came next, first underarm and then gradually faster till match conditions had been replicated. Practicality was more helpful than posturing. Before long I had recovered my reputation and my self-respect and thereafter my nerve did not falter. But a lesson was learnt. Coaches must prepare their charges for the hardest things that lie ahead.

Back at Somerset, my form fell away so much that officials wondered whether sufficient effort was being made. In fact I was trying too hard. Infuriated by these insinuations, I threw the bat the next day and scored 65 in 40 minutes whereupon the chairman said he knew our little conversation would do the trick. In a way he was correct because it had released a lot of pent-up energy. Otherwise, the season was spent none too happily in the Second XI. Not that reserves are supposed to be pleased with their lot. As far as cricket went, it was the first full season that was going to count.

Fortunately, the next season (1977) had its moments. Every year a combined Oxbridge team played in a section of the Benson & Hedges Cup. We had some fine cricketers: Marks, Chris Tavare, Ian Greig, Paul Parker, David Gurr and others less renowned but not much less competent. Worcestershire had been overcome in 1975 and the following season brought two more triumphs and almost qualification for the quarter-finals. Nothing, though, compared with the solitary victory secured in this last year of student life. Driving to Barnsley that spring afternoon did not seem sensible for young men about to take their final examinations. The might of Yorkshire awaited us, besides which our form had been patchy. Boycott was injured and could not play so our hosts depended a good deal upon their other senior men, Jackie Hampshire and Chris Old. To the dismay of a large crowd still recovering from the news that R. LeQ. Savage and A.R. Wingfield-Digby were bowling for the opposition, both scored ducks. Remembering my awful fielding against his team in a recent match, Hampshire took a risky single to mid-on and was run out. Yorkshire did not reach 200 in their 55 overs.

Between innings our captain asked whether Coverdale or our gentle Sri Lankan, Gajan Pathmanathan, should open the innings with me. As a local, Coverdale had been asked to talk about the bowlers and had made them sound like a reincarnation of Alec Bedser and Harold Larwood. Rocker Robinson and Howard Cooper might have been surprised to hear that, besides having cunning changes of pace, a deadly bumper and a lethal yorker, they could move the ball in both directions sometimes, it seemed, at the same time. No point in opening the batting with him. Pathmanathan strode out and promptly hooked and drove Old for 38 runs in four overs, an assault that silenced the crowd and effectively ended the match. Tavare, Marks and Parker finished the job and we drove home feeling more buoyant about our exams.

Oxbridge also played Australia in The Parks. By then news had broken about the Packer rebellion and the tourists did seem distracted. Doug Walters captained the Aussies but did not score any runs. Determined to restore our reputations after a first innings collapse, the students batted well in the second effort, with Marks and I scoring 70 or so apiece. Having bet upon a second wicket falling one evening, Max Walker sent down an extraordinary over of leg-cutters which I was fortunate to survive. Throughout Kerry O'Keeffe was calling the odds from short leg, giving quotes on this bloke reaching 50 and so forth. He had an irreverent sense of humour and would become a close friend. (After cricket, Kerry struggled for years to make his mark, but in the last few years his luck has changed and his humour has been given a wider audience as a colleague on ABC radio.)

Australia chased a target energetically, with Kim Hughes stepping down the pitch to drive the first ball of every over for six. Wickets fell, and the game was drawn. And as far as university cricket went, that was it. The varsity match was also drawn. Parker, Nigel Popplewell, Greig and Matthew Fosh, a lovely young man who died tragically young, strengthened our batting, but wickets were harder to take. Greig was a fine fellow but for years Parker seemed headstrong and his boyish enthusiasm grated. He was too much like Aworth for my taste, too good to be true. Accordingly I teased him mercilessly. University dressing-rooms can be harsh places, with eleven intelligent and competitive young men and no older hands to keep them in their places. Although Paul was a superb batsman, jealousy had nothing to do with it. Indeed it has played no part in my life. Simply, his naturally bounding athleticism and confidence contrasted with my enduring belief in the struggle. Eventually I realised that my judgement had been premature and that the fault was mostly mine—whereupon a healthy respect developed.

In this final year I belatedly began training, a habit that continued till the time came a quarter of a century later to retire from the ranks of competitive cricket. This was largely at the instigation of a mad hatter of a fellow who lived downstairs and went by the name of John James. A cricket fanatic, and desperate to improve, John took the view that if he ran enough miles and lifted enough weights he was bound sooner or later to bowl fast, which was all he ever asked from life. Alas, this admirable eccentric never did propel the ball at speed. The end came when a college wicket-keeper stood up to the stumps when he was trying with all his might. I do not say it broke his heart but it hurt, and a fine man otherwise full of good sense retired from the fray.

Legal studies went better than the cricket. I was awarded first-class honours, news of which arrived at the hotel in Leeds where I was resting en route to Somerset's Sunday league match.

6

GREECE

Ever since he had been ditched by the school he created, R.J.O. Meyer had been urging an assortment of Roebucks to come to Athens to assist him with his new school. As part of his campaign he mentioned that both staff and cricket team needed to be strengthened. No one was surprised to hear that Boss had created a cricket team for he was not a man easily discouraged. In October 1977 the opportunity finally came to leave behind the restrictions of youth. A winter spent with Boss in Greece sounded like a good place to begin.

Boss rang and asked me to bring two new electric kettles. He admitted that, strictly speaking, this transaction was illegal, but added that Greek kettles did not work. A taxi took me through the noisy, dusty streets of the Greek capital to the quiet hotel in Kefelari that served as the school's boarding house. Although not exactly The Ritz, this was not Dotheboys Hall either, for the rooms were adequate and the food reasonable with rice, hunks of meat and crusty white bread, fare that seemed exotic after a boyhood spent amidst fish fingers. It was to be home for the next three months.

Bread was the first surprise. Hitherto a dull part of the diet, it sprang to life with crust, texture, smell and the inner softness that is nowadays so widely recommended. On a trip to Delphi our bus stopped in an old village through which women walked alongside asses carrying piles of sticks. Feeling peckish, I popped into the bakery and asked for some *psomi* which, I had been assured, meant bread. Apart from '*Ena tiropeta parakalo*', which means 'One cheese pastry please', the local language went unmolested. A hunk about the size of the Isle of Man was cut from a loaf and presented to the guest. The bread was mouth watering. No need for butter or cheese. Offers of recompense were rejected on the grounds that the visitor was from the country whose soldiers chased away the Nazis. Apparently Americans were expected to pay the market rate and Germans were sent packing.

The cut and thrust of Greek life appealed to me enormously. Catching a bus was an adventure. Asked to point out the stop most convenient for the school, the lady in the next seat provided an answer that seemed to be satisfactory. However, others were not convinced, a neighbour expressing another point of view with such conviction that the entire bus put aside its concerns and joined the discussion. Soon a heated debate began whose subject might just as easily have been the invasion of Iraq or the tactics of *Panathinaikos*. Voices were raised, arms waved and denunciations made with such emphasis that the puzzled traveller assumed that the argument had taken several unexpected turns. The uproar continued till the bus stopped at the school gates whereupon everyone waved cheerfully, pleased to have been of assistance.

Athens fulfilled my expectations. Dazzling light bounced off whitened stone, children played football in the streets, washing hung from lines, brown skins and large ladies were all around, grizzled veterans sat in cafes drinking small cups of black coffee, discussing football or politics and playing backgammon, slamming down the pieces and otherwise waiting patiently. Often I'd watch these old men as they passed the hours with their friends, sheltering from a sun whose power had survived the arrival of autumn.

Nature played its part, encouraging the rawness, brightness and openness that had been missing in my life.

Occasional nights spent in *tavernas* with water and white bread upon the table, drinking *retsina* and *domestica* and nibbling at kebabs were also a revelation. The Greeks seemed warmer and more generous than the Anglo-Saxons, whose influence was resented among the more vociferous youngsters who were helping Athens to find its voice after years of repression. Most people seemed to think that military rule had been a good idea that had lasted too long. Now the Americans had replaced the Colonels as the main targets of protesting youth, and the English were condemned by association. Not that this prevented the local population enjoying the latest James Bond movie in the outdoor cinema. The cheers of the crowd when Roger Moore jumped off a cliff and promptly opened a parachute were suppressed only when the parachute was revealed to be bearing the colours of the Union Jack.

If nothing else, the intervention of the Colonels reminded a nation of the part its ancestors had played in the creation of democracy. In ordinary times, political debate raged hot as locals enjoyed the restored freedom to speak their minds. During an election campaign Athens became a frenzy of agitation. From every car, child and house billowed flags supporting Karamanlis' Nea Democratia or the PASOK left-wingers led by Papandreou or even the middle party trying to make a mark under the leadership of Mr Mavros. In the last few days before the voting these parties held meetings in Syntagma Square in the centre of the city. Every television channel and radio station carried the leaders' speeches yet hundreds of thousands of supporters arrived from around the country to cheer their man, filling trains, buses, pavements and the vast square with their shouts and celebrations.

I attended one of Mr Papandreou's gatherings with a friend. We parked the motorbike in the hills a mile away and joined the throng as it wended its way to the centre of this ancient city. Already the other opposition party had held its meeting with its leader roared on by a crowd of over a million. PASOK needed to respond. The party faithful grouped in front of the cameras so that television showed only pictures of people as large and happy as a bunch of bananas. Hot chestnuts, peanuts and kebabs could be bought on the roads leading to Syntagma, roads packed as far as the eye could see. We fought our way to the front, jostling like an Australian jockey. Girls fainted, their breath taken away by the crush. Cheerleaders mixed patriotic songs with chanted slogans and as the hour of their leader's appearance approached the songs became more stirring. It was not so much a meeting as a celebration.

Finally Papandreou stood before his crowd and began a slow speech, in which accusations were repeated and promises made, or so the translator indicated, though he may have been guessing. Years later I saw Mr Terreblanche give a similar though more theatrical performance in Bloemfontein, for the incorrigible, and indeed intolerable, old right-winger had clearly studied the methods used by Hitler to build his crowd to rapture: the long wait before beginning, the quiet start, romantic phrases, poetic references, an explosion in the middle counterpointed by a softer period that led inexorably to a resounding climax.

That night motorcyclists roared around town tooting horns and waving flags.

Campion School was full of expatriate Englishmen. Ed Carrick was a big, gruff, bluff, bearded man from Bolton who'd taught in Africa before arriving in Athens and becoming Boss's second-in-command. He'd married a lovely Greek girl and the partnership had produced two daughters. They lived in a noisy house full of relatives. Ed spoke Greek fluently and roamed around at centre-forward for our soccer team, which played matches on dirt fields on Sunday afternoons. It was in those forthright engagements that I discovered that running off the ball meant rushing up and down the left side of the field while everyone else kicked the ball around on the right. Many years later Somerset played soccer in Antigua, where my style and neckerchief won widespread support, though putting through the opposing striker for Antigua's only goal may also have helped. Ed had lost a yard or two of pace over the years, tucking into the kebabs as he did, but he was warm, competitive and loyal to Meyer, in whom he had detected a genius who ought not to be judged in detail but rather in great sweeps.

Dr Bridges was our manager, a correct, taciturn, calm but humorous Scot who served as Director of Studies. He'd stand on the touchline sighing, smiling, shaking his head and, one rather suspected, remembering glorious days at Parkhead. Dr Bridges was also the scorer for our cricket team and I was never so pleased as when he said that a backfoot drive of mine had reminded him of Hammond.

George Graves was our resident wit. A product of the London School of Economics, George was left-wing, generous and outspoken. More importantly, he organised our trip to Corfu as well as restoring relations after the riot. Cricket had been played on Corfu since the British had held the island and a rivalry had begun between the three local teams. Matches were played on a patch of grass near the sea around which bathers and shoppers parked their cars. Boundaries could be long or short depending upon the number and location of parked vehicles, a situation that provoked the sort of opportunities neither W.G. Grace nor the Corcyrans were above appreciating.

Campion had lost its first match after some unusual interpretations of the rules by the local men in white. Accordingly our intrepid leaders decided to contribute our own umpire, by way of balancing the scales. Our opponents were dismissed for 80 or so, by most reckonings around 30 under par. Our response began and one of our sacrificial lambs (traditionally, I believe, referred to as 'opening batsmen') edged the first ball and was caught behind the wicket. The bowler who, unbeknownst to the visiting team, had been banned from local soccer owing to an approach regarded even by the Greeks as hot-headed, appealed with all the conviction he could muster, and he was not a man to be underestimated. It took a brave man to turn him down, or a fool, upon which assessment the author expresses no opinion.

Rather earlier than expected our umpire found himself at the epicentre of attention. Hitherto his contributions had been stronger on the social side than upon the field, for cricket was not quite his game. Now he was in a quandary for an answer to the enquiry was momentarily expected and, so far as the fieldsmen were concerned, eagerly anticipated, and there was not a moment to lose. Somewhere in the depths of his mind he may have recalled the rules of the game and thought that, perhaps, things were not looking too bright for his colleague. In this time of reflection he may also have remembered stirring speeches about justice given by men whose names have survived the ravages of time. Left to his own devices he might have done the honourable thing for he was not entirely without conscience and, in truth, the issue was clear cut. But there were other, more pressing matters, to be considered. His appointment to stand in this match had been accompanied by a briefing from a burly figure resembling his employer who had provided a most helpful discourse on the question of subjectivity and objectivity, shedding light upon an issue that for centuries had been confounding the greatest minds. Moreover, our man remembered well enough the events of the previous afternoon and suspected that in more felicitous circumstances his own contribution might have lasted longer.

After due consideration, taking his courage in his hands and notwithstanding widespread dismay upon the field, its most heartfelt form finding its expression in a bowler upon whose countenance the sun no longer shone, our man shook his head.

Even Campion supporters, a group numbering three and including the aforementioned Bridges, a reserve and a fellow from Blackburn who was hoping to promote a brass band festival on the island, were surprised by this turn of events. Tactically it did not at this time seem sensible to prolong the occupation of a batsman whose elevation had been the merest bluff. An awful lot of conscience had been lost in a dubious cause. Still, scowls and glares complete, the bowler stalked back to his mark and presently the game resumed.

Now had come a time for discretion. A man may survive many blows, outstare numerous disappointments and still hold his head high. It is not the harshness that brings him down but the tiny, unendurable slights that follow. Had our batsman pushed back the next few deliveries the crisis might have passed. Alas, he had found the taste for putting bat on ball and swung violently at the following delivery. What trick of the gods it was that caused a man who had not once before struck a cricket ball further than twenty yards to dispatch this mass of moving leather into a distant cafe cannot be guessed. As the ball crossed the boundary there was a sense around the ground that the plot was thickening. Dr Bridges was sufficiently moved to put aside his *Telegraph* crossword.

The bowler was not pleased to find his best offering rudely treated by an incompetent opponent who had already outstayed his welcome. A few men might have responded to this sequence of events with a shrug of the shoulders. One or two might have managed a rueful grin. Our man was not of this ilk. Suddenly the unfairness of life came upon him, the injustices that throughout had conspired against him. Every man has his breaking point and his had been reached. It was time for action. He took hold of the middle stump at the bowler's end and brandished it in the manner of an enraged chef. Finding himself the focus of attention, our umpire took flight, hotly pursued by the offended party. Fearing that their colleague might not emerge unscathed from the forthcoming fracas, our two batsmen took off in pursuit of the bowler in the hope of imposing some restraint. Finding their compatriot out-numbered, the fieldsmen rallied to his cause, and sought with the urgency demanded by the situation to turn the odds more in favour of the hosts. Campions waiting their turn at the crease thought their presence was now required upon a field that had begun to resemble Brighton on one of those weekends when both mods and rockers thought the time had come to pay their respects.

It would be pleasing to report that your author rushed into the hottest part of the engagement with a view to playing some con-structive role in the proceedings. Alas, the truth is less heroic, for it seemed more conducive to spend the time chatting with the good doctor and trying in vain to solve one of the riddles posed by his newspaper.

No bones were broken, relations were eventually restored and the match was abandoned without any lingering acrimony. Next day Campion was legitimately beaten by a team whose champion kept dispatching deliveries not so much into the hotels as over them. Suffice it to say that everyone suffered under his lash, not least a certain conveyor of fastish off-breaks supposedly well suited to the matting wicket. Boss had remained in Athens and was dismayed, not by the disturbance but by the fact that no one had tried slow leg-breaks against this vigorous Corcyran. In the play-ground he demonstrated his various deceits of spin and suggested that underarm bowling be brought back into the game, arguing that the ball lobbed over the batsman's head and landing on the bails was legitimate, unplayable and neglected. He showed me the grips, subtleties and parabolas of underarm bowling and, as an afterthought, provided a cure for hiccups that has given good service, though it did not help the drunken Pakistani painter with permanent hiccups encountered in Sydney some years later.

Dimi was our only Greek player. Dimi ran a clothes shop in Athens and opened the batting with immense tact. His innings were judged, at any rate by their composer, not by their productivity but by their duration. After a match he'd return to inform his friends that he'd remained at the crease for 53 minutes, defying all the efforts of his eleven opponents to bring him down. It was not considered relevant that a mere handful of runs had come his way, and the topic was never raised by colleagues whose task it was to attend to the minor matter of putting some runs upon the board. Dimi's idea of a scampered single consisted of an edge to third man followed by a long period of contemplation and an abrupt, desperate dash to their other end with his little legs pumping until, at last, safety was reached whereupon a triumphant grin would appear upon his face.

Campion itself was a hubbub of activity. Apart from the afternoon siesta when the shutters went up around the city, there was noise everywhere. Institutions, households, teams, schools, companies can be judged in a minute. If it feels right, walk out, let them get on with it. The search for blueprints is without merit. Indeed it is downright dangerous because it has denied us liberalism, stoicism and much else, and put in their places fuss and the arrogance of those who believe the true course has been found. Bedales and Gordonstoun are shadows of their former selves; West Indian parents send their sons back to the Caribbean for a proper education; drugs and youth suicide are rife; children are happier at fifteen and much more miserable at 21. It is a poor swap.

There were about 500 children in the senior school, most of whom arrived on bicycles or buses, ploughing their way through the smog or the crispness that Athens always promised and sometimes produced. A few of the older pupils arrived in stately though still dusty and dented cars and the teachers turned up proudly in beaten-up Minis. English exams were taken and my task was to help the English Department, for which purpose classes were allocated and something that might otherwise have been mistaken for a cupboard provided. Boss suggested that I help an especially bright girl with aspirations to go to Oxford, an achievement the old rogue felt might give the school a push along. Her English was polite, immaculate and detailed but somewhat stilted. His recommended method of instilling a more carefree outlook was unorthodox.

At breaks for rest and provisions the school remained alive, with basketball, volleyball and five-a-side soccer matches being played by teams of various ages and both genders representing houses named after Greek heroes. Munching our *tiropeta* we'd watch these frantic though well-mannered games, especially enjoying the girls' Under-17 soccer because it was played with bounteous enthusiasm and entirely seriously, except that the girls could laugh at themselves, a gift that has by and large eluded the sporting male. No one teased the girls, or wolf-whistled or demeaned them in any way.

Eventually winter arrived and with it rains for which the drains were unprepared so that water flowed down into the city in torrents, causing mayhem and some casualties. The time had come to leave Greece and fly to Australia, a distant land where a fresh start could be made and preparations could begin for my first full season of professional cricket at Somerset. For the next few autumns I would return to Athens for a few weeks on the way to Sydney, catching up with friends, playing cricket and football, enjoying the clarity of the light. Cricket alone stymied any thoughts of putting down roots in that glorious country. It was odd. People thought me so very English yet I was always uncomfortable in the land of my birth, and felt throughout like a man born in the wrong place or, anyhow, at the wrong time.

7

DOWN UNDER

Australia was a distant land about which I knew little. An image formed of a vast, hostile continent thinly populated by leathery people who spoke with deep voices, a rugged lot able to endure drought, fire and a gruelling sun. But it was a long way away, and a fellow arrived with a blank piece of paper.

Australia has become my homeland. I have spent more time there over the last 25 years than in England, where cricketing satisfaction was found and a living earned. Emotional and financial investments were made down under. Once the first and sporting part of my life was over, the idea was to move lock, stock and barrel to the southern hemisphere. Not that things turned out that way, for Devon CCC provided so many rich characters that cricket lasted a decade longer than anticipated.

From the moment of my arrival in Sydney, to take up a position at Cranbrook School, my adopted country surpassed my expectations. The people were direct and took a fellow as they found him. They tried to look for a man's strong points and were not bothered about trivialities. Much could be told from the newspapers. The Australian variety could be forceful and narrow, but could also distinguish between public and private lives. There are no predatory paparazzi or editors mouthing platitudes about freedom of speech or 'the public's right to know' as they exposed some poor soul's folly. Australian papers are neither as prurient nor as puritanical as their English counterparts. Of course it is wrong to tar all English newspapers with the same brush. After all, alongside the Barmy Army, Reggie Perrin, Inspector Frost, P.G. Wodehouse and 'Yes, Minister', *The Times'* letters page counts among its country's greatest attractions.

'Griffo' was the first Australian properly encountered on that first day in Sydney. He was an eccentric from Tasmania (this may be tautological) whose few remaining locks were swept back and whose clothes had not in recent months spent any time with an iron. Griffo had just returned from Germany, where he had studied Brecht in the original language. Music was his first love and Bach, Rachmaninov and Fauré could constantly be heard roaring from his room, in marked contrast to the predictable tunes blaring from record-players elsewhere in the boarding house. Griffo played piano and organ with gusto and sensitivity and, later, discipline. He had played the organs of many of the great churches and attended and sometimes gave concerts, once inviting me to a performance of Fauré's 'Requiem' that was delayed by the non-arrival of the organist, upon which misfortune light was shed only when the purchase of a programme revealed that the concert was to be given by a certain 'J.W. Griffiths'. Griffo was not the most organised of men. He went fossicking for gold once, found some, stored it in a glass in his room and drank the lot after an especially lively evening.

It was all spur of the moment with him. His Mini Moke was always packed with laughing children. Not unlike its owner, the vehicle would not have passed many inspections. Originally yellow, it spent most of its surprisingly long life half-blue after its owner had decided to paint it one morning. Unfortunately supplies ran out midway.

Griffo was a gentle, gifted man and a wonderful influence on many of the boys in junior school. His cricket practices lasted longer than anyone else's and organised chaos prevailed in his classroom. Although he was inclined to forget various parts of the syllabus (say, multiplication), his students produced superb creative work and were devoted to him. He eventually settled in Germany, where he is still rushing around, constantly late for appointments but also capable of sending the soul soaring.

Our Scottish matron took a less generous view and once upbraided him after cockroaches had been found in his bed. Jonathon defended himself, saying that the cockroach had been a particular friend and would be missed.

Griffo did not quite fill the picture of an Australian but, then, nor did my other friends. Our school's history department included Anthony Anderson, an amusing fellow who in previous incarnations had been a lawyer and a fine schoolboy athlete and who said he had been in 'Lawrence of Arabia' ('I was the one with the beard'). He was not entirely convinced about education or boys and taught history from the supposition that no one was listening, a point he proved by moving from the causes of the First World War to the Mau Mau Uprising and back without anyone noticing. We enjoyed many long lunches and cheap meals with bottles of red wine and conversations about goodness knows what. In the end he left education and built a house in the bush, where he lived a somewhat hermitic life.

Toby was my other close friend, a remarkable fellow at once ruthlessly honest and almost recklessly idealistic. Listening to my tirades, he'd bark, 'Instead of stuffing around, why don't you do something?' It has always seemed a good question. He'd played rugby for Australian Schools and was embarked upon a business career before he suddenly went off to India. On his return he went to work in a library, and set out to play his part in the greening of his country. Along the way he has been chased by gangsters, met and sometimes written about some extraordinary people, lived in a hovel, studied philosophy and read widely. 'Knowing you is a process of disillusionment,' he'd announce, adding, 'What the hell are you doing in Australia?' He accused me of flirting with life and he had a point.

Our fellow boarding tutors were a mixed bunch and included an intemperate Irishman who gambled, a delicate chap who always wanted the first cup of tea from the pot, a medical student who put an empty dustbin outside my room after an especially fierce debate, a demented archaeologist who suddenly revealed he was only in it for the money and several gushing Christians.

Cranbrook's cricket coaches were an unusual lot. Until recently, Edgar Castle had been called upon to take a team (there were about 25 of them, so resources were fairly stretched). Apparently he used to stand on the field reading a book of Robert Frost's poetry. Upon his reverie being interrupted by an appeal, he'd decide the issue by the length of time the batsman had been at the wicket, an approach that did not win universal approval. Not that that worried Edgar. George Gassman, head of foreign languages, instructed his charges to use the back of the bat as then fieldsmen would not know which way the ball was going. Jo, a fiery French-man who had been to Cuba and whose entry to the country had not been entirely orthodox, refused to count byes and recorded figures so that 3/51 meant the fellow had taken three wickets and sent down 51 balls. K.J. came from Korea, resembled Buddha and walked around the field while umpiring. Big Al told his Fourth XI to get out as quickly as possible so that they could all go home. Cranbrook had its share of artists, time-servers, disciplinarians, rugby-heads and dedicated teachers, and the mix seemed to work.

The headmaster and his wife, Mr and Mrs Mark Bishop, were my hosts on that first visit, and together they helped a young graduate appreciate their school and their country. Mark was a small, impish and humble man, as likely to be found pulling weeds from the gardens as parading in the state of a headmaster. He was a compassionate man who spent a good part of his time defending boys from the attacks of teachers inclined, for some mysterious reason, to regard them as louts and illiterates. Not that he was a soft touch—far from it—but he had a sense of humour and did not expect boys to behave well. Like Boss he employed a wide range of characters, and especially appreciated those whose life experience offered something unusual, such as membership of the Salvation Army or experience fighting alongside Che Guevara. Mark's passions were chemistry and cricket, and he was often to be found showing an errant, but pleasantly surprised boy who had been sent to his study for other purposes the intricacies of the off-drive. We left Cranbrook at the same time, but unfortunately he did not long enjoy retirement as his health had been poor for many years. His admirable wife survives him.

My arrival at Cranbrook coincided with a cricket coaching course held there and financed by Kerry Packer to show that he was putting something back into the game. Packer spent a million dollars bringing the most promising youngsters in the region to Sydney, putting them up at the school and providing intensive coaching from English professionals hired for the purpose. John Spencer of Sussex was in charge, an enthusiast who bounded around the field with the spring of the Pink Panther, tirelessly spreading laughter and advice. John Barclay was his main assistant and every session ended with hilarious and eventful rigged cricket matches.

These coaches were paid 250 pounds a week, far more than most earned from their county contracts. Of course that was Packer's point. Professional, and especially international, cricketers had been underpaid since the game began. Packer's rebellion was provoked by poor management and the refusal of the game's authorities even to consider his offer for the television rights over the game. As it happened, one of the coaches, Clive Radley, was called away to play for England in Pakistan, and I was given the opportunity to coach for the last two weeks of the course. Not only was my airfare paid, but the idea of running my own courses in the future was firmly planted.

A few months later, the English Test players tried to persuade their county colleagues to refuse to play against the rebels. Rose and Botham spoke to the Somerset players for an hour. Apparently Brearley and Willis were adamant that Snow, Knott, Amiss, Greig and the rest should not be allowed to play for counties and wanted us to go on strike to press the point. Since some of these gentlemen had considered signing for the World Series, their position did seem hypocritical.

I spoke out against the ban, both at Taunton and at a stormy meeting of the Cricketers' Association at Edgbaston, arguing that professional cricketers should not refuse to play against other professionals, and pointing out that, in any case, what cricketers did in the winter was their own concern. David Shepherd from Gloucestershire also spoke up, as did Greig and several more dubious lieutenants, and this view prevailed. Unfortunately, this did not prevent colleagues treating Dennis Amiss disgracefully.

Of course, Australian television covered the cricket, and this season viewers were given the choice between an official series between India and an obscure Australian side, or the great players of the age battling in almost empty stadiums. Packer's men wore coloured clothes and played extraordinary cricket: Richard, Roberts and Lillee were at their peaks and no prisoners were taken as the West Indians tried to prove themselves against Ian Chappell's Australians. Packer expected nothing less, after all he was paying the bills. Years later, some of the West Indians would regard Packer's insistence on the highest possible standards as the turning point in the making of a mighty team. Cricket had taken a leap forwards.

After a couple of years of coaching at Cranbrook, the school began to offer extra English classes to introduce students to Browning, Austen and others from English literature, as well as modern Australian poets, authors and playwrights. At first, I was responsible for the less gifted boys, those who struggled with dyslexia and other reading difficulties. Constructing sentences and paragraphs was beyond them, so my role was to foster their self-esteem. My own spelling has never been the same. Over the years, more academically inclined classes followed, offering a different stimulus.

After a few years cutting my teeth on younger teams, I was put in charge of the First XI. Under my stewardship, the school team started badly, rose to dominate for three years, with long winning streaks and strong connections with local grade clubs, and then faded. It was a wonderful time and many lasting friendships were made, often with cricketers and their families. Many of the friendships made in these years remain intact and many of my former students are now themselves middle-aged, though few seem to realise it. Australians like being eighteen so much that they are reluctant to abandon the posting without a fight.

At the end of every Somerset season I'd return to Sydney and Cranbrook to resume cooking stews, coaching cricket, catching up with friends on the staff and around the cricket team, running madcap camps for youngsters aged from six to thirteen to pay the airfare and generally enjoying the cheap restaurants, beaches and theatres on offer. Outward Bound was tried and all the worst-behaved boys in the form were put into my group, whereupon they managed to discover short cuts and other schemes calculated to make ten days spent sleeping in the drought-ravaged outdoors (literally, in my case, as the blessed tent refused to open) pass more comfortably. They supplemented our diet of beetroot, sultanas and tuna with tins of stew and soup gathered on expeditions undertaken, it was later understood, mainly for the purpose of smoking cigarettes.

Apart from running cricket camps, I spent the summer holidays visiting chums in the farming area. David Alexander captained Cranbrook in the late 1970s and stayed with me in England in the early 1980s, impressing all and sundry with his left-arm swingers and dry observations. His father wrote that masterpiece 'I'd Like to Have a Beer with Duncan' which Slim Dusty took to the top of the charts. David worked on a farm out in Euchareena, a tiny settlement twenty miles from Orange. Euchareena was a pitiful sight during the drought of the early 1980s. Hardly a blade of grass survived the long dry and owners unable to provide fodder for their animals were forced to watch them decline. Nothing could be done to save land or cattle. Still the sun shone, browning the arms of the farmers, drying the lips of the children and burning the protruding ribs of the animals. Many cows died on David's farm: some were sent away to the coast only to die when the rains finally came, swept away by torrents which could not penetrate the hard, dry surface of the land. A year later the grass was green and water filled reservoirs from which cows gulped.

And so the years passed, eight of them, and always the welcome was warm. Now and then the thought did occur that something more serious and substantial ought to be attempted but perhaps the dogged, defiant opening batsman needed this warm counterpoint. Cricket stretched my character and I have never felt any regrets about accepting its challenges. Dangerously so, it was my life and my measure of self-esteem, but little thought has been given to life thereafter.

Cricket was not a trivial concern but a means of expression and exploration. Some comedians fall into despair, convinced that their abilities should have been put to better use. Others remember the almost incomparable importance of laughter.

Cranbrook provided eight wonderful years, until I was asked by the *Sunday Times* to cover an Ashes tour of Australia. By then I had written several books, had published some articles in

Australian newspapers and my first season as captain of Somerset had ended in a nasty and prolonged power struggle. It is now time to return to Somerset to describe the rise and fall of that fine team, the first in the history of the county to put trophies in the cupboard.

8

SOMERSET RESURGENT: 1978–79

Much had changed at Somerset as the 1978 season began. Viv Richards had emerged as a great batsman with a fierce, combative temperament and an array of shots that did not so much dissect opponents as brutalise them. Here was an uncompromising man who entered the arena with the majesty and power of an African chief and the menace of a heavyweight champion. Aroused by Tony Greig's remark about making the West Indians 'grovel', and helped by a drought that scorched outfields, softened balls and exhausted bowlers, Richards had torn the Englishmen apart in 1976. During the Packer years he confirmed his reputation as one of the most destructive batsmen the game had seen. No longer did Viv cut loose for an hour and then throw away his wicket. Now there was an authority about him, a hunger that could be sensed at the bowler's end. Always he was a great competitor, always he believed in his team, an approach that made him a formidable opponent and a daunting colleague. Nor did he ever underestimate opposing teams. Whereas Botham was inclined to bluster, Richards was respectful because he did not want to be accused of complacency or arrogance. Strutting was reserved for the performance, and afterwards he was often to be found talking quietly in the bar. He chose his company carefully and had a mind that penetrated like a saw through soft wood.

Botham's life had also changed as, to the surprise of all save those raised alongside him, he burst into the England team, taking wickets against the distracted Australians of 1977 and scything down teams weakened by losses to World Series. Relishing the opportunity to represent his country and enjoying stages that others found intimidating, he played for England as he did for pub, club and county. Slowly the cricket fraternity realised that a force had been let loose, a young man without fear or inhibition, an all-rounder more skilful than he appeared. In the guise of a roughneck from a troubled, semi-industrial town located in the least appetising corner of a previously unfashionable county, had appeared a cricketer capable of changing matches and seizing the imagination. Botham craved attention and, armed with bat and ball, he grabbed it.

Richards' strength lay in his determination to set the mood of a match. He was a powerful, sometimes brooding force, a predator with a fierce, pent-up energy. Botham was an extrovert. He relied upon intuition and instinct. Whereas Richards was essentially solitary, an observer in the dressing-room, Botham belonged in a crowd, a joker searching for laughter and warmth. Rejection and isolation were his greatest fears and they drove him towards the light. Accordingly he gathered cronies around him, went to pubs and drank and belched and was outrageous. Enemies had to be destroyed because they threatened, not so much his reputation as his state of mind. Of course he did not argue with them. Instead he took the rest of the world along with him on his journey and used his popularity to turn the tables. He was a master of public relations. Somewhere hidden, though, could still be found the scared young man. His mighty deeds secured the acclaim that alone could silence those voices. Far from being a simpleton, he is a complex character whose actions alone indicate the truths of his personality.

Somerset had also signed a second West Indian cricketer, Joel Garner, a tall fast bowler from Barbados. Roberts and Holding had signed for Kerry Packer. Joel soon joined his contemporaries in the rebel cause and presently his reputation soared as high as his head. Although Holding and Roberts asked Somerset to sign them, Roy Kerslake, our chairman, a Cambridge Blue who captained his county for a single season in 1968, after which he concentrated upon his work as a solicitor in Taunton and captaining the Second XI in his reserved and kindly way, had steadfastly sought Garner and he took the committee along with him. Garner had already helped Somerset to defeat the 1977 Australian touring side in Bath, in an eventful three days during which Brian Close scored a duck and walked through a glass door. Graham Burgess and Ian Botham took wickets and Brian Rose scored runs. For the time being, 'Big Bird' Garner was only available sporadically because he was committed to playing League cricket at weekends. Had he played on Sundays, Somerset could not have been stopped; but, then, the anguish of defeat made victory all the more memorable.

Brian Rose had replaced Close as county captain. He had not been the players' choice. Rightly, club and team wanted to make a leap forwards which meant choosing a captain from the younger brigade. Peter 'Dasher' Denning had a lot of support, because he was popular, stubborn, honest and inclined to regard anyone living outside his county with a mixture of pity and naked hostility. Gruff, intelligent and the son of a butcher from Chewton Mendip, Dasher was well liked and respected. Rose, on the other hand, was an enigma. He seemed to live in his own world and was on that account called 'Dozy Rosey'. Later the players realised that he had merely been thinking and he was rather sharper than had been supposed. In his six-year stint as leader Somerset would win numerous trophies, though not the championship, be turfed out of a competition after declaring at 1/0 and endure internal turmoil as the players started their own business selling clothes, books and other mementoes to supporters.

From the start of the 1978 season there was an ambition within the team that had previously been missing. Partly by chance and partly by design, a tough, gifted and hungry collection of players had come together, a group determined to bring glory to their county and prepared to risk unpopularity in its pursuit. The sense of identity was strong and bound together a diverse bunch of men. Looking back, it must seem surprising that Somerset did not win everything in the four years when the team was at its peak. But winning competitions is not easy, besides which desperation creates pressures of its own. Also Botham was away a good deal playing Test cricket, Garner concentrated on one-day cricket and only once took more than 50 county wickets in a season and Richards was an explosive rather than metronomic player. Moreover, other teams also fielded two overseas players—Clive Rice and Richard Hadlee at Notts, Imran Khan and Javed Miandad at Sussex—and some of them were far more streetwise than the men of the cider county. Finally Somerset just wanted to win something, anything.

Determined to secure a regular place in the side in all forms of the game, I put my head down at the start of that season and kept it down till the last ball was bowled. A century against New Zealand and a run chase in Bath were the highlights, but consistency and fluency were missing. The accolades bestowed upon a raw young batsman owed more to the success of the team than any unusual merit in his game. Of course I was neither ready nor good enough for a higher calling. Watching myself on television for the first time was disconcerting. Who was this tense, angular, awkward creature? Thereafter I avoided doing so, and in the ensuing 26 years have not repeated the experience.

Despite the presence of two foreigners in most teams, and the availability of most of the outstanding players of the era, county cricket was not obviously stronger in the 1970s. It has changed, that is all. Defensive skills and craftsmanship have been replaced by a belligerence that reflects an age in which youth has been given its head.

Somerset fought hard throughout the season and by August still had a chance of winning two trophies: the 40-over Sunday League played before packed crowds and the 60-over Gillette Cup knockout competition, whose final at Lord's had become the climax of the domestic season. Our championship run had petered out in the last few weeks of the season.

Somerset had played superbly in the 60-over matches. Warwickshire had reached 292/5 only to be overwhelmed by an angry, explosive century from Richards. Viv did not like Bob Willis, and he was not alone in that. Still enraged about remarks the fast bowler had supposedly made years before, the Antiguan batted with restrained fury as he struck an unbeaten 145. During the course of the innings he was caught behind the wicket off the paceman, but stood his ground, chewed harder upon his gum and stared down his opponent. No one had chased as many runs before but Somerset romped home. Fortunately I played my part, helping Viv with an attacking innings that took advantage of the tighter fields inevitably set for all his partners, except his friend from Yeovil. Actually Viv and Botham were not all that close. No cricketer was close to Viv. Peter 'Jock' McCombe remained his sole confidant and many times I'd go around to the modest house of the cheery Scotsman to find the greatest batsman alive watching 'Starsky and Hutch' or a cricket video.

Glamorgan were crushed and Kent overcome, which left Somerset facing Essex in a semi-final to be played in Taunton. By then our small ground was packed hours before any one-day match. Players arriving a couple of hours before play was due to begin were obliged to thread their way through long queues. Spectators watched from trees and a bridge spanning the River

Tone, into whose murky waters Botham and I once plunged to satisfy some wager or other. Inside the ground the atmosphere was a mixture of frenzy and expectation, with songs and shouts blending with screams as something went awry. Yet Somerset remained a rural, amateurish club scarcely able to carry the weight of this team. Our committee consisted mainly of amiable but dim farmers, reflecting an ageing membership boosted on Sundays by the arrival of youngsters and workers. Everyone in the county had but a single thought. Somerset had to win something.

Essex were every bit as desperate to secure their first trophy and the meeting of these emerging teams became an epic. Richards scored 116 and Roebuck 57 as Somerset reached 287/6 in its 60 overs. The next few hours were excruciating for all concerned, inside and outside the ground, listening on radios or watching on television. With ten overs to go, Essex were 67 runs adrift with six wickets in hand. It sounds like a doddle but winning is not that easy, especially with Botham and Garner still to complete their allocated overs. Hitherto ineffective, Botham ran out Pont, who had hit two sixes, and then held a stinging return catch to remove Keith Fletcher. Another run out followed and with two overs left the visitors needed 18. Twelve were required from the final over to be bowled, owing to some miscalculation by Colin Dredge, immortalised by Alan Gibson as 'the demon from Frome'. Unfortunately the demon was not especially demonic. An edge eluded our usually reliable wicketkeeper, a no-ball was caught on the boundary by the author and three runs were needed off the last ball as nine fieldsmen protected the boundary and prayed the ball would go elsewhere. The hush around the ground was extraordinary. Dredge looked like he was going to the scaffold. Hardened journalists hardly dared to watch. John Lever sliced the ball to deep cover and the tenth wicket pair ran for their lives. Rose collected the ball at point, threw hard and low, Taylor grabbed the bouncing ball and dived upon the stumps with the Essex man a foot short of his ground. The crowd erupted, Somerset players hugged each other, tears were shed in the visitors' room. For the defeated it was a long drive home. Not that Essex had been beaten for the scores had been tied and Somerset had reached the final on the technicality of fewer wickets lost. It was a match that contained so many of the qualities that allow sport to hold such a prominent place in the minds of those whose lives are otherwise undramatic.

Somerset had reached a Cup Final at Lord's and a young team was within sight of fulfilling its dream. In hindsight this match was our final because we had given our all, and were now weary beyond the reach of recreation. We had been living on our nerves for the past four months, and the strain was showing. Regardless, Somerset reached the climactic weekend of the domestic season with two trophies within our grasp. Moreover, we were favourites to win both trophies. Caveats were voiced only by those familiar with the history of the club and aware of the weariness of the players.

Alas, Somerset did not rise to the occasion at Lord's and were decisively beaten by a fresher, calmer Sussex team. After Rose had driven fourteen runs off Imran Khan's opening over, our innings fell into meek decline. It is one thing to perform in front of cheering supporters on a familiar ground, quite another to play relaxed cricket at this historic ground and in front of the great men of the game. Most particularly it is exposing, so that newcomers feel as if they are lying on a slab with a hundred doctors staring at them. To walk into the ground on Cup Final day is to sense a high-pitched atmosphere calculated to add to any insecurities. To walk out to bat through a hushed Long Room is to follow in the footsteps of Bradman and Armstrong and the rest of them. Most of us shrank from the light that day, and afterwards realised the need to relax on the big occasions. We felt like a rural repertory company let loose in the West End.

My performance was abject, a knee-high full-toss lifted to mid-on, but the failure was valuable and my next 12 finals reached with Somerset and Devon ended in victory. Although Viv scored 44, even he seemed burdened by his responsibilities that day at headquarters and eventually fell hitting out. Botham alone bestrode the occasion. His energy and confidence seemed boundless as he swept sixes over midwicket in an innings of 80 that alone illuminated a tentative effort. Even on a slow pitch, Somerset's 207/7 was inadequate and Botham tried to put matters right with a hostile opening spell, a strategy that backfired as Sussex rushed to 93/0. The beefy allrounder returned and, snorting like a bull, removed first Barclay and then Imran, after first hitting the Pakistani on the head. Garner dismissed Miandad as Sussex slipped to 108/4. Unfortunately the aggression could not be sustained and our opponents romped home, with Paul Parker scoring the important runs.

After accepting our loser's medals and a cheque for 2000 pounds we sat silent and inconsolable in the dressing-room. Eventually we packed our bags and made our way through still cheering supporters to our cars. After all there was another crucial match to play next day, a meeting with Essex at our county ground to decide the John Player League.

Inevitably the ground was abuzz long before the players reported for action. Before the match Somerset made a fateful decision. Garner had returned to Taunton with a view to playing in this match. Hallam Moseley had been a regular member of the 40-over side but counted as the second overseas player. A choice had to be made. Desperate to secure a trophy, most of the players wanted Garner to play. Rose and Kerslake decided otherwise.

Essex reached 180 on another sluggish pitch, a total raised by some expensive overs towards the end as lesser men tried to fill Garner's boots. Our chase went along in fits and starts, with several batsmen scoring 30 or so and no one summoning the decisive innings. Eventually 9 runs were needed from the final six balls with two wickets left. Our tailenders swished and ran and the crowd shrieked and died a thousand deaths but it was not to be.

Afterwards the players sat in the bowels of the pavilion in utter silence, pretending to read papers, anything to help them slip into private worlds. Viv picked up his bat and smashed it against a wall in the room, like a maddened lumberjack attacking a tree. He had tears in his eyes, and he was not the only one. Those cynical about sport and sportsmen, especially professionals, should have been in the Somerset room in that devastating hour. No one was thinking about money or personal glory. A long, exhausting journey had been undertaken, a bond had been formed, a promise made to tens of thousands of supporters and at the last, the very last, and by the narrowest of margins, we had failed. Somerset still had not won a trophy. Not a word was said. There was nothing to say.

Viv was especially distraught for he took each defeat personally, like a death in the family. Perhaps, that day, he took a vow that it was not going to happen again. Subsequently he did much less on the road to Lord's and much more on the day itself. Indeed he used to walk around the players' balcony on the new pavilion in the early rounds saying, 'Take me to Lord's, boys, take me to Lord's.'

Outside the pavilion thousands of supporters were refusing to go home, singing and chanting and demanding that the players take a bow. In the end we dragged ourselves up to the viewing room and responded to their roars. Their loyalty helped to remind us that it had been a wonderful season in which many great battles had been won. Moreover we were a young side still, and nowhere near the end of our road. Slowly spirits returned and players started changing and going home to their families or else out to wakes with friends or each other.

Unable to summon any interest and with nothing at stake in the last match of the season, I rested and then went off to Athens and

Sydney. It is part of a county cricketer's life that he sees the same fellows every day for five months, shares their dreams, dreads, arguments, amusements, bedrooms, cars, baths, meals, joys and despairs and then, suddenly, in mid-September everyone goes their separate ways, calling out 'See you in April' as the door closes. Of course those whose contracts have not been renewed or whose bodies or minds can no longer take the strain will not return. For them the door has closed for the last time. Many never come back to the ground. It is all more fragile than it seems. Players live under a cloak of confidence that hides the nakedness of their insecurity.

Defeat did not harm Somerset. At the time it hurt enormously, but the setbacks led to a fury of effort the following year. Not until years later, as the intensity eased, did the cracks begin to show as hitherto hidden differences between management and players, particularly the top players and their confidants, slowly turned into mutual mistrust and a struggle for power that weakened this same team to such an extent that it finished bottom of the championship in 1985, Botham's second and worst year as captain.

Meanwhile the averages revealed that my wicket had cost the bowlers 31 runs so they had not exactly been shopping in Harrods. Viv finished 13th overall with 45 an innings, behind a distinguished list that captured the strength of the competition and read Rice, Turner (Glenn), Greenidge, Amiss, Hampshire, Davison, Proctor, McEwan, Asif, Lamb and Randall.

Somerset players returned to Taunton for the new season of 1979 as a hungry team approaching its peak. Garner could play the entire summer, which gave the attack a menace missing when Botham was absent. Marks had completed his degree course, in classics he thought, and was also available all season. Soon Somerset signed Nigel Popplewell, an engaging young cricketer currently at Cambridge whose dad was a senior lawyer, a profession Nigel seemed likely to join after his fling in professional cricket. After the university season he stayed in my house, one of many Somerset players to do so.

Strengthened by these fine cricketers, Somerset started the campaign with a succession of victories. Inevitably the Benson & Hedges Cup was our first target, simply because it was the first trophy to be decided. After winning our opening three matches of the division Somerset arrived in Worcester needing to beat our hosts to move into the quarter-finals. Steady rain fell on the first of the two days assigned for the contest. For a day we sat glumly watching the rain come tumbling down. In truth we did not expect to play at all as the forecast was poor. Next morning we returned to the ground to find puddles and a forlorn aspect all around. We had too much time on our hands, time to think about how things could go wrong once again.

In the dressing-room thoughts turned to the various situations that might arise later in the day. Concern was felt about a pitch that had been under covers for several days and was bound to misbehave. Insecurity increased as the hours passed. We just wanted to reach the next round and were aghast to find that our position remained vulnerable. Presently we discovered that defeat in a long match might well cost us a place in the next round on run rate, but that a swift demise meant we'd still advance as our rates would not be harmed. Debate began to rage. After considering the possibilities I pointed out that to avoid losing too much ground, Somerset could declare its innings closed at any convenient moment. Alternatively the bat could be thrown and outrageously aggressive fields set to ensure a quick finish, the approach taken by a rival county in these circumstances.

No sooner had the words been uttered than I wished them back where they belonged, for the discussion became serious and heated, with Viv and Joel insisting that Ian Chappell would not hesitate to take advantage of the rules and that victory must be pursued with complete ruthlessness. Botham was also gung-ho about the idea and not a word was heard against it, although reservations may have been voiced in the private conversations which took place on the balcony throughout the debate. Qualification matches were about qualifying, nothing more or less. Why not declare? At least it was honest and within the rules. Rose went off to ring officials at Lord's and returned with the news that declaring was indeed within the rules but that it was bound to be controversial and to provoke a change of rules for the following year. Lord's would later deny that any conversation along these lines had taken place, in effect calling our captain's word into doubt, which added to our sense of injustice when the sword of Damocles fell.

Accordingly the hotheads, myself included, won the day. Somerset batted first and declared its innings closed after a single over. Afterwards half England claimed to be sitting in the stands. School parties, farmers, members and visitors from near and far were reported to be waxing indignant about this strategy. Suffice it to say that the ground looked miserable and empty on that damp, windswept afternoon in the middle of another dull English week. Those present, and there may have been a dozen, were spared the misery of sitting almost alone on a cold day watching a match of doubtful interest! Instead, they were treated to the sort of self-important drama sport alone seems to provide.

No sooner had our opponents scored the winning runs than we jumped into our cars and went home, still top of the table but suspecting that the last had not been heard of our manoeuvre. Of course, we did not get away with it. A hue and cry broke out across the land. Members resigned and others wrote strong letters of support as the players, and especially the captain, were condemned. Other counties claimed to be outraged, especially Glamorgan, who demanded our place in the quarter-finals. Inevitably ranks closed at Lord's and although some of our rivals expressed sympathy, we were expelled from the competition. Team meetings followed, with players advocating legal action against Lord's for our case was strong. We believed we had acted within rules that had so often been our undoing and were indignant that the truth of the matter was not being told. Fortunately calmer counsel prevailed, with Colin Atkinson, the senior man at the club and also a former captain, managing to persuade the players to put the episode behind them.

If nothing else the declaration showed the sense of desperation within the team. It is not easy to put into words the desire to win that first trophy for the county, or the nagging fear that it might never happen.

By the middle of the season Somerset had only two trophies to think about. Helped by drier weather in the east, Essex had run away with the championship and despite playing incisive cricket for a few months the gap did not close and our interest faded. Fortunately the team was playing superbly in the one-day competitions and gradually the crowds, noise and expectations grew, and a sense that this time no one born of man was going to stop the charge.

Somerset started well in the Sunday League and did not suffer a defeat until the tenth match when Leicestershire once again exploited our weak points. Meanwhile Derbyshire were trounced in the Gillette Cup in a match entirely forgotten until it turned up in a relation's scrapbook. Kent were our opponents in the quarter-final. Unfortunately we batted poorly on a damp pitch and scored only 180 or so. Disappointment hung heavy in the air before a plan was hatched. Garner was not the easiest man to rouse and usually saved his most venomous spells for Lancashire, on the grounds that he had been rejected by them. Otherwise he was too good-natured and professional to allow emotion to interfere with his performance. Something special was needed from him or the cause was lost. Accordingly I sloped up to Joel and expressed surprise about something said by the opposing captain. Joel was interested. 'What dat man say?' he asked, and listened intently as the news was relayed that the visiting skipper thought that 'though Garner gets some bounce you couldn't call him fast'. Joel was stirred and asked, 'He say that?' Several colleagues confirmed that they had heard the remark. Garner sent down thunderbolts and, amidst roars that must have been heard in Bristol, Kent were routed for 60 runs. Of course Alan Ealham had not said anything of the sort.

In between these heady occasions, my 85 not out helped Somerset to save the match against an Indian team that included Sunil Gavaskar, Dillip Vengsarkar, Gundappa Vishwanath, Kapil Dev and the spin twins, Bedi and Chandrasekhar. On a previous tour Chandra had seemed formidable, sending the ball climbing over the batsman's head. Richards regarded him as the best bowler he had faced because he could produce a delivery and sometimes a spell that was unplayable. By 1979 though, Chandra's powers were waning. Bedi remained a master of flight and guile but spin seemed to be in decline. Even five years before men like David Allen and John Mortimer put so much energy on the ball that it dipped in flight. Bedi was almost the last of that school. The ball seemed to be on a string as it made its way down the wicket. A batsman could step forwards without feeling he was getting any closer to the ball. Somehow it dangled and dropped before biting and turning from the pitch. Unable to read his changes of pace and flight, I decided to advance yards down the pitch or else to go right back on the stumps, and to make that decision before each ball was bowled and thereafter not to take any notice of trajectory. At least this way Bedi could not guess where his opponent was going to be, which made the struggle more even. I hit a couple of sixes and I survived a few miscues. Nonetheless, 85 not out against a strong Indian side was encouraging. Trevor Gard, our tiny reserve keeper who also kept ferrets, was my last partner and once stood at the bowler's end staring at the umpire after an appeal for leg before against me with the air of a man saying, 'Well, that was obviously out!', an approach that undermined my attempts to distract the white coat by feigning interest in a quick single. He did not repeat the offence. Mayhem has its uses. Force the umpire to hop around and he might forget about the appeal. Not that it ever worked but a fellow cannot be blamed for trying.

Middlesex were our opponents in the semi-final of the 60-over competition. Rose won the toss on a damp pitch and our pace bowlers dismissed the locals for 185. Thousands of Somerset supporters had turned up, far more than anticipated by the ground authorities so that more gates and stands had to be opened. Somerset had never fielded such a side and these supporters knew that only a few thousand tickets were allocated for the final. Accordingly they caught trains and hired coaches for this midweek match. Garner and Burgess took most of the wickets.

Peter Denning scored 90 not out as the match was won with wickets and time to spare. Accordingly and astonishingly, Somerset approached the decisive weekend of the season in almost exactly the same position as the previous year. This time, though, Kent had an advantage in the Sunday League and the pressure was on them. Beating Northamptonshire at Lord's was our only ambition. Other things could take care of themselves.

Our approach was altogether more relaxed. Rose, Richards and Garner missed the match played in Brighton in the days before the final. The notion that teams arrived at Lord's fresh and ready for the fray is erroneous. One year Somerset played on 33 out of 35 days, the 35th being the final itself. Many of the players were asleep on the floor of the dressing-room as Somerset batted in the match before Lord's.

On this occasion, however, to arrive at our London hotel that night for the final was to find Richards at his most sparkling. At such times his eyes had a brightness about them that spread around the team. Of course the team meeting was a disaster. No helpful points were made. Somerset did not bother much with analysis because we could not see any reason to change our game to accommodate opponents. Our focus was on playing our own game as well as possible. In any case no one had much to say about the Northants players except that they could not play Garner, which was hardly a revelation. Our group was small and consisted only of players, Roy Kerslake and a physiotherapist who had recently replaced a masseur capable of keeping players on the field because he was about eighty and blessed with cold hands. Peter Robinson was the coach and he was mainly involved with the Second XI. Cricket had not yet been taken over by support staff trying to justify inflated wages by demonstrating the importance of their contributions. The dressing-room belonged to the players, and the responsibility for their performances lay with the cricketers themselves. Thank goodness there was no 'team Somerset' or huddles or any other form of poppycock.

Richards was mighty and destructive as he nonchalantly and carefully flicked the ball away on that memorable Saturday morning in St John's Wood. No chances were taken. This was not the overwhelming, risk-taking, brutal Richards seen on so many occasions. He was cool and considered, a soldier picking his way through a bombsite, wary of traps yet pressing forwards with intent. Not until the penultimate over did he cut loose, backing away from his stumps to carve boundaries over cover. It was a towering performance, a statement of greatness, a man bending a match to his will, a repetition of the innings he had constructed in the World Cup Final at the height of that same summer.

Northants chased valiantly and, despite losing early wickets to Garner, stayed in the game until Geoff Cook was run out. Allan Lamb's forceful innings was ended by a superb stumping, where-upon Garner returned as our supporters started to realise that their long wait was over. On the field, those last few minutes were a strange period. Finally the deed had been done. The result was not in doubt. In some way we wanted to rush from the field to begin the celebrations. In other ways we wanted to remain out there for ever because this was the hour. It was not going to get any better. At last the tenth wicket fell and then came the mad dash to the rooms as the crowd invaded the pitch.

Recapturing that moment of victory, finding words to express the elation felt by a group of competitors in the hour of hard-pursued triumph is not the easiest of tasks. It is the sensation for which sportsmen yearn, the sense of meaning and unity obtained at the end of a long and successful campaign fought alongside friends in a common cause, a campaign that had included times of sharp disappointment, times when this hour seemed far distant. It is the feeling of uncomplicated camaraderie, of uncompromised accomplishment, of something shared and binding that had finally been achieved. Players hugged each other, the crowd could scarce forbear to cheer and even the quietest among us felt a profound sense of satisfaction. A sprint from the scene of fulfilment and a stride through the Long Room took the players into the noise of an already filling dressing-room. Champagne flowed and the more emotional players chatted excitably. A vast throng of supporters gathered beneath the balcony, 10 000 Romeos singing, chanting and calling for the players to acknowledge them. After the cup was presented to our captain, the players held it and some kissed it warmly enough to delight any partner. It had taken 104 years but the deed had been done.

Eventually the tumult subsided into a mere hubbub. After an hour or two the ground started to empty for there were journeys to be undertaken, to Nottingham or back to Chewton, babysitters to be relieved, lives to be resumed. Sportsmen feel themselves at the epicentre of a storm but meanwhile traffic lights keep changing. The players began to shower and put on their civvies, but no one wanted to leave the pavilion. We were drunk more upon happiness than alcohol. In some respects those quiet minutes of unwinding were the most rewarding of all, with players alone again and reflecting upon the day in their own ways: Denning puffing on a miniature cigar, Botham horsing around, Richards bubbling away in his exhaustion, Rose hardly saying a word, Burgess, the veteran, sipping and smoking and remembering that he had only one match left to play and then it was over, as it one day ends for us all.

Not that the players could linger in London. As dusk fell across Lord's we carried our kits to our cars and began the long drive through the streets of London and out onto the M1 and towards Nottingham, where professional cricket had been started 130 years before as working men realised the value of their skills with cloth or upon the sporting field. The journey passed in a trance and seemed to take five minutes. Everyone was eager to reach the hotel to resume the celebrations. Many cars bearing Somerset supporters were passed and there was much hooting. These were the unspoilt days. Somerset had won a trophy and the taste was sweet. Now it was a question not of fearing defeat but of pursuing further victories.

Nor was it an especially late night in Nottingham for there was business still to be done. Going to bed directly was a waste of time because the adrenalin was flowing and there was a lot to talk about. In any case some of the players were owls, especially Garner, who preferred five hours of sound sleep to eight hours of tossing and turning. At about 1 a.m. most of us put aside our refreshments and went to bed. Kent might slip up. Certainly we had no intention of losing. Confidence was high.

Inspired by the cheers of our supporters, Somerset reached 185 on a slightly unreliable pitch at Trent Bridge. My 50 was comfortably the top score and indicated an easing of the tension within. In the field Somerset took a couple of wickets, only to be held by a rousing partnership between Tim Robinson and Clive Rice. At last a third wicket fell whereupon Colin Dredge, who had not played the previous day, took another crucial wicket. Meanwhile roars from spectators who were listening to their transistors suggested that Kent were wilting.

As wickets tumbled in Nottingham and Canterbury the noise grew louder as players and supporters realised that a second title was to fall into the safekeeping of a county so long denied. Botham took the last wicket, whereupon everyone charged from the field. Now the room was full of laughter for this second triumph was unexpected and had been more of a team effort than Lord's. The trophy arrived in its helicopter and Rose embraced it and his men were jubilant. Afterwards we settled in the rooms, joy unconfined. Of course we had to drive home that night but the journey could wait. No more matches had to be played. The season was over. Five months and several years of intense effort had been rewarded. Graham Burgess stayed longer than most. Eventually he walked out onto the balcony and hung his capacious boots from a post.

Rose deserves considerable credit for the successes of his team. Captaincy is not as straightforward an occupation as it seems. Admittedly he was leading a highly motivated young team containing great players and numerous intelligent and powerful characters. But he was also presiding over a change in the club that involved the gradual replacing of older players. Moreover, he had to keep his side together for five months while surviving the inevitable setbacks, insecurities and differences and still performing upon the field, for a struggling captain swiftly loses his authority.

Celebrations resumed in Taunton with an open-decker bus ride around town, official recognition from the local authorities and various soccer matches at which the trophies were displayed to large crowds. Somerset took its soccer seriously and debates about selection and strategies were far more intense than occurred with the cricket. Kitchen, Dredge, Richards, Botham and Rose were fine players and some of the veterans could hold their own.

Opponents were surprised by our competitiveness, especially by the crunching tackles produced by Denning and other suspects.

Somerset had enjoyed its best season. Fortunately I had played my part. My batting had improved and I had made satisfactory contributions in both forms of the game. Chasing targets, batting on dodgy pitches and building partnerships had become strong points. An inability to play long innings was my main weak point, a point reflected in figures indicating that I had scored 1273 runs in first-class cricket at an average of 47 with a top score of 89. My name had been mentioned among the candidates to tour Australia but obviously such talk was premature. Of course the high average and the failure to reach three figures were connected. Every fibre in my body, every part of my brain, an entire personality was concentrated upon avoiding failure. Reaching 50 was the aim for then the head could be held high. Every innings was an ordeal. Every innings began with the fear of a low score, especially a duck, and the humiliation and loss of respect that seemed bound to follow. To relax was to risk ignominy. To get out was a calamity to be avoided at all cost. People praised my courage but the truth was that, even in these times of fast bowling and little protection, the fear of failure was stronger than the fear of getting hit. Accordingly, I became hard to dislodge but incapable of taking the steps needed to dictate terms to a tiring attack. Repeatedly I'd fight my way to 50 and then lose my wicket. Only in run chases or when trouble was brewing was the effort sustained, for then I was obliged to leave the cocoon. Not until 1984 did I realise that scoring hundreds was not so difficult, whereupon my game turned on its head as consistency was replaced by rank failures and numerous centuries. By then I had written books and experienced success outside the game so the world had become a different place.

9

MIXED RESULTS:
1980–82

After the highs of 1979 came the flatness of a dull, wet season that contained few moments of illumination, several disappointments, one controversy and not much else. The West Indies were touring so Garner and Richards were missing for most of the summer. Somerset's search for a top-class fast bowler was fruitless and Graeme Pollock reluctantly rejected the county's imaginative approach. Fortunately Sunil Gavaskar was willing to play for a season and his arrival continued the custom of bringing brilliant cricketers to the county. Moreover Ravi Tikkoo, who owned the world's two biggest tankers, was willing to pay his wages.

Gavaskar went quietly about his cricket. Certainly he was not as imposing as Richards. Doubtless on his own patch he was formidable. Among county professionals he preferred to show his impish side, making dry and amusing remarks now and then but otherwise attending to his own affairs. He lived modestly with Pam, his wife, and Rohan, a son named after Kanhai, a batsman held in awe by colleagues and opponents. Gavaskar did not like to practise before play began and instead followed his own rhythms, thinking about his innings and also submitting to the fate bestowed by the Hindu gods to whom he regularly performed *siva*. He did not like to be disturbed in prayer or preparation but otherwise seemed to find his team-mates amusing and the situation more relaxing than in the pressure cooker atmosphere of Bombay or Calcutta. Occasionally he batted in the nets and then I'd watch and marvel at how late he played the ball. At times he did not seem to move until the ball was upon him and then he'd roll his wrists or else tuck it away behind square.

A damp summer brought green pitches and most batsmen struggled to find their best form. Gavaskar was inconsistent and often edged catches to the slip cordon. Perhaps he sensed he was living in Viv's shadow. Sunil had criticised the West Indians in a book and there was some tension between them. Also the routine of county cricket must have been deadening for a man reliant on his spirit. Few Indians have enjoyed the life of the county professional. In any event, Gavaskar experienced mixed fortunes and was a popular member of the side, although he did not seem to appreciate my driving as on several occasions he went as white as a rice pudding.

Hugh Gore was our other overseas player, a left-armer from Antigua recommended by Richards, who arrived several curries over par, bowled superbly on occasion but spent most of the summer on the treatment table. Not until 1982 were counties limited to a single imported player, but those with pre-existing contracts were allowed to continue until their careers were over.

My form was poor and old habits returned. Selected to play for the MCC against the county champions in the traditional opening fixture of the season, I felt out of place and failed miserably. Nor did things improve in Taunton and frustration set in. Before long, and quite rightly, I was dropped from the side. Most cricketers suffer reverses but it's no use telling an intense young batsman that it is all part of growing up. My confidence was in my boots and I became testy.

In hindsight the 1980 season was not so awful, merely forget-
table. Some runs were scored and some victories secured. Indeed
Somerset finished in respectable positions in both Sunday League
and the championship, without ever quite threatening to win
either trophy. But the campaign ended on a sour note. Gavaskar
was obliged to return to India for a meeting a fortnight before the
end of the season. Determined to fulfil his commitments, he flew
back to Taunton to play in the last two championship matches of
the summer. By now the West Indies tour was over and Viv had
returned to help his team out in the absence of his replacement.
Accordingly the prospect loomed of the two greatest batsmen of
the period playing together in a county match. Alas, Viv was reluctant to play alongside the Indian maestro. Naturally Botham took
his side. Meetings were held involving senior players and Roy
Kerslake. Eventually Rose returned to the rooms to mutter that
he'd been outvoted and that Gavaskar was not going to play. It
was a deplorable capitulation and an insult to a great cricketer.
Somerset's cricketing leaders had given way in the most craven
manner. Hardly a murmur was heard. Eventually Somerset paid
the inevitable price for this feebleness of mind. Not that those
responsible accepted any part of the blame for the ensuing
disintegration.

Fortunately the 1981 season was altogether happier in spirit
and deed. Somerset was at full strength, with Moseley able to play
as an Englishman, which meant the attack could survive Botham's
absences with England. Botham had become captain of his
country, a position he was to lose after the Lord's Test. In truth
he had been out of his depth. It had been a romantic appointment.
He became inhibited and resigned after scoring a lame duck at
Lord's, whereupon he was forced to walk back to the dressing-
room through the silence and apparent hostility of the members
in the Long Room, an experience that revived half-forgotten
demons. Ian returned to Taunton and went drinking with his

friends, including some players, letting off steam and ridding himself of the frustrations of his period in office. At such times he was a vulnerable and sympathetic character.

From the start of the season Richards was in majestic form. His 100 on a dangerous pitch at Weston-Super-Mare was as superb a piece of batting as the game has known and confirmed that his skills went far beyond power and domination. His confrontation with Jeff Thompson in a county match at Lord's must count among the most compelling seen on a cricket field. Thommo was playing for Middlesex that summer and on that first morning recaptured the pace, bounce and hostility produced in his prime. Bowling to Viv with only two men in front of the bat, Thommo pounded the West Indian with deliveries that thumped into his body. Stung, Richards responded with a counter-attack full of drives and hooks and savage cuts. His strokes were breathtaking and brutal. Having somehow survived Mike Selvey's subtler offerings I was able to watch these proceedings from the bowler's end. Thommo, and then Wayne Daniel, blazed away, raining shells upon a target that refused to give ground. The epic ended in favour of the Antiguan, who scored 92 before losing his wicket to a medium-pace delivery.

Thommo was a humorous fellow. Finding my batting rather cautious, he asked Mike Brearley whether he could send for a deckchair as nothing seemed likely to come his way at mid-off. Brearley liked to be snooty towards unknown opponents, presumably in an attempt to put them off their game. He appeared from slip, stood in front of me and called out to his distant fast bowler to choose between a mid-off and another slip. Always willing to join in a discussion, I confirmed that the bloke at mid-off was indeed wasting his time. Brearley seemed nonplussed that a young batsman had been cheeky enough to put across his point of view. Apart from the usual encouragements and the occasional remark about a fellow's batting, little was said on the field during county matches. Unpleasantness only seemed to creep into English cricket in the 1990s, and was not limited to the professional game.

I was injured during the Bath festival, staged in June: a leg muscle pulled while fielding after scoring 73 not out in front of a packed crowd on the Sunday. Walking in water was recommended and accordingly the next few days were spent in the vast tub in which rugby players soaked their bodies after matches. Meanwhile Rose was also hobbling around. Eventually Somerset faced the task of saving a championship match. An hour before 'stumps' urgent messages arrived ordering me to return to the pavilion. Since I was naked, wet and far away it took some time to obey the instruction. Wickets were tumbling and I arrived as Rose shuffled out to bat accompanied by a runner. The situation was grim so I strapped on the pads, as did another runner, and limped out to join my captain at the fall of the ninth wicket. The sight of four Somerset men at the crease seemed to amuse the crowd. Since a run-out appeared imminent, the runners were dismissed and a decision taken to ignore runs even when a walk sufficed. Unfortunately Rose kept forgetting the agreement. Spectators found further amusement in the sight of two experienced batsmen standing at the same end, arguing about which man should attempt to reach the other popping crease. However, the match was saved.

Somerset fought its way into the final of the Benson & Hedges Cup, scraping home against Kent in the semi-final after the usual suspects had taken the opposition's wickets. A sturdy partnership of 67 with my housemate Popplewell settled a low-scoring contest. Popplewell was not so much a fine cricketer as an outstanding competitor. His bowling was serviceable but his batting had an edge about it; he created runs by hitting the ball to unlikely places and running hard. After several seasons as a valuable allrounder his batting had improved, especially his backfoot game, and he became a player of substance and an opening bat to boot.

He left the game in his prime because it was no longer worth playing for Somerset. An intelligent man, he had wanted to delay his entrance into more respected professions in order both to test himself and to pursue an enthusiasm for cricket that his conscience never quite managed to persuade him was serious. We had in common a desire to prove that playing professional cricket was a worthwhile and demanding endeavour. Accordingly the collapse, when it came, had a more profound effect upon us than it did on our contemporaries.

Much happened in the fortnight before the final. Released from the captaincy of his country and the tensions it had caused, Botham became a massive figure, cutting a swathe through the serried ranks of Australians. Lashing about, hurling down his bolts and between times guffawing, he played an enormous and thrilling part in turning individual matches and the whole Ashes series upon their heads. A quarter of a century later those days of transformation are remembered whenever the thoughts of Englishmen turn to cricket. Truth to tell, there has not been much to celebrate in the intervening years. Not that Botham's county colleagues saw much of the action, for players live in their own cocoons and Somerset had matches of its own to think about. But he had left with heavy tread and returned as a national hero.

Botham's stamina was extraordinary, as was his appetite for life and the game. Playing Test cricket must be exhausting and that summer of 1981 must have taken its toll, yet he returned to Somerset apparently fresh and committed to the cause. Not even a first-round defeat at Northampton in the Gillette Cup could dampen his spirits, or those of his county colleagues. These things happen. By now Somerset did not even contemplate defeat at Lord's. The team believed in itself in a way recaptured by the Devon sides of the 1990s. These teams won twelve finals in a row and not one of these results came as a surprise. Looking around the room, contemplating the abilities of the players and their hunger, I did not think it possible to lose. Both sides were as vulnerable as any opponent in the early rounds of a competition, but take them to Lord's and they had the men and resources required to carry the day.

As usual, Joel Garner bowled magnificently in the final of the Benson & Hedges Cup, removing five Surrey batsmen in his eleven overs at a cost of only fourteen runs. He could easily have won the 'Man of the Match' award in all of the finals he played in Somerset colours, but he did not win any of them. He was a great and gentle giant and, among the West Indians, stands behind only the incomparable Marshall and Roberts, for these men led the attack and therefore deserve special credit. Also as usual, Marks bowled splendidly and despite a defiant 92 from the secretary of the MCC, Surrey were dismissed for 194, a total well within our grasp on a benign pitch.

The loss of two wickets for five runs put the proverbial cat among the pigeons. Fortunately Richards remained and we constructed the decisive partnership—taking the score to 110 before my clip was held by David Smith, who seemed quite pleased. As usual my contribution was important but my batting was cramped.

The only press cutting I have kept throughout my career was a report of a benefit match played in Northumberland in which I decided to provide the entertainment myself in a contest more competitive than it sounds, and promptly scored a brilliant 100 off an attack including Courtney Walsh. Despite relaxing more as the years went along, despite accepting more responsibility for playing decisive as well as useful innings, I did not really let go until I was playing as an amateur for Devon, at which point the constant desire to hit straight sixes was at last released. Of course it was much easier in the middle order and by then a few wickets had generally come my way, which eased the burden. As a professional batsman I concentrated on eliminating error. Scoring runs and surviving were stronger driving forces than the exploration of character or talent. Was this a mistake? Could things have turned out otherwise? Cricket may reveal character but it does not tell the whole story. To protect my position it was necessary to suppress myself. Perhaps that explains my happiness with Devon and down under.

Richards was masterful as he produced his third consecutive century in finals played on the hallowed turf. Afterwards he said he had dreamed of playing at Lord's as a child growing up in Antigua and the sense of excitement had not dimmed. After my dismissal, Viv and Botham brought the match to a spectacular conclusion with a withering assault full of explosive and audacious strokes. As a rule they did not bat well together, but this partnership of 87 from only thirteen overs was an exception. Somerset had won its third trophy in as many summers.

Attention turned to the Sunday League and the Championship. Despite slipping to eighth in the three-day competition Somerset was only two wins behind the leaders and now did not have the Gillette Cup to think about. Our position in the Sunday League was even less promising but a late charge was not out of the question. Somerset was at its peak. Anything was possible.

Over the next six weeks Somerset played outstandingly. The charge up the Sunday League table was so impressive that by the end of the campaign only Essex had secured more points. It was a fruitful, invigorating period that alarmed opponents and suggested that in mind, body and spirit the side remained intact. To my mind the team was at its peak, with Jeremy Lloyds taking his place at the top of the batting order, fielding at first slip and also turning his off-breaks sharply to give his schoolmate Marks the support he needed. Popplewell was also playing some telling cricket and from top to bottom the team was full of character and ability. Most particularly there was a balance between the great players and the hungry, intelligent men also determined to play their parts. Somerset were formidable.

Significantly Garner was fit for most of the championship matches and ended the season with 88 wickets, only seventeen fewer than Richard Hadlee and taken at a rate almost as miserly. Opposing teams tried to thwart him with slow and low-bouncing pitches but he liked bowling on them as the ball could hit the wicket. Bouncy surfaces could be frustrating because the ball kept flying past the batsman's nostrils and thudding into the gloves of the distant gloveman. Of course, batsmen did not see things in quite the same light. Joel could be endearing and enjoyed sleeping too much to relish the sight of a well-grassed pitch. At such times he was inclined to walk mournfully out before the start of play to inform his captain that, 'This wicket not as green as it looks.'

Had Joel played in every match the championship might have been won. Alas, he missed the two matches at the annual festival in Weston-Super-Mare and although Worcestershire were beaten, Northants prevailed by two wickets in a contest that turned upon a leg before decision awarded by Bill Alley against Botham as he stretched forwards to Tim Lamb's medium-pacers. A month later Essex were forced to follow on, but were saved by a combination of Gooch and rain. Nonetheless Garner was magnificent and well-nigh irresistible. Unfortunately Notts and Sussex also kept winning, with Imran Khan, Garth le Roux, Clive Rice and Hadlee playing their parts to the utmost.

Ultimately, Somerset suffered for not thinking about the championship at the start of the summer. Planning was not our strong point. The team had a maverick spirit which took a while to awaken. That is not to say that discipline or dedication were lacking. Despite an inspired run, Somerset knew the championship was beyond its reach by the time of the last match of the season, to be played in Taunton. Warwickshire were our opponents and, as usual, something smouldered beneath the surface. Joel did not play and by lunch on the third day the visitors had taken advantage of lacklustre bowling to reach 375. Long interruptions for rain had been appreciated by players whose minds were elsewhere. During the breaks some became engaged in the sort of frolics more often seen on end-of-season tours. Accordingly the news that the sun had appeared and that the ground had dried out was greeted with general dismay. Eventually a run chase was arranged and we found ourselves needing to score 376 in 65 overs. The fellows marched out and belted the ball around. Several of the batsmen needed to pass 60 or so to reach 1000 runs for the championship season, not an easy task in those days of pitches prepared for the seamers. Rose, Denning, Richards and Botham moved the score along and I contributed an unbeaten 89 so that Somerset won with several overs to spare. Given all the circumstances it was an astonishing performance.

It had been the most satisfying summer of them all for me. Somerset, though, was never quite the same again. The rot began to set in the following summer as players previously united fell into conflict, whereupon the danger of having a club within the club was confirmed. For the time being, however, troubles seemed far away.

After the disappointments of the previous summer my return to form came as a relief. Although not yet a top-class professional batsman, my game was improving and my confidence was rising. No longer regarded as a promising youngster, I had played my part in both campaigns, averaging around 43 in the championship and Sunday League.

10

DECLINE AND FALL

When Somerset retained the Benson & Hedges Cup on 24 July 1982, it seemed that the good times were going to last for ever. Although the season had started poorly, with four defeats in eight days, recovery had been swift and another trophy had been put in the cupboard. Somerset had become the most glamorous cricket team in the land. Richards had been hailed as the greatest batsman to appear since Bradman, Botham was a sporting hero, Garner was an immense influence, Rose and Marks had played for England, membership was rising, a new pavilion had been built, players were clamouring to join and actors, comedians, novelists and rock stars mixed with the players. What could possibly go wrong? Two years later Martin Crowe would be widely praised for bringing a fresh spirit to the team. Three years later Somerset would finish bottom of the table, a deterioration that prompted my appointment as captain of the club. Critics can squeak and squawk but must find in their explanation some place for these inconvenient facts.

Our victory at Lord's was comprehensive. Even before the match began we were convinced that victory was more or less inevitable. By now even our shyest players were comfortable on these public occasions. Walking out to bat did not feel quite so lonely an experience. By contrast the Nottinghamshire players were full of anxiety. Doubtless we had been just as tense in 1978. They walked across Lords to practise in the nets at the Nursery End with the air of a team doomed to defeat. Hadlee was not properly fit, which hardly helped their cause. Not that Somerset had been thinking about him or any other opponent. Apart from a brief discussion over a dinner memorable for Denning's rather violent recommendations, the match was not debated. There was nothing to talk about. If Somerset played well the rest was inevitable. If this sounds arrogant, so be it. A lot of time and energy is wasted on words.

Our assessment of the state of mind of our opponents proved to be correct. Aghast at losing the toss on an uneven pitch, Notts were dismissed for 130. Although Dredge, Botham and Moseley took wickets, Garner and Marks did most of the damage. Joel took three wickets for thirteen runs in another towering perform-ance, while Marks' spell of 2/24 from eleven overs won him recognition as 'Man of the Match'.

Between innings at Lord's, Richards was both delighted with the prospect of victory and dismayed that he could not score a century. He was not exactly burdened with self-doubt. In the event he reached the 40s, waited until my 50 had been acknowl-edged and then finished with a blaze of strokes. Somerset had won by nine wickets and with 22 overs to spare. It had been an intim-idating performance.

Next day Somerset narrowly defeated Worcestershire in a 40-over match played before a jubilant crowd in Taunton. Buoyed by our efforts at Lord's, Marks and I added 115 in fifteen overs. And then the team drove to Bournemouth to play Hampshire in the County Championship.

Something happened on the morning of the match about which all save those intimately involved remain in the dark. Viv

Richards did not play in the match. He looked fit and well and would turn out in the 40-over match a few days later, but after long and apparently tense meetings before the match he did not take part in the three-day contest. Inevitably his withdrawal provoked suggestions about disciplinary measures and so forth. Just as inevitably, Rose mentioned illness and a slight leg strain. No one in the team believed either story. Nothing had occurred to warrant any action being taken against Viv, who had been a constant source of strength to the team. Nor was it usual for him to miss a day, let alone an entire match. Moreover, this was his benefit year. He did not withdraw lightly. Something was building and the atmosphere had become uneasy.

Viv's absence was the first sign of the strain within club and team. Hitherto the divisions between the players and those running the club had not mattered because the team was a united force intent upon glory. Measures had been taken to bridge the gap between management and senior players. A position had been found for Jock McCombe, Viv's batman, who worked variously on the club lottery and as a general factotum. A compromise had been reached over the selling of club merchandise. Kerslake, a man popular with and respected by the players, was filling the roles of cricket chairman and, effectively, team manager. Sensing something awry, Robin Marlar, cricket correspondent of the *Sunday Times*, wrote about 'unhappy rumblings' at the club, described McCombe as 'the every day nanny for the players' and said that in Kerslake the 'Somerset cricketers knew they had another who rain or shine, night or day, would give his all for them'. Marlar added that it is a 'fortunate group who can have one of a County Town's leading solicitors as a special events nanny'. Of course, in his characteristically robust way, he went too far. Typically he took my no less forthright defence of the arrangements in his stride. In hindsight he was right. The situation contained the seeds of its own destruction. Somerset and Essex had risen side by side, country cousins determined to prove themselves against the high and mighty. Essex lasted longer because they built a club. Somerset built a team.

Rose had been captain for five years and in a side full of strong characters was bound sooner or later to feel his control slipping away. He needed the consent of his players to continue as their leader and he could no longer depend upon it. Once it began to falter, his authority could not be recovered. In fact, he did not really try for he was not a confrontational man and also possibly realised the game was up. By now Rose was regarded with suspicion by the committee and by sections of the team. Because he did not say much people thought him cunning. Perhaps, though, he was merely quiet.

Meanwhile Botham had secured an appointment as vice-captain, a position available because Denning had resigned after falling out with Rose. Of course Botham had ambitions of his own. Naturally he wanted to lead his country again, both for its own sake and to prove that he could succeed in the role. A feeling may also have developed that Rose had been praised for the deeds of his players. If so, it was a foolish notion because cricket captains are invariably blamed and lauded more than they deserve.

Whatever the cause of the disturbance, the decline of Somerset began on that day. It was caused not by any individual action, but by strains that had not mattered in the days of scrumpy and roses. And there were plenty of people gathered around the great players who were prepared to stoke the fires.

Somerset lost that match in Bournemouth. Needing to score 81 runs in the fourth innings of a low-scoring match played on a dreadful pitch with a hole just short of a length at which the fast bowlers aimed enthusiastically, Somerset collapsed from 38/2 to 72 all out. Forty might have been too many because our minds were elsewhere. Alan Gibson was covering the match for *The Times* and at its conclusion I asked him whether he had detected any change within the team. 'Hubris,' he replied, and his diagnosis was correct. Alan wrote beautifully and amusingly and often about trains and cider, both of which played important parts in his day at the cricket. Although in decline, he remained an astute judge of character and had a particular fondness for staunch locals such as Denning, Dredge, Marks, David Shepherd and Jack Davey.

Defeat in the 60-over Cup followed a few days later. It was another lacklustre performance. By now I was contributing a regular column to the *Sunday Independent* and that week mentioned the 'staleness in the air', observing that 'everyone has noticed there is not nearly as much passion in Taunton these days'. As best as I could without breaching the confidence of the dressing-room, I was drawing attention to a problem. The column ended with the suggestion that Somerset might 'seize the opportunity to invite Roy Kerslake or someone of equal knowledge and business sense to fill the vacant club secretary position'.

In the event, the troubles within the team worsened and the club did nothing of the sort. Kerslake was interested in the job but withdrew when Somerset did not respond quickly enough to give him time to withdraw gracefully from his current employment as a solicitor. Feeling slighted, Kerslake resigned as cricket chairman. For their part, officials expressed astonishment that he had not persisted with his application. Kerslake had a lot of support in the dressing-room, especially among the great players, and his loss was keenly felt. Others regretted that his sensitivities had prevented him fighting harder for the secretaryship. Thereafter he became an outsider at the club. His closeness to the players had been resented.

Instead Tony Brown, formerly captain and secretary of Gloucestershire, was appointed, an act regarded within the dressing-room as provocative as Brown was viewed as an establishment man. He also arrived bearing the residue of past conflicts between the neighbouring counties. Later the committee said that it had merely wanted to find a cricket man capable of bridging the widening gulf between players and officials.

Somerset's season petered out. The next row occurred during the Weston-Super-Mare festival, when the senior players complained furiously about the pitch and demanded an explanation from the chairman of the club, summoning him to the decrepit dressing-room. Although unreliable, the surface had not struck me as dangerous and the fuss came as a surprise. Indeed Somerset had fought its way to 147/2 on the first day until, trying to push the score along, I played a loose stroke and was caught in the covers. Gibson recorded that 'Roebuck, so austere that you could envisage him in a gown about to take his doctorate in Philosophy, reached his 50 in the 64th over. Then the undergraduate that lurks within him had his say; he drove impetuously at Cowans, did not get it quite right, and was caught'.

Somerset collapsed to 187 all out, Middlesex reached 319 against Garner and Botham, a lead that proved sufficient as our second effort was brief, wild and unproductive. After the match hysterical words were said in the rooms as relationships soured further.

Our season ended in disarray. At stumps on the penultimate day of the last match, our opponents were still 56 runs behind with only six second innings wickets remaining. Suffice it to say that little interest was shown thereafter, with bowlers taking to the field in sandshoes and so forth. Needing to score 134 to win after letting Lancashire off the hook, Somerset subsided for 119. Rose missed the match, giving Botham a chance to prove his worth, but he did not impress. Somerset finished sixth in the championship and ninth in the Sunday League; hardly disastrous but well below the team's capabilities.

From my point of view, an undistinguished season was saved by two developments. Rose had explained over supper one evening in Yorkshire that he wanted to drop down the order and thought that I had all the attributes required to take his place as an opening batsman. Doubtless a few words of flattery were thrown in. I accepted the challenge and although my results had been uninspiring there were indications that better days lay ahead.

Also, my first book had been published to some acclaim. *Slices of Cricket* contained mostly light-hearted studies, most of which had previously been published in the *Cricketer* magazine. Becoming a cricket writer had not been part of any plan. There was no plan. The discovery of this second talent came as a surprise and helped to improve my cricket and settle my character. Of course it was ridiculous that my self-esteem should ever have depended so much upon a constant flow of runs. But there is no reasoning with such things. Recognition as a promising performer with the pen eased the pressure and allowed a broader, more confident character to emerge.

Pretty soon, in response to an invitation from David Robson, the sports editor of the *Sunday Times*, I began to contribute to that newspaper. Before long, and on a whim born of boredom on a wet afternoon in Sydney, I sent an article to the *Sydney Morning Herald*, whose hard-bitten Scottish sports editor somehow deciphered it. Some measure of success had fallen on my life. Not that this sudden maturing was obvious to colleagues in Taunton, for we had all been assigned our roles. Perhaps that was the problem. We were all changing. The past was not enough.

11

LEARNING TO LEAD

Captaincy came into my life in 1983 as an unexpected guest. Retirements, World Cup calls, injury and disgruntlement gave me—a player ranked only eighth a few months before—an opportunity to lead the team onto the field. Somerset had made a dismal start in the championship and were floundering. Rose, the official captain, was incapacitated; Richards, Marks, Botham and Garner were representing their countries, Taylor had emigrated and Denning was growling. Eric Hill, a former player and war hero who presided over the tatty press box at the county ground in Taunton with the air of a man not entirely convinced that modern contraptions were all they were cracked up to be, wrote that Somerset had 'recently endured some of the bleakest days in their history'. A few early victories in the Sunday League did not provide sufficient comfort.

After only 40 minutes in charge I realised that captaining a cricket team without bowlers was like driving a car without brakes. By then Gloucestershire had reached 84/0, most of them scored by Andy Stovold, a batsman whose style had earned him the nickname of 'The Helicopter'. Somerset had a threadbare attack and precious little experience. By stumps on that first day our rivals had declared at 375/8 and we had reached 23/3, with the temporary captain among the fallen. Significantly, though, Somerset fought back to draw that match and Hill reported that 'Somerset's bowlers and fieldsmen took their hiding magnificently, never giving up and riding over their many disappointments in praiseworthy fashion'.

Subsequently Glamorgan were forced to follow on and were beaten in the Sunday League as Popplewell, still my housemate, scored 84, whereupon the Demon of Frome and I scrambled the 47 needed from the final seven overs. A large crowd basking in sunshine at the Recreation Ground in Bath roared its approval. Playing cricket for Somerset was fun again. Derbyshire proved too strong but Gloucestershire were almost beaten in the return match as Popplewell struck one of the fastest centuries in cricketing history, reaching three figures in 41 minutes and 60 balls, a remarkable display unjustly dismissed by historians as one scored against the lob bowling that had come into vogue as a way of reviving dying matches. David Graveney was bowling throughout.

I found leadership invigorating. Parts previously subdued were released, including concern for other players and commitment to the cause. Colleagues were surprised to find warmth buried beneath the frost. Of course it is always easier to captain a fresh young side. Still, the responsibilities of leadership and the opportunity to put a mark upon the team were appreciated. Hill wrote that my captaincy during this three-week hiatus had 'impressed [him] enormously'. I had never expected to captain the county, and did not anticipate doing so again.

Towards the end of the festival Somerset officials asked for a private meeting. They were in a pickle. Rose was standing down as captain at the end of the season and Botham was next in line. They outlined their misgivings about his ability to lead a county club and asked if I'd be prepared to continue as skipper for the rest of the summer. In an attempt to avoid a future that was not going to work, they were prepared to reject Botham and disregard his supporters. It was an extraordinary notion. Astonished, I replied that Somerset had a properly appointed captain and a vice-captain and it was up to the committee to support them or remove them. If they did not think Botham was the right man to replace Rose then he should not be appointed. The committee was responsible for the future of the club. It was not up to a junior player to fight battles on its behalf.

Neither party ever raised the question again. Obviously the privacy of these discussions was respected. Sniffing the way the wind was blowing, David Foot wrote that 'Peter Roebuck has suddenly become the strong favourite to be the next captain of Somerset'. I disagreed and regarded Botham's appointment as inevitable. The decision had been taken when he was named as Rose's deputy. As far as the players were concerned, Botham deserved his chance and he might make a fist of it. We all tried to believe that. Not that there seemed such an awful hurry to be rid of Rose. In any case Botham resembled an irresistible force. Scrapbooks reveal that further opportunities arose for me to captain the side later in the season, and that Garner and Marks played under my leadership, facts that I had forgotten though the matches went well. Indeed at one point a row broke out between Joel and myself. Two matches had to be played before the Lord's final. Joel wanted to play against Hampshire but not Glamorgan. I wanted him to play against the Welsh because a fast pitch had been prepared for that game, which gave Somerset much more chance of recording a victory. On the other hand, the surface for the Hampshire game was slow and even Joel could not get much life from it. I refused to give ground and the matter had to be settled by officials, who supported their captain. Glamorgan were beaten in a tight match and Hampshire held to a draw. Perhaps the committee took notice of my fearlessness and determination, but it was not an attempt to impress them or anyone else. Rather it was a matter of doing the right thing.

Botham was not willing to wait until the end of the season to press his case. Rose returned to the team for the championship match in Leicester and made the mistake of calling out 'Come on, boys!' after another fielding error during a feeble performance as our hosts reached 137/2. Offence was taken, with senior players asking, 'Who are you calling boys?' A change came over the contest. Somerset started playing flat out and Leicestershire were dismissed for 180. By the close we were powerfully placed. That night most of the players gathered in the bar. Rose, Marks and myself were attending to our own affairs. A lackey knocked on my door and said, 'The lads are in the bar downstairs and we are going to have a meeting tomorrow and tell Rosey to resign.' It was a coup. I replied that I did not speak to messengers and that anyone wanting my support had better come themselves. Apparently Marks said he was not in favour of changing horses midstream. Accordingly the uprising petered out. The next day Richards and Botham added 172 for the eighth wicket—Botham was batting down the list—and Somerset won by an innings. Complaining of an injury, Rose did not play again that summer. It was his last match as leader of the club.

If anything these tensions improved our cricket. Although lacking the energy to sustain a challenge for the championship, Somerset remained a formidable one-day side and the team ended the season with the same number of points as Yorkshire, only to be placed second for the sixth time in ten years, once again on a technicality. Tenth place in the three-day competition was, perhaps, a better indication of the team's prospects and the lack of depth in a growing squad.

But it was the 60-over knockout competition that most held our attention because Botham could play in every round and had a full-strength team at his command. Somerset put its mind to winning this Cup, restricting Lancashire to 163 and dismissing Sussex for 65 to set up another semi-final with Middlesex. Botham played an extraordinary innings in the semi-final, perhaps the most impressive of his career. Desperate to take his team to Lord's and to lift a trophy as captain, he imposed his will upon the proceedings to a degree equalled only, in my experience, by Steve Waugh. In the rush of events this mountainous performance has been almost forgotten by all save those closest to the action.

Despite sound efforts from Garner, Richards and Popplewell, Middlesex reached 222 and in reply Somerset stumbled to 52/5. Usually exuberant and sometimes mischievous, Botham had been quiet all day, as if summoning from the depths of his character the strength needed to carry this team upon his shoulders. He watched the wickets falling with disappointment rather than dismay for he did not doubt his own ability to turn the contest around. Botham knew he had been blessed with a special talent and understood that, properly applied, this gift could achieve almost anything on a cricket field. Of course he could not reach into his innermost being every time he seized the ball or strode out armed with a bat. No man could sustain such an effort. Instead he chose his moments and then called upon his sporting gods. At last he found an ally in Popplewell and the pair took the team to tea without any further losses. Nonetheless the situation remained dire and the rooms were silent. Botham sat in his corner, puffing on a small cigar, showing none of the usual swagger but quietly contemplating the work still to be done. Watching him during this break in play was to see a performer demanding greatness from himself and hoping for assistance from his colleagues. It was compelling.

Somerset's sixth-wicket pair took the score to 156/6 but, despite their resourcefulness, the result remained in the balance. One mistake from Botham and it would all be over, a fact that he had known for several hours. He did not make a mistake, however, nor did he ever look like making one. Bear in mind that the ball was moving around sufficiently to disconcert many accomplished batsmen. Marks joined his captain and took the total to 218/7 before falling with a few balls and an over left to play. Twenty years later the task of scoring a handful of runs with eight balls and three wickets in hand sounds straightforward but this was a day of almost indescribable tension, a day upon which powerful forces came into conflict. Another wicket fell and Botham was left to face the last over of the match with the scores level and in the knowledge that, provided no further casualties were suffered, Somerset were through on the basis of fewer wickets lost. John Emburey was the bowler. Dare Botham go for the winning run? Dare he take the risk of blocking the last six balls? He decided to defend and did so with every part of his anatomy and a bat so broad that he resembled Trevor Bailey in one of his 'Thou shalt not pass' moods.

Many who were present will go to their graves swearing that Botham was plumb leg before to the last ball of the match but by then both he and the umpires had grabbed stumps and were running for their lives towards the pavilion as an enormous crowd released its pent-up emotion.

Botham returned to the rooms both exhausted and exhilarated but the dressing-room was strangely subdued. Officials and employees new to the club were amazed to find the atmosphere so restrained. In truth many players had mixed feelings about the outcome. It had been an almost miraculous win and most felt they had not played their parts. But there was also something deeper at work. Everyone knew that the issue of the captaincy had been decided. Although the sun of victory burned bright, dark clouds were gathering upon the horizon. While celebrating the present it was possible to fear for the future.

Of course the final was won. Despite losing the toss on a damp pitch Somerset beat Kent easily enough in a match shortened by rain to 50 overs each. Admirable bowling from Garner, Botham and Marks meant that a score of 193 was sufficient, with 24 runs to spare. Richards scored 50, an innings that proved decisive. He had fallen for 41 as the West Indies lost the World Cup Final, a defeat and a 'failure' that upset him, though it took an astonishing outfield catch to bring him down. On both occasions he was his team's top scorer. Although his mortality had been revealed, he was still a wonderful batsman and a fine competitor.

Somerset had won its fifth trophy. Botham was duly appointed captain of the club and the West Indians said their farewells, for they were touring in 1984, which meant that Somerset had to start looking for another overseas player.

Botham chose a bright-faced young batsman from New Zealand as his overseas player. Only one foreign player was allowed under new regulations designed to give more opportunities to locals. Martin Crowe arrived as a man on a quest, a cricketer searching for the refined expression of his abilities. As a batsman he was a classicist and played with a beauty born of simplicity. It was not his game that worried him but his mind, for he felt the need to be in constant and absolute command of his brain or else failure was inevitable. His standards were high and the polishing and self-scrutiny were unceasing.

Crowe was an idealist and wanted both his life and game to take their perfect forms. For such men there can be no relaxing. He was a mixture of naivety and expectation, and had within a darkness that was both a driving force and a weak point for it contained emotion, even anger, and he strove to be in absolute control. Accordingly he fought against his temper and, therefore, against the stubbornness and aggression that sat by its side. Crowe tried to bat without emotion for he believed that greatness could not be achieved until the self had been conquered.

Paradoxically, I liked his anger and was less drawn to the geniality he tried to capture as if it were a butterfly to be put in a container.

Always with Martin there was the search. The journey drove him on, held him in its thrall. He could not arrive at his destination for it was not a fixed point but an idea, a form of self-expression. Accordingly he tended to fall a fraction short of his hopes. He did not quite know himself or trust himself sufficiently to complete the maturing process. Rather, he remained young and slightly unfinished. But he was a glorious batsman and proved to be an astute signing for he brought to the team the freshness that had been missing.

From the start Martin took the younger players under his wing. He could see that they lacked leadership and formed them into a group that met in a local pub every Thursday. Also he coached and trained them, trying to instil techniques and attitudes that might help them. Some detected a demagogic streak in Crowe but he was merely intolerant of nonsense and hated to see younger players spurning their chances. Not that any of the group subsequently prospered. Viv Richards thought that only a rugged local lad called Richard Harden had the wherewithal to succeed as a professional cricketer and events proved him right. Crowe did not know the players as well and did not attempt to judge them. Perhaps, though, he was inclined to value those most enthusiastic about his teachings.

After a shaky start Martin batted superbly and produced numerous memorable innings. At first he did not take one-day cricket seriously, dismissing it as the merest biff and bash. Only the pure forms of the game interested him. Later he realised that a professional cannot pick and choose and he also grasped the point that the game presents many challenges and that a fellow must be adaptable enough to meet them. He learned to compartmentalise his mind and his game, seeking mastery of himself and his game in championship innings and cutting loose in the briefer engagements.

Crowe was an amusing and intelligent member of the side. Although he had been playing Test cricket for some time, he remained an inexperienced and impressionable young man. By now Richards and Garner had become senior players, so the shift within the team was considerable. Wisely, Martin did not involve himself in the struggles behind the scenes and concentrated instead on scoring runs and taking wickets. Accordingly the tensions eased and the summer was happier, though not quite as successful as its immediate predecessors. Martin took 50 wickets, scored 1500 runs, caught numerous catches at slip and helped other players with their games. His insights into batting technique were much appreciated, especially his emphasis on staying side-on and leading with the left shoulder, an approach that has fallen from favour in England but seems to appeal to Sachin Tendulkar and Steve Waugh.

Certainly Crowe improved my game. Whereas Viv's strong point had been the mind, Martin could detect technical flaws and suggest remedies. Not that his approach suited everyone, and those with technical failings but more competitive outlooks kept their distance. Harden was wary, and Marks was not affected by him or anyone else.

Not until midway through the season did Crowe find a way through my defences. Somerset had been going through a bad patch and encountered further difficulties against Leicestershire in Taunton. He had lost his temper with Andy Roberts in the first innings, charging down the pitch and hooking and driving with abandon after the smouldering fast bowler had peppered some of the lower order men. Crowe was furious with himself and quite inconsolable, though he had played with panache and courage. Overnight he wrote to his mother and said he could not control himself and was thinking about giving up.

Next day Somerset found itself needing to score around 320 to win the match and, as usual, a couple of early wickets were lost. Crowe strode to the crease and gave as clinical an exhibition of stroke play as it has been my privilege to watch. Resisting the desperate attacks mounted by Roberts, Jonathon Agnew and others, we added over 300 and took the team to within a few runs of a victory secured with time and wickets to spare. My innings has not lingered in the memory. Doubtless it consisted of the customary dogged defiance and edges to third man. Curiously my first innings dismissal remains clear, a lovely ball from Agnew that lifted and moved away. Afterwards he said he'd been surprised by the touch because the ball was unplayable, a remark that confirmed suspicions that my game was at its peak. Also I can remember getting myself out with only a handful of runs needed and expressing not pleasure at the partnership, but annoyance with my new partner's dreaminess, a feeble reaction to a fine moment. Apart from Crowe's peerless stroke play, nothing else remains from this superb victory.

Crowe and I enjoyed many other excellent collaborations and Marks also found his best form, as was to be expected from accomplished cricketers given added responsibilities by the absence of several great players. Vic also captained the team when Botham was away. He was an unthreatening fellow, and Botham had chosen him as his vice-captain. Now and then Marks would be away on international duty, whereupon my turn came. Crowe thought Vic was the best of the three captains, with myself placed second, which was also my opinion.

Fortunately Somerset found a young pace bowler that summer of 1984. Unfortunately he did not last long. Mark Davies was a hustling and bustling left-armer whose deliveries cut away and often took batsmen by surprise. Apparently he had been chased around the hills outside Taunton by a mother-in-law familiar with his fondness for the easy life. Repeatedly Davies took wickets with the new ball, which made life easier for captains and colleagues alike. Had his second spells been as effective he might have played for his country, for the West Indians were running riot and a change of angle had its merits. Alas, Davies lacked stamina, athleticism and dedication and swiftly faded. Whether he blamed himself or others for his decline is hard to say. But it was his fault. Later he became one of four former Somerset players closely involved in the matters that would cast a pall over my life for 26 months.

Throughout the season Somerset played spirited cricket. Indeed that summer sits beside that of 1981 and most of my years with Devon as the most enjoyable of my cricketing life. Of course it helped that the barriers holding back my batting were finally broken. Before the season began I spent many hours in the nets with my friend Peter Robinson, trying to reconstruct my batting technique with the assistance of a bowling machine. A study of the previous year's dismissals had revealed that in 52 innings I had been caught 39 times, many of them edges into the slip cordon. Too many balls were being played away from the body. Clearly the front foot game had to be abandoned and the ball played later, under the chin and, preferably, off the back foot. Robinson would arrive early every morning and patiently fill the buckets and send down the balls. An outstanding man with a fondness for gardening and opera, but without much sense of leadership and reliant on the forms of communication favoured in the Black Country, he remains my only friend in Somerset.

By the start of the season I had developed a solid backfoot technique and thereafter I was caught in the slips or at short leg only about twice a year. On the other hand, dismissals by being clean bowled or caught leg-before increased. Fortunately it took bowlers years to realise that Roebuck had become a different batsman, and was now scoring not through the leg side but past point. At last I had built a game that could withstand the demands of opening an innings in top-class cricket. Previously my batting had been praised beyond its desserts. From this time onwards I was a competent professional batsman. Alas, I had not been taught how to use my feet against spinners and was often bogged down and sometimes dismissed by modest practitioners of this admirable craft. My students are encouraged to step down the pitch to spinners in their first lesson.

Somerset's first match of the season was against Oxford University and, on a sunny day, on a friendly pitch and against an attack that, in the judgement of the harsher critics, lacked menace, I batted all day and scored 150 or so. Though hardly the most difficult it was, in some respects, the most significant innings of my career. For once 50 was not the top of the mountain. Taking a fresh guard upon reaching that landmark, a habit that would continue for the rest of my time in professional cricket, I concentrated on adding another 50 and was thunderstruck by the ease with which this target was accomplished. At last, realisation dawned that moving from 50 to 100 was, comparatively speaking, a piece of cake. In my ensuing years of county cricket I had an almost unequalled record for taking 50s to three figures. It was quite a transformation.

Of course it was not merely a matter of the proverbial penny dropping. By now I was entirely happy with the direction of my life, a contentment that has subsequently seldom been shaken. Many things had fallen into place. My school team had won 34 of its last 36 matches, my books had been well received, my households were flourishing and my batting commanded a certain respect. By the end of the summer I had scored seven centuries and 1702 runs. Somehow those figures have stayed in the mind. Playing for Somerset had been an enjoyable experience and there did not seem to be much to worry about. Admittedly Denning had retired and men of his calibre are always missed. Nonetheless, spirits were high and everyone was looking forward to the return of the West Indians in 1985. Botham had not been such a poor captain and, in any case, had been away for most of the season. Crowe went back to New Zealand, and although Somerset kept his registration we did not expect to see him again, or not in Somerset colours anyhow.

In 1985 Somerset suffered one of the worst seasons in its history. A team containing two great West Indian cricketers, two other men with recent experience in Test cricket and captained by the most inspiring all-rounder England has produced since the Second World War finished bottom of the championship. At the end of the summer the captain was duly removed from office. Patently the team had lost its way. The journey from idealism to cynicism had not taken long. A battle had broken out between the top players and the management of the club, a battle that distracted the players' attention from the cricket and demoralised the team. Both sides were to blame for the debacle, the committee for its inability to sustain healthy relations within the club, and the players for becoming ungovernable. Nor did it help that the senior men had around them people hostile to those in charge. It was a recipe for disaster. Nor was any effort made by either side to confront the difficulties, either through meetings or concerted action.

Somerset started badly and did not recover. Resting after a gruelling winter, Richards and Garner missed the first few matches. Botham pretended he could not get hold of them and shrugged his shoulders. In fact he was speaking to them every day and understood their need for a break. Unfortunately Somerset played Hampshire in that first month and found Malcom Marshall and Gordon Greenidge included in the opposing ranks. Later the West Indians admitted that their late return had been a mistake, but pointed out that it was not typical of their characters or conduct at the county. Inevitably the issue became a hot topic during the uprising that occurred a year later when Somerset members were called upon to resolve the impasse. Too much was made of absences that were merely symptomatic of a wider malaise. Regarding it as a minor matter, I did not once mention it during the exchanges that followed the club's decision, taken eighteen months later, not to renew their contracts.

Rather, the point was that, after being away for nineteen months, Joel and Viv did not feel like hurrying back to rejoin their comrades. In the past every player had looked forward to the season, and to catching up with friends, but things had changed. Jock McCombe had died of a heart attack. Determined to lead his life in his own way, and ignoring warnings about his health, he had continued to eat chips and drink lager till the end. His coffin had been carried by the players judged closest to him. Kerslake remained popular with the top players but had washed his hands of the club. Taylor, Denning and Hallam Mosley had gone, under-estimated men who played a considerable part in the balancing act to be found in a cricket dressing-room. Jeremy Lloyds had joined Gloucestershire, where he hoped his talents might be better appreciated. These players were not adequately replaced and the staff, though larger, became weaker. Botham was not interested in signing outsiders and would not approach David Smith or Bill Athey, arguing that the former was a handful while the latter was limited. Both played for England.

Respect had been lost both in the dressing-rooms and between club and players. To hold the West Indians responsible for this collapse is as ridiculous as it is gutless. They were merely caught up in a mood that was destroying the club. No one can escape blame. None of us did much to turn things around. Heads were buried in the sand until it was too late. Botham took his team to Barbados on a pre-season tour and none of the older players was willing to accompany him. Not that he was unpopular, far from it. Most of us were, at that time, fond of him, but the trip fulfilled our worst fears.

Botham thought he could carry the team and club along with him but he was mistaken. People laughed along with him but wanted something to believe in. Also he lacked judgement. Short of players for a 40-over match against Glamorgan, he decided to call up one of his drinking partners, a reasonable club cricketer. He asked Marks and Rose for their opinions and both murmured sceptically. My response was more forthright. Alas the newcomer was to be found on the treatment table before the match had even begun. He bowled an undistinguished over containing several no-balls, chased the ball without ever quite catching up with it and could not find the reflexes required to counter a visiting medium-pacer. Worse, Somerset lost by the narrowest of margins. Botham's credibility was lost. By the end of the season Caligula's horse could have beaten him for the captaincy. In some opinions, it did.

Somewhere amidst these shenanigans, Ian and I found time to write a book called *It Sort of Clicks* after a phrase he had used during our conversations. For contractual reasons he needed to produce a book quickly and he had asked for my assistance. As eager as most professionals for a payday I had accepted the brief. Hereabouts Botham sacked his manager, replacing him with Tim Hudson, whose offbeat way of life tickled his new client's fancy. Botham found himself wearing striped blazers and sporting straggling locks as the new man tried to portray him as a latterday Errol Flynn. My work of realism did not fit in with his plans and attempts were made to suppress it. A row broke out between Hudson and myself in the farmhouse his client was renting, but the book was eventually published and others must decide its merits.

Somerset's first match in Oxford was more damaging than the late arrival of the West Indians. One night, several young players were encouraged by a senior colleague to try cocaine. One among them rang his wife, who promptly drove through the night to Oxford to rescue her husband. Before long, news of the escapade reached the ears of committee and reporters alike. Statements were taken and the story was written but withdrawn at the last moment, after the screamers had been sent to the newsagents. Somerset officials interviewed all the players by turn in Weston-Super-Mare. Everyone held their tongues. Some of us had not been present and, even if so inclined, could not assist the enquiry. Among the players only Rose thought the matter should be taken further. My view was that this episode, though unacceptable, was out of character. Upon my taking over as captain, those involved were advised that the past did not matter but nothing of the sort could happen again. My hostility to drugs was well known. If, among all the joys to be found in nature, music, friendship, literature and humour, substances were needed to make life worth living then the imagination had failed in its duties.

This episode was merely another indication of the deterioration within the club. Somerset finished the season where it belonged, occupying the seventeenth and last place in the championship. Botham could not survive the debacle. Of course he did not see things that way, and was encouraged in his opinions by the coterie of comrades who hung around him, a number of whom, including Breakwell and Richard Lines (and his wife), are still among his closest friends.

Inevitably the Somerset committee decided to try someone else as their captain. Over the course of the previous few weeks approaches had been made by various intermediaries to ask whether my position on the captaincy had changed. Of course it had. Botham seemed incapable of restoring either the spirit or performance of the team. Somerset had become a lazy and headstrong team. Nor was there any sign of improvement. Young players were suffering, the team was losing, members were resigning in droves, outsiders were becoming reluctant to join and valuable players were leaving. It was not going to work.

At the end of the season Popplewell announced his retirement. It was a major blow, because he had the fighting spirit and honesty that alone could halt the slide. Nigel had never been committed to cricket as a career so it was easier for him to go elsewhere, in his case to a law firm in town. Had Somerset been remotely its old self he would have stayed, because he had become a fine batsman as well as a useful bowler.

Somerset needed a new captain and the end of the season was the right time to make the change. Accordingly my hat was thrown into the ring. Somerset was no longer a worthwhile team and something had to be done about this. Why my name rose to the top of the list of candidates is a question I cannot answer. There were no discussions. No plans were made. At the end of the season the players went their separate ways and then the club announced my appointment as captain for the 1986 season. Of course it was an honour. A month earlier it would also have been a surprise.

As soon as Botham realised that he was to be removed from office he rang Viv Richards to say that he had been sacked, Roebuck was taking over and they were both leaving at the end of the next season, or so a secretary in the office told me. Alarmed, I wrote to Viv expressing my hopes that the good name of Somerset could be restored and asking him to accept the position as vice-captain. No reply to this letter was ever received and not until Viv returned for the first match of the new season was the identity of the vice-captain confirmed. A year later this letter was produced as proof of my double-dealing. I was accused of reassuring Richards while secretly plotting his downfall. A child could not have believed this nonsense. Clearly the letter was sincere or it could not have been sent. It was a heartfelt plea to an influential player for his assistance in turning the team around.

Within a few days of my promotion, I flew to Australia to catch up with the companions and way of life that had proved so fulfilling. Captaining Somerset was far beyond my expectations. Although often frustrated with myself, I had been quite happy playing under Rose, Richards and Marks. Presented with a sharp decline in the morale and performance of their team, the committee had promoted its team's most singular character. Only a coward could have rejected their offer. In some respects it was not much of an inheritance, an ageing team patently in decline, young players struggling to make their mark, a side with a poor reputation among other counties, a committee lacking calibre and a power vacuum that could not last. On the other hand it was a challenge. Perhaps the spirit of the glory years could be rekindled. Not yet 30, and with limited experience, I did not realise that the past cannot be recovered.

12

THE SOMERSET
AFFAIR

At first, things went along quite well in the summer of 1986, and a spring could be detected in the step of the players. Even then, it was not easy. Viv had been persuaded to accept the vice-captaincy but was not prepared to bat at first wicket down, saying that he was 'done with all that bravery ignorance thing'. This was a setback to the attempt to rekindle the spirit of yesteryear. Nonetheless, the results and the mood in the opening weeks of the season were satisfactory and there was no reason to suppose that collapse was around the corner.

Soon, though, a series of events started to undermine the team. On 18 May, Botham admitted smoking marijuana in an article that appeared on the front page of the *Mail on Sunday*. He had previously taken action against the same paper for saying as much, and this humiliating climbdown hurt him badly. As is the way with these things, there had been no warning. The story was splashed across three pages. Having no interest in anyone else's private life, I found the piece melodramatic and barely skimmed through it. Journalists swarmed all over Hove that Sunday morning, and I responded to their enquiries by suggesting that the all-rounder should join a campaign to persuade youngsters to say 'No' to illegal substances, an idea that was not taken up. When I got back to Taunton I wrote to *The Times*, pointing out that if every player who had ever smoked grass was to be dropped, some difficulty might be found in raising a team. Fortunately, the letter was not published, for Lord's could hardly have ignored it.

Botham was banned for two months. He was furious. His lawyer rang Brian Langford to say that his client was threatening to take legal action against Lord's. Botham himself rang later, complaining that the club had been hounding younger players for information and threatening to join Gloucestershire if he was demoted to the Second XI. According to the notes that the chairman made at the time, Botham also talked about refusing to play for England, and going to Australia to meet with Greg Chappell and discuss qualifying to play for that country, a process he claimed would take only two years. He added that Viv and Joel would leave with him, and that none of them had any confidence in the club's secretary, Tony Brown. Langford himself captained the country in the 1960s and early 1970s and remains the club's longest-serving player. He took Botham's threats with the proverbial pinch of salt.

Shortly before Botham's ban expired, Somerset ignored my advice and insisted that Botham play in a Second XI match which, by chance, was taking place in his hometown of Yeovil. To my mind this was an insult, an instance of the club trying to assert its authority when it was far too late for it to do so. When Botham returned to his rightful place in the team he was his old thundering self, not bowling much but blasting the ball around in the manner of a man who had missed the spotlight and was eager to reaffirm his abilities.

Before long, however, the atmosphere began to deteriorate, Numerous ugly scenes took place in the rooms and on the field, with frenzied outpourings and other furies being unleashed on a young and struggling team. Our failure to challenge in any of the competitions added to the tension, as did the uneven nature of a side in which great cricketers whose hunger for county cricket had been diminished by the passing of time played alongside, and were supposed to respect, vastly inferior colleagues. Once Richards cried out, 'Give me the West Indies any day!' whereupon a cheeky youngster retorted, 'Give my granny the West Indies!' or so I was told. Had Popplewell and Lloyd still been around, had better players been sought out and signed, such an imbalance might have been avoided. Instead, those responsible showed blind faith in local youngsters and, by doing so, invited weakness and demoralisation in through the front door. Then they led the rebellion against a decision made almost inevitable by their arrogance and complacency.

There was an edge to the outbursts that was hard to understand. Only much later did I realise that Viv, in particular, was surrounded by people warning him about the club's intentions regarding his contract. It must have been extremely unsettling for him. During our only conversation subsequent to the event, a fraught occasion, Viv said that several outcasts from the club had been telling him that he was going to be thrown out. It had been a self-fulfilling prophecy and I tried to tell him as much, but by then no one's ears were working. Viv was especially paranoid about Martin Crowe, and no one dared to mention the New Zealander's name in front of the Antiguan. Test matches were normally followed avidly on a television in the rooms, but discretion dictated that the screen remained blank whenever New Zealand were batting. Had Viv been remotely his old self, Crowe would not have been signed. The idea that any county would have considered releasing the Richards of 1981 was preposterous. If Viv's advisers had been calming influences, it is doubtful that the situation would have arisen. Instead, and in some cases for their own purposes, they stirred up a man already unsettled by other matters.

My main regret about the Somerset affair is that the lines of communication had long since broken down and no one was prepared to rebuild them. There were no intermediaries in those days, no one in the rooms to calm things down or offer advice. County clubs did not have a manager or anyone else to bridge the gap between the players and their intensities and the committee and its responsibilities. Our coach spent most of his time trying to help the reserves. Our club doctor, chosen to replace a predecessor whom I scorned as vain and immature, was still playing himself in. Our cricket chairman had a full-time job and other officials were barely on speaking terms with the players. In hindsight, all of this makes the explosions easier to understand, Unfortunately, at the time, the barriers between management and the players, and the players themselves, were beyond my power to dismantle.

More sympathy is due to Richards than to any of the other nine players who left the club that year. After all, Joel had not taken 50 wickets in a season since 1981, and had raised the possibility of only playing one-day cricket in 1987. Botham left of his own accord and the youngsters who were dismissed were let go because they could not maintain the standard required. Viv was another matter entirely: a great competitor whose cricket might have been past his peak, but who was still a player of price and passion. Not that Viv can be absolved of all blame. After all, he was 34 years old, a vastly experienced cricketer, the captain of his country, a father, a husband and a hero to many of the youngsters around him. Newcomers were entitled to take him at face value.

At any rate, the season went from bad to worse and the team continued to tear itself apart. Somerset started sinking towards the bottom of the table. And then, on 21 July, Michael Hill, chairman of Somerset CCC, rang to invite me to a special meeting of the cricket committee he had called for that evening. No indication was given of the subject matter to be discussed or the reason for haste. As it happened, a finger injury had prevented me from playing the three-day match in Bristol that had begun a couple of days earlier. Accordingly, I could accept the invitation. Completely in the dark, I reported to the county ground at the appointed hour and sat quietly as various members of the committee took their seats. I had been captain of the county for twelve weeks.

Hill explained both the need for urgency and secrecy. Martin Crowe had rung on the morning of 15 July to say that he intended to accept a contract offered by Doug Insole on behalf of Essex to join that county as its overseas player for the 1987 season. Allan Border had unexpectedly decided not to fulfil the second year of his contract with the county and Crowe seemed an obvious replacement. These were the unforeseen circumstances which now forced Somerset's hand.

Since Somerset held his registration, Crowe's call was both a courtesy and a necessity. He assumed that his former employers intended to retain their current overseas players for another season and merely sought confirmation of the fact. He had enjoyed his season in the West Country, knew the county and the players well and was keen to return. But he was eager to play more county cricket and could not be expected to wait for long.

Hill said he had reminded Crowe of his promise not to join anyone else without giving Somerset time to respond. Crowe had shown his commitment to the county by playing a match for the Second XI before the start of the New Zealand tour. Hill had intended to speak to him during the next match, but Crowe had withdrawn. Concerned that the rising batsman might accept Essex's offer, and acting in a personal capacity, Hill wrote to him to say that he would call a committee meeting as soon as possible and added that, in his opinion, Somerset's long-term future lay with Crowe.

Now it was up to Somerset to determine its position. After describing this sequence of events, Hill informed the eight men present that he had called this impromptu gathering because he did not think Somerset could afford to lose Crowe. He pointed out that the team had fallen into decline and that the situation was deteriorating. He thought the West Indians had changed, and not for the better. He did not think that a responsible committee could allow the situation to continue. He realised that releasing the West Indians was bound to provoke an outcry, and possibly a rebellion, but those present should not be intimidated and must instead concentrate on making the right decision.

Later, Hill remained curiously immune from the venom that was otherwise freely dispensed. Dismissing him as a bumbling farmer whose heart was in the right place, the rebels absolved him from all responsibility. Dropping his notes at the special general meeting that was the climax of the dispute only added to the impression of innocence. He was puzzled and somewhat embarrassed to be so gently treated. Of course, belabouring men like him and Popplewell only weakened the rebels' case that it was a rotten decision taken by rotten people. More vulnerable targets had to be found. In fact, Hill was the driving force behind the removal of the established players and the signing of the enthusiastic New Zealander. More than anyone else in the room he had a clear mind on the subject, not least because he had given it a lot of thought.

Afterwards, Hill was justifiably criticised for omitting to invite the management of the club to a meeting that was of the utmost importance. The task of the cricket committee was to make cricketing decisions.

Of course, the implications of Hill's opinion were immediately apparent. If Crowe was to stay with the club then Richards and Garner must be released. It was a momentous decision and one this depleted body was incompetent to take. More time was required for reflection and deliberation. Certainly, the matter had not entered my head. Crowe and I had not spoken since the end of the 1984 season.

After speaking for some time, Hill asked everyone present for their opinions. Needing time to think, wanting to hear the other points of view and mindful of my responsibilities, I asked to speak last, a custom I would follow at all subsequent meetings. From the start it was clear where fingers would be pointed were such a decision to be taken, and it was not at men blessed with the luxury of anonymity. They had to address only the issue of right and wrong. My life would be affected. No one familiar with the characters involved in the case could think otherwise.

Most of those present spoke directly and to the point. Seven of the ad hoc committee favoured change. Among the former cricketers, Roy Marshall, a former West Indian Test cricketer who now ran a pub in town and was widely regarded as an astute judge of a player, said he believed the team had fallen apart and that something fresh was needed. His only reservation was about the bowling. He thought Somerset needed to sign a pace bowler rather than an outstanding batsman. Brian Langford, chairman of the cricket sub-committee, said that his hands were tied as he had indicated to Richards that his position was secure. In other circumstances he'd argue for signing Crowe. His was the sole dissenting voice in the room. At a later meeting, Peter Robinson pointed out that Richards had given excellent service over the years. Although he was well liked, nothing much was said about Garner. Botham's name was hardly mentioned. Indeed, it was generally agreed that no account should be taken of his likely reaction. Subsequently, Botham was offered another two-year contract.

My turn came. Patently, the desired course of action could not be followed without the consent of the captain. Later, it was hard to convince cricketing friends that the club had the conviction needed to take such a step. One colleague said 'they haven't got the guts', and was nonplussed to be told that he was much mistaken. A large majority of the senior officials at the club believed the time had come to rebuild the team, and they were prepared to take the consequences. As captain, I was the only person capable of changing their minds.

At this and all subsequent meetings I supported their proposal. The cost has been enormous. Among the most bewildering aspects of the rebel case was the oft-repeated statement that Roebuck was a ruthlessly ambitious man determined to build a club he could dominate. It was an extraordinary notion. Actually, I was impatient to return to Australia. Moreover, it was obvious that any captain agreeing to the release from his squad of two, eventually three, such popular and gifted champions was signing his own death warrant. Of course I did not expect to survive such a controversy for long. It was not a career move.

My survival was beside the point. My responsibilities were clear and they were not to the past but to the future. Later, John Woodcock, the finest of cricket writers, pointed out that it had been an unsentimental decision. His words touched a nerve, for this was the part that worried me, the part that lay behind the weeks of contemplation and the confidential consultations with players present and past. Sentiment plays little part in my character. Throughout I wanted to know not the cricketing merits of the decision—my mind was made up about that—but the moral viewpoint.

Realising the price that was to be paid, I did not lightly support the release of the mighty West Indians, but by the end of that first meeting the die had been cast. Perhaps the other item on the agenda contributed to the decision.

Viv had refused to take a drugs test a few days earlier in Bristol, a refusal that was bound to provoke an investigation. Drug tests were not yet part of the routine of professional cricket. In eighteen years as a Somerset cricketer I cannot recall any other times when samples were taken from players. In the following decade, Devon players were tested on three occasions and, much to the amusement of the players, my name was picked out of the hat every time.

Realising the consequences of refusal, Langford tried to persuade Richards to provide the sample, but Viv would not oblige. After the match he came around to ask for assistance in writing a letter to Lord's, giving the reasons for his action. He explained that he had not seen the names being pulled from the hat and was suspicious because the other player named was among those given cocaine in Oxford a year before, a fact known to the authorities. Viv smelt a conspiracy. A letter along these lines was written and dispatched. Lord's admitted that the names were supposed to be drawn in public and let the matter rest.

Upon this point I could defend Viv to the utmost. In all his years at Somerset I did not once hear him talking about drugs and I know that he would not dream of encouraging others to try them. Moreover, cricket had no business checking him or anyone else for recreational drugs. That was a matter between the individual and the forces of law and order. Richards was a proud and private man and highly responsible in this area, as was Garner. Later a distinguished journalist asked what part drugs had played in the decision to release these players. 'None' was the reply, but it was not a foolish question, because drugs were plainly part of the cancer affecting the club.

Obviously the decision taken on 21 July put me in an unenviable position, despite the fact that it could be reversed. Every county captain is obliged to respect the confidentiality of private meetings or else no serious discussions could take place. Nonetheless the obligation to pretend that nothing was happening behind the scenes while confidential discussions were taking place created an impression of dissimulation. Readers must decide for themselves the correct course of action to take in these circumstances. Having supported the changing of the guard I held my tongue. Apart from resigning, nothing else seemed feasible.

Astonishingly the secrecy of this and subsequent meetings was maintained. Not a word was heard about the impending move until the announcement itself was made. It was not as if committee members alone were aware of the situation. Searching for wisdom, I raised the matter with friends and colleagues and none of them breathed a word. Only once did the story look like breaking before Somerset had completed its deliberations. Out of the blue Matthew Engel, then the cricket correspondent of the *Guardian* newspaper, rang to say that he had been covering a match in Essex and upon asking about the prospects of signing Crowe had been told that he was going to play for Somerset. Accordingly he was obliged to ask what, in that case, was going to happen to Richards and Garner? 'Matthew,' I replied, 'that is a question I wish you had not asked and which I cannot possibly answer.' He said that he'd always thought exclusives were over-rated and let the matter rest.

A week after the impromptu meeting in Taunton, Crowe informed the county, through his agent, that he had decided to accept the opportunity to play for his old club in 1987. Clearly another meeting of the committee was required because the gathering on 21 July had been informal, unanticipated and unsat-isfactory. The handling of the entire affair reflected Hill's desire to push the matter through as quickly as possible lest the New Zealander decide to try his luck elsewhere.

On 8 August the management and cricket sub-committees met for the first time to discuss the issue. By 9 votes to 3 the view of the first meeting was endorsed. Of course Brian Langford again voted against the move, as did my friend Peter Robinson, who said that Crowe could not replace two men. John Gardner, a wet fish from Weston-Super-Mare, argued that Botham would inevitably walk out in sympathy and that the better course of action would be to release the West Indians at the end of the 1987 season on the grounds that they'd be touring with their national team the following year. Although this position sounded sensible it meant another year of turmoil and merely delayed the inevitable. It was agreed that secrecy should be maintained for otherwise neither the team nor the club could function for the remainder of the season.

It was decided that nothing would be announced until after the normal contracts meeting scheduled for 26 August.

Despite the formality of this meeting and the majority of senior figures in the club in favour of the move, the subject remained a matter for debate. Nothing had been set in stone. If my position changed then the decision could and would be overturned. Since the original meeting, held 18 days earlier, I had been trying to change my mind but had been unable to do so. Throughout the day the issue tossed and turned in my brain, with all possible points considered at length. By nightfall I'd be tired and uncertain. Sleep always seemed to bring clarity. Every morning I'd wake up convinced that this action had to be taken.

In a further attempt to find reasons to swap sides, the subject was raised with tried and trusted friends. Vic Marks and Brian Rose were among those privately consulted. Neither spoke against the move. Rose said he thought the change would be 'bad in the short run and good in the long run'. As the final confirmation approached the pair became nervous. Later Rose was accused in the newspapers of sitting on the fence and responded from his holiday home in Spain by telling reporters that he supported the move but thought Somerset needed a bowler rather than a batsman. As ever, Marks' position remained elusive. When the rebels named him as their vice-captain it was taken as a sign of his support, but he had not spoken to them and, from Perth, said he knew nothing of their intentions.

Peter Denning and Dudley Doust, the respected senior sportswriter on the *Sunday Times*, were contacted, as was an artist friend who lived near Taunton and upon whose hospitality I occasionally imposed myself with a bottle of wine and too many words. Among all these concerned observers, only the artist spoke against the move. Alas, this man let himself down by seeking a confidential conversation by way of finding a compromise then breaking that confidence. He stood up at the public meeting and repeated everything said in that conversation, cleansing his conscience with the words 'the truth must come out'. Our friendship did not survive this manoeuvre. Although these people wore halos most of them were unpleasant, and their brave new world wasn't going to work.

Throughout the consultations the search was for an argument capable of changing my mind. None was forthcoming.

By now the pressure was growing within the team for September was not far away and everyone knew that was the time for hirings and firings. With nothing to think about except the end of the season the atmosphere in the team deteriorated further. Botham was back in the England side and playing alongside Graham Gooch, captain of Essex, in the Oval Test. The Crowe situation seemed bound to crop up. It did not seem right or proper that long-standing players should learn of their fate not from the club itself but through a phone call from a friend. Accordingly I drove to the county ground and interrupted a management meeting to ask that a final and formal decision be taken about the overseas players and that immediately thereafter the players be informed of the club's position.

Somerset could have avoided a lot of trouble by announcing the news in the dead of winter. Hampshire released Gordon Greenidge long after players and supporters had gone their separate ways and barely a murmur was heard. My view was that the county should be more forthright. Later the club was criticised as much for the mechanics of the decision as its merits, unfairly so in my opinion. There is no easy way to tell a man his time is up. At least the announcement was made openly and with sufficient time given to all concerned to try to overturn the decision or else remove from office those responsible for taking it. No one can say that Somerset acted in a cowardly way.

After my intervention, a meeting was arranged for the following Friday, 22 August. By a majority reduced by the absence of the treasurer and the abstentions of C.R.M. Atkinson, a former Somerset captain and still headmaster of Millfield, and myself, the decision was taken to release the West Indians and offer terms to Crowe. In their capacities as Chief Executive and Chairman of Cricket, Brown and Langford were to inform the players of the decision next morning.

Now there was no turning back. My reason for abstaining was simple. This decision could only be taken by the committee. As always I had insisted on speaking last. It was a form of self-defence. When the death threats started coming, as was inevitable, I could with justice point out that this was a decision taken not by an individual but by a group of men elected by the members and presented with the task of promoting the well-being and good name of the club. Whereas a captain might or might not feel loyalties towards his players, these committeemen were duty bound to think only of the club. No one could accuse me of exerting undue influence. Of course both sides tried to do so, the rebels because a target was needed, the club officials because they were worried about the verdict of history. Despite these efforts, the point remains valid. Viv and Joel were not sacked by any individual. Beyond a desire to restore health to Somerset cricket there was no malice or agenda involved. Only outsiders found the decision incomprehensible. Insiders were entitled to regard it as mistaken or even reprehensible, but not shocking.

Somerset had sunk to the bottom and there was no sign of recovery. As far as I was concerned it was as simple as that. My struggle had been not with the judgement itself but with the human element, a question resolved when a friend pointed out that my primary responsibility was to play my part in building a club and team that could work. Throughout the ensuing debate I argued only about the merits of the decision and never about the personalities involved. Throughout the months of furious and sometimes bitter disputation officials regularly asked and sometimes urged me to spill the beans by way of counter-attack. Although some players and committeemen did brief reporters about various incidents, I refused to get involved in name calling. Apart from anything else, I liked Viv and Joel and disliked some of those arguing for the club. One of the rebels asked me, 'Can't you see the sort of men you are surrounded by?' By then some of the rebels had emerged in their true colours and I was able to reply, 'Take a look at your lot. It is not a pretty sight.' The issue was not my captaincy or character but the direction of the club. The team had finished bottom under Botham in 1985 and many members, the owners of the club, had resigned in disgust not so much at the results as the lack of spirit. The contrast with the spirit shown when Crowe was around in 1984 stayed in many minds. Of course these supporters were not entitled to vote at the special general meeting held in November because they had already voted with their feet.

In many ways I was ambivalent about the outcome of the battle between the senior players and the club. Rather, I wanted the matter to be resolved because this demoralisation and destruction could not be allowed to continue. Unfortunately in these disputes a man, and especially a leader, is forced to take sides and cannot thereafter choose his company. The decision was taken on its merits and, in all the circumstances, it was the correct one. How Somerset came to be in such a poor way has been the subject of previous chapters. Arresting the fall was beyond my powers; starting again was the only option. My opinion has not changed. It was nothing personal.

At the end of the momentous meeting I told the committee they had condemned me to a rotten few months and then drove to a nearby village to attend a party given by one of our opening batsmen, Nigel Felton. Of course, I was not much in the mood for company, but Vic Marks was going to be there and he had to be told that the announcement was going to be made the following morning. None of the other players were to know anything about it. Vic looked shocked.

After our brief conversation, I went home. Dudley Doust rang to ask for information. Seeking his counsel had meant revealing both the meeting and its probable outcome. I remember him saying, 'I am wearing two hats in this conversation.' Of course, as a journalist, he scented a story and he wanted to write it. Even though we worked on the same paper, it did not seem right that he should be handed the news on a plate twelve hours before anyone else. Accordingly, I let him think that the issue had been fudged, but arranged a telephone call for the following morning so that his call could be recognised and answered. I knew that my line would be hot and that torrid days, months and perhaps years lay ahead. John Barclay, a lovely man, good friend and then captain of Sussex, had warned that the repercussions would be enormous and that I'd be booed on cricket grounds around the country. On that basis, he'd advised against the move. He was right about the reaction, but it did not seem much of a reason to refuse to take a step regarded as necessary by most responsible men and, as it turned out, by the great majority of the members.

Unsurprisingly Somerset officials were worried by the response of the Sunday supporters to the decision, for this was the group that had seen the stars at their best and was therefore most likely to be upset about their ejection. The next match was only 48 hours away, and demonstrations were anticipated. In the end the atmosphere was eerily quiet both within the team and at the ground. Inevitably, the players' minds were elsewhere. Not that the results could get any worse. Seeing the extra players, Viv produced a high-pitched laugh and asked, 'Did you think we wouldn't come?' Otherwise he did not say much. Everyone was digesting the information and pondering the next move.

Nor was the crowd as vociferous as had been feared. Of course they knew nothing beyond the bare facts and merely greeted Garner and Richards with especial warmth and left it at that. Somerset lost the match but that hardly seemed to matter.

Back in Taunton the letters were flooding in. Naturally, many were expressions of sympathy and appreciation for the West Indians. My pile was also large. Most of the correspondents were hostile and some were abusive. A few were nasty and for the next twelve months a regular supply of threats to my life dropped on my doormat. When Crowe arrived the following April I tried to intercept the more vicious messages. No one was told about these letters, and their existence was only revealed when Tony Brown came across one I had put down and forgotten about whereupon the police were called in. They could not help much. Not that the threats were worrying. Life comes and it goes. But the thought did occur that the rebels might not be as nice as they imagined.

Although many of the most faithful had previously resigned in disgust and could not take part, Somerset officials were confident of the support of the majority of the members. Admittedly some would vote for the club regardless but there was a groundswell of support from regulars dismayed by the collapse of their side. Alarmed by the reporting of the local newspaper and by the contents of its letters page, some committeemen did panic but these arguments were unlikely to change the opinions of those who had witnessed the deterioration.

Before long, Botham started throwing his weight around. He did not think he could overturn the decision but he intended to try. His reason for doubting his influence was that he had been born far from the county he had represented since 1969 and was accordingly regarded as an outsider. When this reservation reached my ears I was flabbergasted. Of all the reasons supporters might reject the England all-rounder, this seemed the least likely.

Botham started by calling the sackings 'disgraceful' and saying that he'd leave with the West Indians. Next he called a meeting of the players and said I could not attend. Whenever I had spoken to the team I had made sure every player was invited. Plainly he was trying to isolate me but it did not work for he had lost the players long before. In his fury he defaced pictures of me and wrote 'Judas' on a piece of paper and pinned it above my place in the changing room. None of the players had the guts to remove the placard, which was more disappointing than the hotheaded reaction of a former friend. If these men wanted to play for a club worth something then they, too, had to start fighting.

Far from taking the sign down, I let it hang in its place. Botham's opinions did not bother me, and anyhow the placard told outsiders something about the state of play in the room and the nature of one of its inhabitants. Eventually a local photographer heard about the sign and took a picture that was published in several national newspapers.

My argument with Botham was not about the sign but the timing of its posting. My younger brother had come down to the club for some treatment on his back and was in the rooms when Botham wrote his message. As far as I was concerned, families were off limits.

Before these events I had intended to fly to Australia as soon as possible to resume the warm way of life that had proved so fulfilling. Moreover, there was the small matter of contracts with the *Sydney Morning Herald* and Melbourne *Age* and an English paper to cover the forthcoming Ashes series. These attacks and the urgings of committeemen forced me to stay to the bitter end.

Botham's supporters were concerned for the reputation of their man. A businessman in town contacted a mutual friend and warned that anything said about Botham's private life would provoke repercussions in the form of attacks upon mine. When the news was relayed to me, I laughed. The deal seemed to be that they would not tell lies about my life provided I did not tell the truth about someone else's. A reply was sent through the same emissary, a member of the committee, along the lines that I had no intention of saying anything about anyone's private affairs and that I did not appreciate threats of this sort.

Later the matter was raised again in a phone call indicating that the rebels intended to push hard at a press conference. Reasoning that I was, after all, a journalist and that no one involved was listening to anything said by the other side, I decided to attend the conference. Characteristically I went first to the wrong venue, Creech Castle rather than the Castle Hotel. Accordingly I arrived late and made an unintentionally dramatic entrance. Fortunately the rebels did not stoop that low and instead made some hostile though entirely legitimate points.

Nor was this the end of the diversion. Soon two journalists approached asking for a private word. Both were evidently embarrassed and clearly hated every second of the ensuing conversation. They explained that they had been instructed by their editors to ask certain questions about my personal life. One of the papers involved was Botham's tabloid, not that this proves he knew anything about it. The reporters were delighted and relieved when I declined to admit or deny anything. From experience I knew that the only way to kill a story is to make no comment. 'Thank goodness for that,' said the late Colin Price, one of the number and a man with whom I had no quarrel.

Actually I have no quarrel with any newspaper. Throughout this and subsequent matters I have always been treated fairly. Inevitably some journalists are more kindly disposed than others but few have been unprofessional or personal. More often than not I have been pleasantly surprised by the mature nature of even the most critical piece. My dislike of most English newspapers is founded not upon grievance but upon a longstanding rejection of the puritanism, prurience and downright nastiness to be found therein. Unfortunately the nastiness was reflected both in the characters of the editors and the relevant cricket reporters, whose company I avoided whenever possible. Although much better paid than their colleagues overseas, they spent most of their time fiddling their expenses in the English way. I did not allow these newspapers into my house because I did not want my charges to be affected by them. Whenever their editors appeared on television to defend their latest tawdry manoeuvre I felt sick. Later, one of the journalists admitted that he did not allow his own paper into his house because he did not want his daughter to read it. My dislike of this debasement has come to include reality television, a lesser evil altogether but also a depressing spectacle. Life seems to offer so much more.

My contempt for the more unpleasant tabloids was and remains founded upon a belief that they had played a large part in destroying the culture of their country. I have always believed that every institution, team and nation has a prevailing culture. England's had become cheap, mean, narrow and vindictive. These papers excuse themselves on the ground that they merely reflect the thinking of the general public. If so, then God help the old England. Maybe I was taking those papers too seriously, overrating their effect, but sometimes I did forget to laugh. But I do not think so. In the noble cause of freedom of speech they indulge themselves in crassness and racism, all covered with a thin veneer of humour. Inevitably, their poison has spread. Mr Murdoch has had his revenge. His papers in Australia do not work along such lines.

Of course, some of the tabloids were fine, and some of the broadsheet writers were themselves beneath contempt, especially Auberon Waugh and Matthew Parris. Fortunately, there were compensations in the writings of John Woodcock and Libby Purves.

Before long I stopped reading English newspapers altogether. Regarding them as enfeebled, I also rejected any invitations to visit schools and so forth. It is not that I did not care about England; quite the contrary. I admired its sometime greatness and contribution to the world. Persuaded that the contemporary could not work I scorned England more, perhaps, than it deserved and was accordingly surprised whenever youngsters showed the guts that alone command respect. Regardless, though, I set out to become as Australian as possible.

As might have been expected Viv Richards did not lower himself in those months of ferocious argument. Although he could be shrill, dignity and pride were never lost. He confronted me during a match in Worcester played in that awkward period between the announcement of the decision and the end of the season. He was aggressive and spoke with passion, saying that he'd been hearing all these rumours but had not believed them. Pointing his finger into my chest he accused me of sickness, treachery and much else. If my life was limited by Somerset or England or cricket it might have been intimidating. I tried to tell him that the decision had been made inevitable only by events during the summer. He was not for listening and dismissed my remarks as the clever words of a manipulative man. He wrote a letter to the local paper saying all he wanted to do was to play cricket for Somerset and made an appearance on television so outspoken that some supporters were shocked. Not having read the letter or seen the interview I cannot comment.

In October the West Indies went on tour to the sub-continent. Interviewed by a reporter for *The Times*, Viv called me selfish and accused the committee of shooting him like a dog. It was all fair comment. He did not cross the line.

Throughout the months of debate that led to the final meeting I was nonplussed by the ease with which other former friends were able to condemn as wicked someone they had known for years. Afterwards only two friends remained in Taunton, Phillip Squire, the new club doctor, a fine man, and Peter Robinson. The rest were consumed by the hatred created by this affair. They were besotted with something that no longer existed, the old Somerset team with all its character, excitement and glory.

Joel was likewise impressive. A man without malice, he was uncomfortable amidst all this name-calling. Alone among the three great players, and the all-rounder who took up their cause, he would stay in the county until the matter was resolved. Beyond accusing me of also wanting to get rid of the club's management lock, stock and barrel, he did not have much to say. Of course he was telling the truth, for he is a truthful fellow and moves around with a Bible in his bag. Fortunately he included in his list officials I respected, a mistake that allowed me to issue a denial.

Obviously I wanted to change both the way the club was run and the people running it. Mismanagement had played its part in its decline and fall. If Somerset was to be a proper club then strong foundations had to be put in place. In the event a consultant was asked to prepare a report but, as should have been expected, nothing much changed. Of course a streamlined committee was needed (39 members did seem a lot) and younger, more gifted men and women were required for positions of responsibility. But a man cannot fight a battle on two fronts.

Those last few matches of the summer were tense. Essex arrived in Taunton with a championship to win, and the contrast between their sustained success and our disintegration was stark. The match also contained an incident that lingers in the mind. Botham was bowling and, for the first time in memory, asked for a man to be placed close at silly point. To be specific, he asked his captain to occupy this hot spot. Before long he sent down the juiciest of half-volleys, which Brian Hardie smashed through my legs. A bone could easily have been broken. I glared at Botham but said nothing. I thought there was a look in his eye. Of course, it might have been my imagination.

Once the season reached its unhappy conclusion the players

went their separate ways and I was left in Taunton, three doors up from Garner. By now both sides had formed committees to run their campaigns. A petition was produced demanding a special general meeting and letters were sent to members with both sides putting their case. Apart from appearing a couple of times on local television, I held my tongue. The phone kept ringing with rumours and offers of support. A national paper rang to say that it wanted to back our side but the editor thought the rebel cause more likely to boost sales. It was all part of the process in an imperfect world.

Autumn arrived and still this bird could not fly south. By mutual consent the special general meeting was arranged for 8 November and was to take place on the Bath and West showground near Shepton Mallet, an appropriately rural setting. Against the wishes of the rebels, the ballot was to be secret. Meanwhile I kept myself occupied by fulfilling engagements, seeing my few remaining friends and running around the ground. Since university days I had kept fit by going for runs a few times a week. Now a picture was taken and shown in the papers under the headline: 'The Loneliness of the Long-distance Runner'!

At last, the day of the meeting arrived. Impatient to get to Australia I had booked a flight for the next day. On Saturday morning the membership, committee and disenchanted of Somerset drove to the showground site, where a large hall and countless reporters and cameramen awaited them.

Decorum was maintained throughout. There was no catcalling or shouts or other interruptions. It was a strangely muted and generous affair. Both sides listened respectfully to the other point of view. For the first time in years the lines of communication were open. There did not appear to be any rancour. Beforehand it was even possible to chat amiably with supposedly bitter opponents. Afterwards the same applied. With a few documented exceptions, the fight had been conducted along the proper lines which meant that, regardless of the result, there could still be a club and team to support.

At last the votes were taken and the club secured a decisive victory. Nigel Popplewell delivered the crucial speech, in which he described his disillusionment with the West Indians and his support for the changes. And he had retired before I was made captain. The leaders of the rebels did not complain. Some indicated their intention to accept the judgement of the members and to continue supporting their club. A press conference was held in which advocates of the two cases sat side by side to answer questions. A man with long hair in a ponytail suggested that it had been a defeat for individuality. My reply was the merest waffle. Already my mind was on the journey back to Taunton and then, the next day, to Sydney.

There were no celebrations. There was nothing to celebrate. A job had been done, that was all. Dr Squire drove the car home and the evening was spent sipping beer and enjoying a quiet meal in a pub. After all it was a parting of the ways for five months. The adrenalin was flowing because it had been quite an occasion, especially for Philip. My mood was one of relief that it had not been worse. Of course the attacks upon my character and captaincy had been fierce but that was to be expected, and anyhow some of the points made had merit. Undoubtedly there was a lot to learn. Perhaps the temptation to try to put things right in the first year as leader had been too strong. Nonetheless there had been too much harking on about 1986. Popplewell had set that right. I had been an easy and convenient smokescreen behind which the truth could be concealed. The fact was that Somerset had fallen apart and that all concerned, including the leaders of the rebellion, were partly to blame. Lacking the courage to take responsibility, reluctant to admit their mistakes and depending upon the support of the besotted Sunday crowd, the complainants had pointed the finger at an admittedly flawed new captain and an anonymous committee.

Next morning Brian Langford drove me to Heathrow, where reporters and cameras were waiting. Overnight Botham had warned me that I had better keep away from him. Since I was covering the Test series in which he was playing, this was going to be difficult. After responding disdainfully, I climbed aboard the plane bound for Australia.

One small incident remains from those months of fury. Stopping for petrol on the journey back from Manchester, I was approached by a soldier in uniform. He introduced himself, wished me well and then, as he walked away, he stopped, turned and said, 'The closer you get to men of substance the more they seem like shadows.'

13

INTO THE
PRESS BOX

Writing for Australian newspapers for the last eighteen years has been a stimulating and satisfying experience. From the start, the company of colleagues covering matches proved convivial. I have made many friends. Warmth and honesty prevail. No grudges are held, no petty jealousies or meanness pollute the atmosphere. A bloke could have an argument one minute and a beer the next. The press box had no pretension or pecking order and this newcomer was treated on his merits, and never mind that he was from the Old Dart, had been to Cambridge and had spent most of his cricket career blocking furiously. Contrastingly the English press corps seemed narrow, a trait that emerged more starkly on a subsequent tour to Pakistan when its more dismal members let themselves down.

By and large the English cricket writers were unpleasant and miserable. Of course, not everyone was affected by the mob. Christopher Martin-Jenkins retained his dignity and, among the retired players, only those commenting on the Sky Channel sank into the trough.

In his playing days, Michael Atherton was considered disdainful and aloof, but he attacked the grubbier tabloids after they stuck their snouts into his private life, for which he had been hauled over the coals by people who should have known better. He obviously did not lack courage. Unsurprisingly, he has become a considerable journalist. Between them, past players and uncynical youngsters might yet rescue cricket writing in England.

Of course it helped that from the start I liked my adopted country and most of its inhabitants. In some respects it is odd that an apparently archetypal Englishman should feel at home in a distant land with a different culture, but from boyhood I had wanted to find a place with clear skies where a man could hope to lead an uncluttered life. Australia seemed bright and young and raw and challenging, whereas the country of my birth appeared grey, tired and cynical.

Further travel helped to broaden the mind and, as time went by, I tried to combine the best things I came across in these wanderings—Africa's tribal ways and respect for elders, the sub-continent's warmth and intimacy, New Zealand's sense of independence, Australia's straightforwardness and belief that sport is an outlet for aggression and adventure and that the field is a separate place, England's wonderful stoicism. Of course, I fell far short. Of course, all these cultures also had their faults. Moreover, all and sundry were victims of an age in which youth had been promoted until it had become a market. As the years went by, the sales pitch was directed at ever younger ages, until childhood with its scrapes and bruises scarcely existed at all. Of course unhappiness followed.

Past customs did not arise by accident and cannot be abandoned on a whim. Now everyone complains that their children are obese, transfixed by computer games and utterly unruly. Well, there's a surprise. Political leaders have begun to talk about the crisis in young masculinity, which seems torn between emasculation and over-assertion. Inevitably, the abandonment of the rites of passage has come at a cost. Inevitably, over-protection has led to a loss of self-esteem. Meanwhile, those responsible for this debacle complain the loudest about the results they lacked the wits to foresee and now blame on others.

Fortunately all is not lost. Boys are still climbing onto surf-boards, fighting, dancing, singing and playing the fool. My youngsters lead a simple and natural life, with strong structures and secure foundations. Almost without exception, they are making the most of their abilities.

Australia offered hope, toughness and enterprise. Even the local sayings struck a chord, especially 'Cop it sweet'. Australians sat in the front seat of taxis, alongside the driver. It might sound corny, but taking the oath of allegiance and becoming an Australian citizen counts among the happiest days of my life. Of course Australia had its surprises. Considering their maverick reputation it came as a surprise to see locals standing obediently at traffic lights, waiting for the little man in green to give them permission to cross the road. High taxes also seemed to clash with the supposed rugged individualism but did confirm a willingness to give everyone a 'fair go'. Soon it became apparent that Australians were not as individualistic as had been imagined. Their sense of identity and desire to belong was pronounced and did allow much room for manoeuvre.

Becoming a citizen was only a step on the path to absorption into the country that had put out the welcome mat. Further information was needed. Not long afterwards a conversation arose on the ABC with fellow commentator and friend Jim Maxwell about what it meant to be a typical Aussie. Jim, who has a fair crack at fitting the bill, produced a list of the qualities required which was long and without blemish. Eventually the necessity arose to interrupt the discourse with the question, 'Do Australians have any faults?' The thought had not occurred. Pride in their country is widespread but behind the swagger can be found a hint of uncertainty. Australians count among the least tactile people around.

Traditionally they talk in deep voices and call everyone 'mate', sometimes even the females. Fortunately confidence has risen in recent times and, as in South Africa, humourists are making locals laugh at themselves.

But Australia does have its weak points, including self-obsession, the need to feel that it matters. Accordingly, minor sporting triumphs receive rapturous acclaim and sporting stars are glorified above all others. Australia does not, as it turns out, cut down its tall poppies but waters them, protects them and admires them uncritically. In 2003 I was dismayed by the attention paid to Steve Waugh, Shane Warne and Brett Lee, and saddened by the glorification of the individual. Perhaps it was the fault of the newspapers and television stations, for cricket is a small community.

By 1986/87 I had spent eight summers in Sydney, teaching, coaching, running holiday camps, going to movies and plays, drinking wine and eventually catching waves. Few young men are able to lead such a life, the life of their choice. Still, it could not last forever and at last the time came to leave education and to plunge into the world of antipodean journalism. During previous visits I had contributed to the *Sydney Morning Herald* (*SMH*) and the Melbourne *Age* and the articles had been well received. Australia and its newspapers seemed capable of accepting my entire self. A six-month contract was offered for that Ashes summer, the idea being that colour pieces should be written in support of Michael Coward and Bill O'Reilly, the senior men in the cricket writing team. Eventually Bill retired and ever since it has been my task to provide cricket columns for the Fairfax group.

O'Reilly was a great man and a wonderful writer. A fierce patriarch from the deepest bush, he had red hair, Irish blood, a fondness for beer, a penetrating mind, unwavering contempt for one-day cricket and absolute faith that sooner or later leg-spin would return. Unfortunately he did not live long enough to see

Shane Warne prove him right. Authority did not intimidate him and his love of language shone through every piece he wrote.

Bill's working routine was simple. In the mornings he'd arrive and take up his seat in the press box in the Monty Noble Stand. Until lunch he'd yarn with anyone within earshot, and his remarks were generally ripe and rich. Sometimes Steve Waugh sat by his side, listening to his tales and picking his brain. Few lunch breaks passed without a glass of beer being consumed, a custom also followed towards the end of his career by John Woodcock, the other great cricket writer of the era. Between lunch and tea, O'Reilly would follow proceedings with an eagle eye. Not that he ever missed a ball for his concentration was remarkable. Around tea-time he'd open his school exercise book, produce a pen and start composing his piece. He wrote in a copperplate hand and did not seem to pause until the last sentence had been constructed, whereupon he'd ring the copy-takers, dictate his 750 words, collect his papers and go home. On away trips he stayed in pubs and, like his old foe Harold Larwood, led a simple and modest life in a suburb of Sydney.

Mike Coward was and remains a skilful and committed journalist with firm principles and a fine singing voice. He has become the senior and most respected cricket writer in the country and also finds time to produce films on cricket history, write books, compère numerous events and appear on radio. Only a handful of reporters accompany an Australian tour because money is tight, deadlines difficult and newspapers thin on the ground. Fortunately a friendly atmosphere exists between journos, photographers and commentators so these trips are enjoyable, though too long in the opinion of most wives and some husbands.

A budding journalist could not have wished for better mentors. Third writers must think laterally and my time was spent in scoreboards and on The Hill, or interviewing umpires and curators, or simply giving the flavour of a day whose significant moments were covered by my elders.

Until a year or so ago my articles were written in an illegible longhand and dictated over the phone, an arrangement that seemed to amuse some of my contemporaries. Writing this way had its advantages. Whenever a copy-taker could not understand a sentence it was crossed out. It is not a journalist's task to confuse his reader. Often these hidden ladies would suggest a word or fill a gap. Now and then things did go haywire but I enjoyed the personal touch and the advantages were considerable. During the riot in Calcutta I was able to dictate as events unfolded, with the match starting and stopping, baton-wielding police charging and retreating, fires blazing or subsiding, match referee marching on and off the field, and all of it with deadlines coming and going. As events unfolded the *Age* held over its last edition and a few hours later a description of a colourful and changing scene landed on the doorsteps of inner Melbourne.

Among my regrets as a cricket writer was my failure to do justice to the century in Sydney that prolonged Steve Waugh's Test career. Although superb as far as spectators, television viewers and dramatists are concerned, in the opinion of reporters his timing was poor. Steve reached three figures at about 6.45 p.m., roughly 45 minutes after our usual Friday deadline, itself a product of the extra time needed to produce the vast slabs of paper bestowed on readers of the Saturday editions. By now writing on computer, I had the piece more or less completed and only trimming appeared possible. For the later editions, I should have picked up the phone to dictate 1000 words off the cuff, as had happened before on numerous occasions when immediacy was required.

The *Sunday Times* had also asked for full coverage of the series. No sooner had the plane reached Sydney than it was time to hurry to Brisbane to report on the first Test. Botham and I remained far apart at practice, which did not prevent a television crew showing film of him spitting in my direction. Foreshortening made it appear personal. Years later an Australian fast bowler and a Kiwi batsman went after each other like a pair of enraged bulls. Television directors in remote studios noticed the paceman spitting towards his foe. Soon the phones were ringing. Fortunately my sports editors, including the estimable Patrick Smithers, were prepared to rely on my judgement, which was that nothing had happened and, if it had, no one present at the ground was aware of it. To the contrary, the confrontation had been compelling and enjoyable.

Of course it was impossible to approach Botham in public. Nonetheless Somerset had not entirely given up hope that he might remain at the club. At any rate it was worth putting the ball in his court. After giving time for tempers to settle, I visited his hotel room. It was a quiet evening. Kath answered the knock on the door and said that her husband was out. A message was left. Doubtless news of the visit was relayed but nothing further was heard from the all-rounder and soon news arrived that he had joined his friend Duncan Fearnley at Worcestershire.

Weakened by tours to South Africa and demoralised by repeated defeats, the Australians were in disarray. Allan Border was captain and the selectors were searching for men with heart, and bowlers capable of taking wickets. Brisbane confirmed their worst fears as Botham scored a typically belligerent century that set the tone for the rest of the summer. A frail-looking young man batted in the middle order for Australia, and played alongside a rough-looking fellow with a beer belly and a flourishing moustache who might have been collected from a nearby pub. Not even the sagacious Mr Woodcock could have foretold the deeds to be done by Stephen Waugh and Mervyn Hughes.

England won the series. Nothing on the field of play indicated that English cricket was about to enter a long, dark night or that the Australians would recapture the Ashes in 1989 and hold them with almost contemptuous ease for the following seven series.

Michael Gatting captained England and, apart from oversleeping one night and reporting late for play in a friendly with Victoria, his work was praised. His mishap provoked one of those bursts of indignation that remain such an improbable part of the English experience. Even so, he seemed likely to be captaining a strong England team for several more years. During the Adelaide Test, I criticised Mike Gatting's team for dawdling over a drinks break. Afterwards the team manager, a useless fellow, was overheard to say that 'Roebuck will never play for England'. It did not bother me. A journalist has obligations to fulfil.

In hindsight, however, the seeds of self-destruction had already been sown. No leaders had emerged from the group of senior players into whose hands the team had fallen on the retirement of Mike Brearley. Most of them had tried their luck as captains and none had been able to impose himself upon his contemporaries. The premature death of Ken Barrington years before had left a hole that had not been filled, for he represented the best of England and cricket. Had he been spared, the disintegration of a talented team might have been avoided.

As it was, Gatting was sacked after losing his head in Pakistan. Of course this was not the reason given for his removal, the authorities preferring to rely upon some supposed liaison with a barmaid, a ruse that merely made them appear ridiculous. Gatting went off in a huff, which hardly helped matters. Further damage was done by an ill-timed rebel tour to South Africa, led by the deposed captain and managed by the current Chairman of selectors. At one stage the entire England selection committee had participated in rebel tours to the land of white supremacy. According to Ali Bacher, Graham Gooch and Jack Bannister, Botham was interested in joining a tour to South Africa, a suggestion the former Somerset all-rounder denied, saying with characteristic bravado that he could not have looked 'Viv Richards in the eye' had he taken the money. Someone is not telling the truth. My contempt for those who had taken the money offered by repre-sentatives of the South African regime remains intact. Even now their voices can be heard and their articles can be read. Only in the last decade has cricket begun to confront its white racism.

England lost its way, and its reputation. Although the World Cup was almost won in 1991 a slide had begun that has proved hard to arrest. As usual the authorities were blamed but players and coaches must also accept responsibility, including those of us running around in county cricket who indulged ourselves in donkey drop bowling, arranged declarations and other devices cal-culated to compromise the first-class game. Nor did it help that the old universities were allowed to retain their first-class status although their teams consisted largely of over-rated schoolboys. England's decline was reflected in the rush of appointments made from overseas, including numerous county coaches and captains chosen because our thinking was emaciated and theirs was stringent.

Meanwhile Australian cricket proceeded in the opposite direc-tion, with an unflinching analysis of the problem leading to the execution of an uncompromising plan. It might seem that great cricketers simply turned up at the right time, including a certain leg-spinner and some fine fast bowlers, but the system was in place to identify these players and to get the best out of them. Cricketers like Warne, Hughes, McGrath and Gillespie could easily have been lost to the game. There was no inevitability about their rise. Strong coaches, shrewd selectors and proud captains were appointed. Appropriate roles were found for men like Rod Marsh and Dennis Lillee, and more obscure thinkers of high calibre were also put to work. The cricket community had, and retains, a strong sense of service. Ambition and ego are not allowed to stand in the way of the game.

My contributions to the *Sunday Times* were well received and secured an award reserved for promising newcomers. Alas, no other gongs have come my way. Flying around the country covering cricket matches proved to be stimulating. Domestic bliss had never appealed. From the outset it was obvious that a way had to be found to turn a dislocating lifestyle into an enjoyable experience. Already established in Sydney, the opportunity now arose to build friendships and activities elsewhere. These relationships have sustained a career on the road. Matches in Brisbane meant a chance to catch up with the Nothlings, a family encountered while writing an article on Dr Otto Nothling, the only man for whom Don Bradman was dropped from a cricket team. He turned out to be a remarkable man with a colourful history. The Nothlings' middle son stayed at my house in Sydney while studying medicine, a process that seemed to demand watching a great deal of rugby on television. Brisbane also offers the Brants, with whom a friendship began in Harare while I was coaching Scott, their eldest son, at one of many African schools visited along the way.

14

TO REGROUP
AND REBUILD

Apart from my writing, the main concern that summer in Australia was Somerset's attempt to sign some bowlers. Many felt that bolstering the bowling was the top priority and that the overseas player should have been chosen with that in mind. My reply was that the attack was toothless and that one good bowler would not make much difference. Better to reinforce the batting, so that at least part of the team was competitive. Of course club, players and captain were going to be under enormous pressure and a powerful batting order might hold the fort by winning some one-day matches, and thus buying the time required to start the slower process of developing an attack capable of inconveniencing opponents.

In the event Brian Rose made more progress than anticipated. Assisted by funds made available by a club anxious to avoid ignominy the following summer, the newly installed manager of the county team signed Adrian Jones, a red-faced, huffing and puffing fast bowler from Sussex. Jones was an unusual man, an energetic but unpredictable bowler with an ability to take wickets at the sort of cost generally associated with Harrods. He had a strong presence in the rooms largely because he could say things hovering in the backs of the minds of more discreet colleagues. We clashed many times, but he took wickets and sent a warm letter when news of my retirement appeared in the newspapers.

Neil Mallender was the county's other main signing, an opening bowler raised in Yorkshire, currently playing in Northampton but tired of bowling on dreary pitches. Rose flew to New Zealand to offer him terms, a gesture that impressed a man from the old school of county cricket. Mallender commanded respect as a committed cricketer, and was invariably described as honest and reliable by reporters seeking to sum a man up in a couple of words. Both characteristics could be found within this splendid colleague, but he was also as mad as a hatter. Like most fast bowlers he considered the bouncer to be not only a top-class delivery but also an essential part of the armoury, to be dispatched once or twice an over. Now and then, when his rhythm was right and there was nothing in the pitch, Neil would sustain long spells of line and length delivered with pace and bounce, and then he was a formidable opponent. Always he was a loyal supporter and an admirable professional whose weakest point, apart from the penchant already mentioned, was a groin that occasionally demanded rest and recuperation.

Graham Rose and Neil Burns had also joined the club, so the winter had been productive. Accordingly there was reason to hope that Somerset might rise from the lowly position occupied in the previous two seasons. No one was expecting miracles, least of all the beleaguered captain. A careful campaign was planned, the pursuit of results respectable enough to give the team time to settle and the manager the opportunity to strengthen the staff. About the only blot on the landscape was the news that New Zealand was to tour Sri Lanka and that our overseas player would miss the first few matches of the summer. A replacement was needed and thoughts turned to the pale-faced fellow recently seen vainly and valiantly trying to keep the rampant Englishmen at bay.

In the event, Martin Crowe returned to Taunton earlier than expected because a bomb planted by the Tamil Tigers exploded outside the New Zealand team's hotel in Colombo, causing carnage and the cancellation of the rest of the tour. He missed only the opening match of the campaign, played against Lancashire and lost after a generous declaration had been set by a captain pressing for a result and impressed with the new bowlers in the first innings. Unlike characters in the novels of Kingsley Amis, pitches in Taunton calm down with age. Before the season began I had announced that Somerset was pursuing a five-year plan, always a wise precaution for a leader to take. In fact we were merely hoping for a couple of early victories to keep the wolves off our backs. Accordingly this defeat was discouraging, though not devastating.

Somerset won its opening one-day matches, beating Essex twice, victories that instilled confidence and hope. Unfortunately Crowe had been weakened by a mysterious ailment that affected his back and his strength and prevented him bowling much. Eventually salmonella poisoning was diagnosed. Doubtless stress also played its part for the quest for perfection was constant and exhausting. A replacement was needed and Brian Rose was dispatched to Birmingham, where Stephen Waugh was widening his experience and earning his keep.

An arrangement was made whereby the Australian was able to play for the county as needed and Somerset was obliged to send someone to take his place on Saturday afternoons. Accordingly Matthew Cleal was dispatched to the Midlands. Cleal was a young all-rounder from Yeovil whose career would be cut short by a back injury. Having left school early with a chequered report, he had put all his eggs in the cricketing basket. Not until bad luck befell him did his true character emerge. Undaunted, he went back to school, studied alongside boys five years younger than him, passed his exams, advanced to college, took his degree and proceeded with a master's course which was passed with flying colours. He stayed in touch and most conversations begin with, 'Roeby, you're never going to believe this but . . .', whereupon he'd outline his latest academic endeavour. In his playing days he had been dismissed as a dimwit, a role he seemed happy to fill. As a cricketer he had his days, once winning a match at Old Trafford with a straight six. As his character inspires warmth, so his achievements command respect. Suggestions of an allergy towards all-rounders from Yeovil are wide of the mark!

Waugh proved to be an intriguing character. A slight, pale, apparently frail young man, he did not say much but his words cut to the bone. Nor was there anything fancy about his cricket. Everything was reduced to its essentials and then rebuilt by an original mind uninterested in frills and intent upon productivity. He liked to get on with the job and was the sort of matter-of-fact cricketer long associated with his country. Whereas Richards had been a performer and Crowe a stylist, Waugh was a competitor. By his reckoning a bloke was there to score runs and take wickets, and all else was tomfoolery. He'd walk out to bat in that shy way of his, take guard and get to work. Waugh was sustained by an inner drive that was rarely revealed, pushed along by an unwavering commitment to winning. In pursuit of his goals, and always aware of the hostile forces around him, he refused to give ground or show any sign of vulnerability. Always he was digging inside himself, searching for the gold that gradually emerged. He was not, though, as calm as he appeared. Mere blood flowed through his veins. Rather he was a poker player determined not to betray a flicker of doubt. Nonetheless, nerves affected him as much as anyone else and he could be quite inconsistent. He learned to overcome them, that is all, applied his mind to the task and came up with an answer.

From the outset Waugh was popular with the Somerset players. Lacking Richards' explosive temperament and Crowe's zeal, he went quietly about his cricket and remained honest and straight-forward. He had reduced life to its simplicities, which is harder than it sounds. In those days there was a lot of Doug Walters and Stan McCabe about him. These former champions and bushies were his cricketing heroes, men who could play stirring innings apparently off the cuff. Usually it is easy to tell apart boys raised in the Australian bush and the city. With Waugh it was difficult, because there was a lot of the country in him and little of urban sophistication. Even then he was a dogged fighter and determined to finish on top.

Despite seeing him play from his school days when the latest deeds of the Bankstown twins were a regular feature of cricketing conversation, I had not previously met him. Both his cricket and character made immediate impressions. Humour could be found in his Charlie Chaplin walk and terse way of talking. Waugh and Bob Dylan count among the driest, funniest fellows around.

Of course it was not all cheese and pickles. Now and then differences of opinion arose. Waugh rescued our innings against Gloucestershire with a coruscating assault upon Courtney Walsh, an attack full of thrilling, powerful shots played with a sudden thrash of arm and wrist. In this mood he could make the danger-ous appear safe, and seemed capable of striking any ball to the boundary. Having stormed past 100 he was in full flight until, 30 minutes before stumps, his benighted captain unexpectedly declared. Waugh tossed his bat in the air, stalked from the field looking like Monty after a double bogey, strode into the dressing-room and growled, 'What does a bloke have to do to get a decent hit around here?' He was frustrated that Somerset had closed its innings just as he was cutting loose and did not seem convinced by the observation that declaring had seemed the best way of winning the match.

After a few overs in the field, Waugh wandered across and, from the corner of his mouth, muttered, 'Geez, sorry skip, got a bit carried away!' At least he cared. Fortunately three wickets fell that evening and the tactic might have worked even better had not a crucial slip catch been dropped by a certain gentleman from Australia!

Although inconsistent, Waugh proved to be an astonishing winner of cricket matches. In those days he was not nearly as much use when a match was taking shape, a weakness he gradually overcame. When his blood was up, though, when there was a match to win or a fast bowler to tame, a change came over him; the introverted accumulator trying to find the way forward was replaced by an elemental force of nature. It was as if a typhoon had suddenly taken the place of an ordinary breeze. Even now, sixteen years later, several of his innings remain vivid in the memory. An apparently lost cause was saved in a 40-over match as the Northamptonshire bowlers were torn apart. Centuries were scored in adversity and in the face of ferocious bowling from Walsh and Silvester Clarke. For a long time Waugh regarded his innings against Clarke at the Oval as the best he had played, and recorded the fact in a book. It was an extraordinary effort from a brilliant batsman. It is no small thing to be both pragmatic and inspired.

Waugh had not yet learnt about averages and churning out runs, the characteristics later regarded as the main features of his game. Then he did not think in terms of careers or posterity, concentrating his entire being upon matters in hand. On his quiet days he did not catch the eye. No one could have picked him out in a crowd or even from a net. He was not a pretty or pleasing player, the sort whose talent expressed itself in every manoeuvre. Not until effectiveness was taken into account did respect for his cricket grow.

Failure proved instructive. Dropped from the Australian Test side after a bad spell, he made a private vow that it was not going to happen again. To that end he analysed his performances, realised the umpires were not, as he had originally thought, entirely to blame and that parts of his game required attention. Determined to recapture his place in the Australian side, he set about eradicating error and risk. The cart to leg disappeared for a decade as, more permanently, did the back foot exuberance at deliveries wide of the stumps. Instead, Waugh built a wall around his wicket. Years before the opportunity had arisen to bat with Ken Barrington in a charity match played in Melbourne. A lot can be seen from the bowler's end. In Barrington's case, there was this broad bat and this body moving behind the ball and knocking it away in a manner reminiscent of the Australian champions of the 1920s. It was hard to see how any ball could get past. Indeed it hardly seemed worth trying.

Searching for the same effect, Waugh moved back behind every ball, kept his bat straight and waited for the loose delivery. He batted and batted until the figures spoke for themselves, and then he batted some more. Only in his dotage, with time running out, did flamboyance return to his game, whereupon he said he felt young again. Jon, one of my students, lists his favourite last words as, 'My only regret in life is that I did not drink more alcohol.' Waugh will understand the sentiment. Perforce reason had taken over his game. Part of him regretted this conquest of instinct, though it could not have been otherwise for a man must be able to live with himself.

Thanks to Crowe, Waugh, the newcomers and the remnants of the old guard, Somerset had a satisfactory season, finishing five places higher in the Championship than the previous year; fourth in the Sunday League and reaching the semi-final of a knockout competition. Avoiding humiliation had meant taking a conservative approach. Few chances were taken against other weak teams. Eleventh was a respectable but hardly exciting position. Unsurprisingly there were some bad days and then players could sense the vultures hovering. An embarrassing defeat was suffered against a minor county in a Gillette Cup match played on a plasticine pitch. The next morning Botham was gloating about it in the papers. Our match with Worcestershire attracted a large crowd but was spoilt by rain. All eyes were on the antagonists. Facing an attack weakened by injury, Botham scored 100 and gesticulated towards the committee balcony. And then we all went home.

Before the match, Botham had walked out to the square and loudly predicted that the pitch would be bald. Among the more absurd of the accusations made the previous year was that I had prepared pitches to suit myself, rather than Garner and the other fast bowlers. The match with Surrey was mentioned, when the grass was, admittedly, removed, which did not stop our mighty batting order being swept aside in the second innings. If there is a captain around who has prepared a greentop for Silvester Clarke, I have not met him. In that match Botham refused to face Clarke in his only innings, instead standing at the other end and hitting hard till he was out and between times refusing all singles.

The criticism was wrong. The matches with Gloucestershire (Walsh) and Hampshire (Marshall) were played on pitches lively enough to encourage the captain winning the toss to bowl first. As ever the point did not survive a moment's scrutiny from the fair-minded, yet it is repeated as gospel.

My form was satisfactory, and unaffected by the constant threats and denigrations. During the winter *Wisden* announced that I had been chosen by the editor as one of its five players of the year. It was an honour keenly appreciated, especially as Mr Woodcock was responsible for the nominations. Nowadays *Wisden* is dismissed as a book of statistics with an overblown reputation as the conscience of the game. Then it was highly respected and this recognition counts among the highpoints of my career in professional cricket.

Inevitably the pressures started to take a toll and by the end of the following summer it was clear that the time had come to put the team into fresh hands. From the moment the decision was taken to release the West Indians it was obvious that my days were numbered. Vic Marks had been a loyal deputy and deserved his chance to lead the county team. Moreover, rumours had reached our ears that Jackie Birkenshaw night be interested in putting aside his white coat and becoming a county coach and that, furthermore, Chris Tavare was ready to leave Kent after one of those upsets that arise in all clubs. Vic was friendly with both men and was well placed to lure them to Taunton. In the event the gossip proved correct and both men would join Somerset for the 1989 season.

Not that 1988 was at all bad. Somerset finished eleventh again but the highlight of the summer was an innings played by a visiting batsman, Graeme Hick of Harare and Worcester. Hick had arrived from Zimbabwe intent upon cricketing plunder. Hitherto he had led a sheltered life on a tobacco farm before attending a highly disciplined school not far from Harare Sports Club and the President's House. His reputation as a prolific batsman preceded him and he had justified his reviews with numerous commanding innings. His 405 not out was the highest score in county cricket since Archie MacLaren mauled a somewhat depleted Somerset attack almost 100 years before. Had Hick been allowed to continue batting after tea on the second day the record must have fallen. It was a tireless, remorseless effort against an attack strong enough to reduce the visitors to 189/5 on the first afternoon and to concede only 308 runs on the opening day.

Somerset lost the match by an innings but fought back manfully to beat the same opponents a week later. By then Hick seemed capable of reaching 1000 runs in May, a landmark that had been regarded as impossible. Hating the fuss, he batted poorly in the return match and was dismissed cheaply. It was a rare failure. As far as the Somerset players were concerned, he was an outstanding batsman. Other counties might have detected a chink in his armour but only steel was encountered by Somerset's floundering leather-flingers. Tom Cartwright, the county coach of the 1970s and a wonderful medium-pacer in his time, pointed out that his bat swung like a pendulum and predicted difficulties against top-class bowlers in Test cricket. Lacking extreme pace or devious spin, as well as a strategy, Somerset could not bring him down.

In hindsight, his limitations were apparent. Hick seemed to prosper only when he felt comfortable. He had not encountered adversity often enough in his early days for a protective shell to be erected. Accordingly he was vulnerable against bowlers and captains capable of challenging his authority. Hick worked in straight lines. Not that he lacked intelligence, for he had been a middle-ranking student at Prince Edward's School. Rather his game and life had been built upon certain parameters and he was not flexible enough to survive outside them.

At the end of the season, my third as captain, I stood down and the mantle passed to Vic Marks. My life had found its path, writing for the Australian newspapers in the English winter, playing cricket for a few more seasons and then settling in Sydney. By now I had written three books: a diary of a season, a collection of articles and the book written with Botham. Over the course of the next few years another three would briefly appear upon the shelves: another collection of pieces, a book on great innings and a history of Somerset CCC. The last efforts were fun because research was needed and many hours were spent in the archives, browsing through old newspapers.

My batting had responded to this newfound certainty and maturity had brought solidity of temperament and technique. Most professional batsmen reach their peaks between the ages of 28 and 34, when experience has bestowed its lessons but the eye retains its youthful vigour. Exceptions can be found among the great players, whose most substantial innings were often played at the start of their careers. Like Alexander they conquered the world at a tender age and then tried to find meaning in their lives.

In this period between youthful folly and heavy-footed decline some reasonable innings were played. Somerset went to Trent Bridge in 1986 to face Richard Hadlee, Clive Rice and the rest of the men of Nottinghamshire. Infuriated by my ungenerous portrayal of him in an article, Hadlee was reputedly baying for my blood. As it happened my highest score came along in this match, 221 not out. Apparently Hadlee tells the story against himself in his after dinner speeches, how he tried with all his might to exact revenge, how he hit the body, found the edge but somehow could not remove the obstruction. My recollection of the innings last no longer than the first ball of the match which swung away, cut back and somehow missed the wickets. As it passed I can remember thinking, 'Well, that was fun while it lasted!' Then, astonished to find the stumps intact, I batted for another nine hours! It was another lesson in life. The line between success and failure can be wafer thin. Hadlee may have tried too hard. Later I came to understand that he needed to remove himself from the swirl of events around him because he bowled much better cold than hot. Botham was the opposite, thriving on engagement, denying his opponents the luxury of living within the patterns developed over the years. Hadlee was a craftsman, Botham an antagonist.

Two other innings linger in the mind. Weston-Super-Mare had not been a favourite hunting ground because the festival was played towards the end of the summer, by which time emotional energy was in short supply, besides which the pitches were usually horribly slow and low. Eventually one of the sponsors, John Luff, rescued the situation. We had played together for the Downside Ravens, a loose collection of characters raised by Father Martin Salmon to play friendlies at the school in the holidays. Martin was a wonderful man and a teacher of stern disposition who promised to become a monk while drowning in the seas off Japan during the war and kept his word. Jack Fingleton, Siegfried Sassoon and various rough-and-tumble characters had turned out over the years, and Father Martin usually managed his resources with sufficient dexterity to produce a close finish a few minutes before the Angelus was rung. One opposing team was led by an 82-year-old called Austin Wookey, who batted without a runner and walked up and down the pitch depending upon the merits of the shot. One keen newcomer tried to throw him out whereupon our captain called out, 'The Ravens do not run out Mr Wookey.'

Luff had also served in the war, though his naval career barely survived a visit from an admiral who, wanting to test the initiative of the cadets, tossed his hat upon the ground, said it was on fire and, turning to Luff, asked what he was going to do about it? Luff seized the headgear and threw it into the water.

His strategy for improving my record at the seaside town consisted of providing a cheerful supper during the course of the match. Several hundreds were scored after that, some in run chases and one against Malcolm Marshall when I carried my bat through the innings and reached 165 not out. Marshall was the supreme fast bowler of the period. Intelligent, sleek, skilful and committed, he took wickets all around the world, adapting his game to the conditions and thinking batsmen out when the simple approach did not work. In retirement he coached Hampshire. By then Sanath Jayassuriya, one of the game's finest men, was cutting and carving his way into the record books. Asked how he would have bowled to him, Marshall replied in his sing-song voice, 'I bowled to him once. First ball in-swinger outside off-stump and he threw the bat. Next ball, same thing and it flew over the head of the man at cover. I think to myself, "This fellow likes that ball" so after that I just bowl out-swingers starting on his legs and swinging across. He couldn't hit those.' Marshall could not understand why other bowlers did not follow this course of action and we had to explain that not so many bowlers could swing the ball both ways at 90 mph, and none had the wit to change tack in the first over of a match.

Marshall tried his hardest that day but the pitch was disposed towards batsmen and my game was in its best shape. His response to defeat was magnificent. Overnight he analysed the innings, found a flaw and exploited it. Noticing that rising deliveries had been cut hard and high backward of point, he placed a man in this unusual position, went around the wicket to cramp the stroke and sent down a lifter. Robin Smith hung on the ball and the first innings centurion departed for 19. It is my favourite dismissal because it confirmed the professionalism, imagination and humility of a great competitor. It was just another county match played towards the end of a long season. And still he found the answer.

My other memorable innings was at the same venue, a crucial, resilient, patient and decisive 48 not out compiled on a turning track. Nothing is more satisfying than playing a match-winning innings. Overnight the contest hung in the balance. Replaying every possible ball in my mind, and constructing the correct response, I hardly slept. Next morning it was merely a matter of applying the conclusions. Subduing deliveries that turned and bounced sharply was the best part of my game. Belief is half the battle. Nothing can be achieved without it.

Forgive these recollections of a few battles won. Far more were lost. And I never saw a great bowler give up.

15

TOWARDS RETIREMENT

Having stepped down as Somerset captain it seemed that the time had come to contemplate the part of life ignored by rising sportsmen and feared by established performers—retirement. Musicians, actors artists, even rock stars can wear greasepaint until bus fares are half-price again. Sportsmen know that their days are numbered. Like the cicada, they live for years underground, flourish for a brief period and then are lost for ever.

Professional cricket consumes a player's time, removes him from daily life to an almost monastic degree. In other respects the comparison does not work quite as well. Many sportsmen have difficulty in readjusting to ordinary life. Dennis Lillee and Geoff Marsh have spoken about the emptiness that entered their lives when the dressing-room door closed on them for the last time. Suddenly they were no longer members of that secret world of humour and tribulation in which character emerges as clearly as chalk upon a blackboard. No one knows a sportsman as well as longstanding colleagues for among them he stands naked. In those rooms and sometimes upon the field the sportsman feels important, a member of a group yet also an individual, taken to his limits in a manner nowadays unfashionable and absent in other walks of life. Once he has left that circle, the player cannot return because he no longer belongs. Not that those remaining reject the departed. On the contrary, they are often puzzled by their withdrawal.

Some retiring players immediately immerse themselves in commentary or journalism. Others seek entrancement in domestic bliss. Allan Border belonged to the latter school of thought. At the end of his career he announced that hereafter he intended to spend more time at home with his wife and family. Doubtless he pictured a happy scene with father Border mowing the lawn, sipping a mug of tea, playing in the garden with his offspring and perhaps even helping wash the dishes. Now and then he might be dragged away for a game of golf with his mates. About one thing he was certain—his travelling days were over. Border is an honest man and plainly believed every word he spoke. No one else took it seriously, least of all his better half. Whether Border tired of domestic bliss before or after lunch on the first day can be revealed only by members of that splendid household. Suffice it to say that he was soon coaching youth sides, serving on boards, commentating, selecting teams and occasionally popping home.

I didn't expect much from the last few years of my career in cricket. A benefit was not far away, and the prospect of a couple of seasons spent playing under Vic Marks in a team strengthened by Chris Tavare was not unattractive. My benefit was overdue but had been delayed so that Breakwell and Gard could be rewarded for their long service. Moreover the idea of going around cap in hand had little appeal. It is an outdated system, a throwback to a time when professional cricketers were poorly paid and had few openings outside the game. It has become a scam. Not that it is as widely abused as the insurance scheme designed to assist those forced by injury into early retirement.

In the event, 1989 counts among the most eventful seasons of my eighteen years as a paid player. It began with a century scored against the touring Australians, a team regarded as among the feeblest to leave those shores. Border's side had lost its first match in Worcester and arrived in Taunton determined to make amends. Somerset had a weak side, which was further depleted when Marks was forced to withdraw for personal reasons. Unable to imagine our motley crew winning the match, I resolved to prevent the visitors raising their flag. Australia dominated the opening days of the match but did not enforce the follow-on. In the first innings I had been dismissed by a couple of moustachioed adversaries. Watching from the safety of the press box, it was sometimes difficult to see how Mervyn Hughes took his wickets. Facing him on a slow pitch cleared the matter up. Blessed with the heart of a bullock and the strength of an ox, Merv soon produced a delivery whose bounce and pace surprised your correspondent. I could only fend it to short-leg where a silent man from Tasmania moved across to take the catch.

After being dismissed there was plenty of time to reflect upon the amusement friends and opponents would take from my misfortune. Not even carrying my bat against the 1985 Australians had stopped the teasing, though admittedly survival was made possible by a flawed performance in the slip cordon from Mr Dirk Wellham. Playing as a fully fledged journalist was another matter. Cricketers are not often given the chance to exact retribution upon their critics. In the event nothing much was said in the first innings. Carl Rackemann bowled his best spells of the tour, or so reporters later insisted, and the thought did occur that perhaps he remembered some remarks to the effect that he was a little fragile. Rackers had retorted that though this opinionated Pom might know something about English cricket he was clearly in the dark about its antipodean counterpart, whereupon I denied knowing anything about English cricket either. The rest of the second day passed without incident except that Mark Taylor sportingly hit one of my offerings to deep cover and Rackemann contrived to direct a full-toss into my hands at silly point.

Australia declared overnight, thereby giving themselves a day to dismiss their rural opponents. Somerset need to score 340 or so on a turning pitch to win the match. In the event the match was saved for the loss of three wickets. Afterwards we were condemned for playing for the draw. From the outset survival was the height of our ambitions. Providing encouragement for the Australians was not part of our brief. Our batting was as short as Twiggy's miniskirt and the wicket was deteriorating. When only two wickets fell before tea the thought did occur to go for the win. Already my vigil had lasted four hours and I was keen to have a stab at it. Tavare thought the task beyond our reach. Accordingly Somerset shut up the shop. I reached my century with a few minutes remaining.

Among the Australians only Hughes and Border took a dim view of my efforts, but the fast bowler did shake hands afterwards. Border seemed to find my batting dull, and he had a point. A range of opinions were expressed in the newspapers. Graham Otway described the innings as selfish and its perpetrator as the most boring batsman in the county game. Several colleagues suggested suing the blighter but he had been helpful in Pakistan and, anyhow, was entitled to his opinion. At such times it is worth bearing in mind Mr Mandela's observation that he, too, was sometimes upset by things said in the papers, but only when they were true.

At the end of the season Robert Baddeley Simpson, an Australian coach of Scottish extraction and dark disposition, found himself obliged to nominate the best hundred made against his team by a county player. Given the unenviable task of choosing between Mark Nicholas and myself, he rightly plumped for the imperious captain of Hampshire.

Simpson and I fell out over a misprint in an article published in Australia. During the course of a generally favourable article the point was made that some observers frowned upon Simpson in victory and defeat. As usual the article was scrawled upon a loose piece of paper and dictated over the phone, a medieval custom now in abeyance. A copy-taking mistake that survived the scrutiny of subs and editors led 'defeat' to appear as 'deceit', thereby casting an unintended aspersion. Simpson instructed his solicitors to commence action for damages. Correcting the mistake was not enough. Furious at the suggestion that I would deliberately malign the reputation of another man without making any attempt to substantiate the point, I decided to take action to protect my reputation. Accordingly, Simpson and I found ourselves suing each other. Fortunately common sense prevailed and only the action against the newspaper proceeded. The *SMH* asked me to fly to Australia to help them to defend the case but professional commitments in England made this impossible. In the event the matter was settled out of court.

Nicholas was not on my Christmas card list either, for he seemed to represent the unacceptable face of England. Charming, smooth, debonair and confident, he spent much of his time talking to important people and was highly regarded in all the right places. Like David Graveney, he was also adept at briefing reporters. We were chalk and cheese. As rival captains we had fallen out over the use of a fast runner by his slowest batsman. My suggestion that Nicholas, who was not fleet of foot, should take the place of Carl Lewis, or whoever it was running for the slowcoach of the side, was ignored. On another occasion Nicholas sauntered across the committee balcony after both camps had reluctantly accepted that insufficient time remained to set up a declaration, complaining about his opposite number. To add insult to injury, his team promptly insulted the spectators and the game itself by bowling tripe for the last hours of a dying match. Far and away the most annoying thing about Mark, though, is that familiarity softens the hostility. He can be warm, amusing and thoroughly disarming.

Towards the end of the summer the announcement was made that I was to captain a strong England XI to play a couple of matches in Holland. Too much was read into it. Doubtless it was intended as a gesture towards an older player who had never quite been called to higher things. Alec Stewart and Nasser Hussain were in the side, as was Keith Medleycott, who would become the successful coach of Surrey CCC. Obviously they all learnt from the experience! Mickey Stewart managed the side. Over the years the Stewarts have not been my favourite family because their sincerity seemed to be overdone. Nonetheless the trip was memorable and entertaining.

England lost the first match. After catching a morning flight from Heathrow, we found ourselves playing on an artificial surface, asked our hosts to bat first in a 40-over match and were surprised to discover that a 55-minute delay for rain did not entail a reduction in the number of overs to be bowled. Chasing 180 or so, we had reached around 120/1 before darkness fell across the land, whereupon wickets started to tumble. Passionately led by my close friend Roland Lefebvre, Holland bowled accurately, fielded like men possessed and secured a deserved triumph. After the match I told the players to bounce back next day. Later the players confessed to being amused by the holes in my shoes noticed as the address reached its climax.

Naturally the large accompanying press corps wanted comments from those responsible for this embarrassment. In those days no one knew the Dutch played the game so the loss was regarded as a humiliation. As the players were chatting over a glass of beer that evening Matthew Engel wandered across and asked, 'Do you realise that Mickey Stewart has gone around contradicting everything you said?' He seemed bothered about it.

The next day the side fought back to secure a victory that better reflected the capabilities of the teams. John Stephenson and I added 120 for the first wicket and the rest was inevitable. Then we flew back to England, taking care not to read the newspapers for it had been raining and there was precious little else for the boys to write about! Four years later Mark Benson would also lead an England team to defeat in Holland but no one seems to remember that!

Of course the trip was regarded as a disaster. As far as I was concerned it had been enjoyable and illuminating. It was exhausting, though, and respect for those constantly in the spotlight was enhanced. Supposedly my hopes of higher honours were ended by this fiasco. In fact they remained bafflingly high.

Twice that season my name was mentioned as a candidate for the Test team. England's batting failed miserably against Australia and no one could be found to hold up the side. A batsman was needed for the Test in Birmingham and the choice lay between myself and Tavare. Chris was a much more accomplished player and the decision did not seem to be all that difficult. In the event he was summoned, whereupon he called me into a back room to break the news. He was downcast, because he felt he had done his bit and nowadays was entitled to peace and quiet. Indeed he apologised for being picked and I told him not to be so daft as he was the superior player by a distance.

As the curtain fell upon the 1989 summer my name sprang up again as a possible captain of the England team due to tour the West Indies that winter. Ray Illingworth supported my candidacy, arguing that someone tough and independent was needed, besides which alternatives were thin on the ground, which was true. In the event Graham Gooch was appointed. On the day of my exclusion from the touring party I found myself facing Walsh at his most venomous and managed to score 100.

Vic Marks broke his arm in that match, his last as a professional cricketer. Vic had been offered the position of cricket correspondent of the *Observer* newspaper on a take it or leave it basis. It was time to go. As a farewell present the players tried in vain to find a picture of him leaving a ball alone but, thwarted, were obliged to settle for a rocking chair. His retirement brought to an end a cricketing relationship that had involved many car journeys in vehicles ranging from the disintegrating to the new, numerous shared rooms and evening meals, much laughter and occasional differences of opinion. We played golf but seldom encountered each other on the course as I'd be tearing after my ball while Vic pottered along. As close friends must, though, we had a lot in common, more that might have been guessed by an outsider, not least a sense of humour and leftist opinions on most matters (Vic goes so far as to read the *Guardian*). In his quiet way he was competitive and ambitious. People are comfortable in his company. Nowadays we lead separate lives in different parts of the world and our paths seldom cross.

Marks had captained the team well and his main innovation had been the discovery that I could bowl. Called to arms to relieve an attack in which energy played a greater part than accuracy, and bearing in mind that over the last ten years all sorts of styles had been tried in the first-class game, none of them successfully, I decided to try a combination of medium-pace and off-spin. It worked. Many times in these last few seasons the opportunity came to deliver the last, crucial overs of an innings. Cultivating an air of mystery that belied the predictability of the fare to be sent down, and relying upon the bemusement of the batsmen and their anxiety not to lose their wickets to this awkward customer, I managed to turn a few matches around. It was fun to be in the thick of things. Not until the chance arose to play for Devon as an amateur throughout the 1990s were my bowling skills properly explored and then, for a handful of summers, I was a pretty good operator.

My friend's departure, and his replacement as captain by Chris Tavare, hastened the end of my career. It only remained to try to end on a high note and to enjoy the takings of a benefit, accepted in 1990. In the event my last two seasons were not especially enjoyable. 1990 was ghastly because authorities alarmed by the wretchedness of the wickets prepared for county matches had instructed groundsmen to produce pitches as dull as rice pudding, and about as bouncy. In addition, softer and almost seamless balls were used. Boring cricket was the result. The fascination of cricket relies on the struggle between bat and ball and these changes upset the balance. My benefit was hindered by my refusal to stay in England longer than was needed for cricketing purposes. Apart from anything else there was a job waiting in Australia.

Tavare was an extraordinary fellow. He commanded respect and affection and was a brilliant batsman held back by a desire to retain control of every aspect of his life. He liked to plan things and was extremely tidy so that everything was always in its place. Upon removal his socks were folded and put neatly away. On motorways a machine was activated that made his car tootle along at exactly 70 mph. It used to drive me crazy. Nonetheless he was a fine attacking batsman and had all the qualities needed to be a great player, except extroversion. The players nicknamed him 'Blakey' after a character from 'On the Buses' who spoke in the same downbeat manner.

Marks's unexpected retirement had several repercussions. After years of involvement in the direction of the team, I found myself reduced to the ranks. Jimmy Cook had arrived as the county's foreign player. We were not on the same wavelength. A superb technician with an old-fashioned game that sat well beside his Edwardian manners, Cook lacked the force of character and competitiveness evident in previous overseas players at the club. He was an efficient rather than an inspirational or influential player. At the end of the 1989 season both Marks and Brian Rose were far from convinced he was the right man for this team. But Cook was strongly supported by Tavare, most of the players, and by Peter Anderson, the new chief executive of the club, a bossy former policeman.

Moreover our politics were far apart. Cook was convinced that, fearing for his life outside, Mr Mandela wanted to stay in prison, an opinion presumably instilled at an early age. As a member of anti-apartheid groups, I had written on the subject in national newspapers and magazines. Not that Jimmy was untypical of white cricketers in his country. An impression has been created that white cricketers in South Africa were in the forefront of anti-apartheid thinking. It is a self-serving view. None was ever arrested, let alone charged or imprisoned for challenging the system. A brief walk-out at Newlands was as far as it went. Dr Ali Bacher has admitted as much over the dinner table. Cook was a product of his times. No wonder those nowadays in power in South African cricket take the observations of past players with a pinch of salt.

Towards the end of the 1991 season I decided to retire and took no part in further matches. Tavare urged a change of heart or at least a farewell match but the first was far-fetched and the second an indulgence. Enough was enough. By and large the last few seasons had been productive, but the pressures had not eased and were not widely understood. Before a match against Worcestershire Chris Lander, a tabloid journalist with more charm than scruples, rang to say that Botham was also tired of the conflict and wanted to bury the hatchet but was not prepared to take the first step. A friendly approach next morning would be welcomed. Not wanting to let pride stand in the way of peace, I agreed to make the first move and next morning strode across and held out my hand. Lander and his photographer were hovering. Botham was nonplussed. He knew nothing about it. It was a trap and I had walked into it. Lander was Botham's man. Whatever happened, rebuff or reconciliation, he had his story. I was tired of all that. Somerset had been fun but it was time to move on.

Now that my cricketing days were over, the time had come to start thinking about the future. A cricketer lives day by day, month by month, and cannot act otherwise for a career might last a decade or a single, fleeting summer. Only the survivors appear in the daily newspapers with numbers against their names. Others suffer injuries or fall short or are in the wrong place at the wrong time. Such men must come to terms with disappointment early in life. County cricketers are the survivors of a long and hazardous journey and lead a privileged and, in some respects, protected life. But it has its harshnesses and its rivalries, and the pressure is unrelenting. Eventually it ends, often a year earlier than antici- pated so that a bitter aftertaste remains. Many former Somerset players never set foot in the ground again. There are too many ghosts around, and the faces of the men who rejected them. Retiring while still in demand meant that there was no hangover. Every player and official could still be looked in the eye. Visits could still be made to the broken-down old pavilion where the best rock cakes in the world are sold.

My time in cricket had exceeded all my expectations. Of course mistakes were made. My character was both a driving force and a hindrance. For too long the shadow of failure was allowed to cramp my batting. Adventure was sacrificed to the great god of productivity. Too late I learnt about scoring centuries and using my feet to spinners and bowling. Put the clock back a quarter of a century and give the youth the knowledge gathered over the years and a fine cricketer would emerge. But it does not work like that. Instead a sportsman serves as best he can, always fighting for his place, often looking over his shoulder. Critics can make their pro- nouncements but it's a lot of nonsense really for there is always just the next ball. A career is merely a word used to describe countless small actions, a thousand minor decisions taken every day. To go forward or back, to wear studs or ripple soles, to put a man at third man or fourth slip, to bowl another spinner or an armball, to select this fellow or that, these concerns are the stuff of the professional player. Mistakes are made, defeats endured, triumphs enjoyed and then the next day comes, and then the next season, until it is someone else's turn.

Cricket began as a challenge and became a way of life and a means of earning a living. Nothing had existed beyond it. Nothing had been invested. From those early appearances in youth teams, the boy hidden under a red cap, until the last match against Yorkshire when Darren Gough was hooked for six, the game had retained its hold. It was fun to be important, to be mentioned in the papers, to be watched and sometimes applauded, and to be tested and respected but it was only a game and one reserved for youth with its nerve and eyesight. Now it was over.

I felt no emptiness, just the satisfaction to be taken from a job reasonably well done added to a certain relief at the release from the pressure of scoring runs for a living. Not everyone escapes unscathed from professional sport. Not once in retirement would I yearn to be back on the field in Somerset colours. I did not expect even to play the game again. Most former professionals stop playing altogether once their county careers are over. Some have simply had enough. Others are not prepared to risk the humiliation of failing in lesser company. Moreover, first-class players are inclined to scorn the amateur game. In the end I did continue playing competitively because cricket is fun and not to be taken to heart, besides which I found a convivial team. On the other hand Botham's decision never to play cricket again was understood for he was a big name and a prized scalp.

After eighteen years on their books I had left Somerset County Cricket Club and could now concentrate upon building a career in cricket journalism. It was a change easily made. Words flowed with a felicity absent in my batting. No longer was it a matter of wrenching every last ounce from limited resources. A style developed that reflected my character for there was nothing to fear, no reason to hold back. Nor was there any financial hardship because journalists were better paid than cricketers, and the expenses were generous.

Reporters spend a good deal of their time filling in expense forms.

Loud as the antipodes called there was not, for the time being at any rate, any need to choose between the hemispheres because the cricket seasons dovetailed conveniently. Accordingly southern summers were spent following the Australian team around and fulfilling an obligation to contribute four articles a week. April through September was passed covering Test and county matches for an English Sunday paper.

I was offered a position by the *Sunday Times* as its cricket correspondent. Later it emerged that Robin Marlar, the incumbent, had not been informed about his changed circumstances. Not that it mattered because Marlar continued as a columnist for several more years and neither of us bothered about titles. Marlar was bellicose, intelligent to the point of obscurity and helpful. Of course, arguments broke out now and then, and Robin did once bellow that his junior was as mad as a hatter. He had the grace to laugh when it was pointed out that this, coming from him, was a bit rich.

The older writers were a colourful lot. Henry Blofeld used to scrawl his articles on the back of a packet of cigars and once summed up a long dissertation on the role pressure plays in the minds of sportsmen by saying 'pressure is a funny old thing'. Before long he announced that he had fallen head over heels in love with his current partner and future wife, an announcement slightly undermined by his inability to remember her name. Pat Gibson was my favourite of the seasoned campaigners, a dour, discreet independent man with a fondness for beer and jazz. Not thinking much of them, he avoided most of the other journalists, preferring the company of a handful of chums or, failing that, his own.

Despite the fellowship of these veterans, England remained a place to work and leave. Not until Devon and Devonians were discovered did anything change on this front. Australia promised friendship, relaxation and appreciation. Buying a house in Sydney was the next step to be taken. Nor was it merely a matter for forking out lots of dollars. Permission had to be obtained from the Foreign Investment Review Board. Ignoring the advice of numerous friends and the reputation of the suburb, I decided to settle near the beach in Bondi. In those days Bondi was supposedly full of drugs and undesirables but the air felt free and the waves were exhilarating. Moreover it was unpretentious and remained a stronghold of the Labor party.

My chosen home was an old house built in the federation style and situated in a quiet street a few hundred yards from the beach. Of course I did not bother to inspect the place properly or might otherwise have discovered that the only toilet was placed outside in the backyard in the old-fashioned way. A lady had lived in the house for 50 years and had not seen fit to remove the green linoleum or bright yellow paint that adorned the tin shack added to the back of the property. No one else seemed to be interested in the place. Only one other bidder joined the fray and he was surely a stooge. In the event, the house was bought for a song. The old lady's furniture was also purchased because there was nothing else. So life began where it will probably end, in a friendly street not far from the sea with its numerous attractions. In the intervening years Bondi has been discovered by the cosmopolitan set and the house has proved to be a bargain, which cannot be said of the various stocks in my portfolio.

Work as a full-time cricket writer had begun. It has proved to be enormously rewarding. Life has improved with every decade, has found a shape compatible with my character. Over a quarter of a century has been spent in Australia. Africa awaited but leaving England took a decade longer than anticipated for which Farmer, Folly, Gobbler, Donners and the rest of my fellow Devonians can take the blame.

16

THE AUSTRALIAN RENAISSANCE

B ill O'Reilly's retirement and subsequent passing created an opportunity to move into a more responsible position within Australian cricket writing. Although I mourned the loss of a respected and popular man, the opening could not have come along at a better time, as the Australians were about to challenge and eventually topple the mighty West Indians. Writing about a winning team is more fun than describing endless defeats. The Australians triumphed by recognising, confronting and correcting their weak points. Meanwhile the West Indians took little notice of the characters of their youngsters, especially those from the new powerhouses in Antigua and Jamaica. Hubris took hold and laziness followed, bringing about an inability to win away from home that has lingered. Basketball and other innocent parties were blamed for a deterioration whose causes were human and commonplace. Nothing lasts long that has self-indulgence at its core. The notion that things move in cycles is an excuse used by the incompetent.

Not that the rise of the Australians seemed inevitable in the late 1980s. A trip to the Cricket Academy in Adelaide was not then the equivalent of a visit to a guru. An academy had been opened as part of a much broader plan for the recovery of cricket across the country. Realising that youth was losing its way between the ages of eighteen and 22, the Australian Cricket Board decided to gather the cream of the crop and train them hard so that they were properly prepared for the challenges ahead. There was nothing hi-tech about the training. Outsiders assumed that the academy was a state-of-the-art construction with every facility provided. In fact it did not exist, so far as concrete is concerned anyhow. These obscure and unpaid teenagers slept at the nearby university, trained at its gym and practised at the main cricket ground in the city. They were pushed hard and given next to nothing. Jack Potter was their coach, a dry, intelligent off-beat former State player who also ran an ice-cream kiosk at the nearby Glenelg Beach. An impression has been created, not least by former colleagues on television, that Rod Marsh ran the academy more or less from its inception. In fact by the time he took over its best days were behind it for the culture of Australian cricket had been restored and the finishing school was not needed.

No surprise need be felt at the rudimentary nature of the academy. Australia is seldom swept away by the latest fad. Certainly there are fewer pretenders hovering around the fringes of sporting teams, trying to turn their minor contribution into a full-scale industry. When the Australians climbed off the team bus one murky morning in Taunton, the locals were astonished to be told that the players would be ready to practise in the nets in ten minutes. Observers of the Australian approach tend to take away the wrong bits.

Not that the Australians are admirable in every way. Aggression periodically spills over into unpleasantness, drugs have been detected within the sporting community and locals sometimes ignore the contributions made by immigrants in swimming, boxing, football and other disciplines.

Anyway, towards the end of the 1980s I paid a visit to Adelaide to examine this new-fangled creation. That year's intake included a determined, muscular young man from the West by the name of Justin Langer, a talented, headstrong leader called Damien Martyn, a skinny rake of a local who worked in a bank between sessions and called himself Greg Blewett, a mild left-hander from Deniliquin by the name of Laurie Harper and a portly leg-spinner with danger in his eyes and power in his fingers called Shane Warne. None of them had made an impression in men's cricket. All of them had a story to tell.

Langer finished first in every exercise, practised in the nets at Adelaide Oval at every opportunity and was regarded as an honest trier. Sincere, physical, squat, dedicated and feisty, he had broad shoulders and a broader bat but seemed to lack the special abilities required to stand out in a crowd. He was a man on a mission, though, and everyone wished him well. Langer's intensity found expression in the fierceness of his eyes and the fanaticism with which he lifted weights and climbed ropes.

Martyn had captained the national Under-19 side and was regarded as the most brilliant of the intake. He was fit and stylish and full of bravado and scorn. But he had the empty look of those unfamiliar with struggle. Like most flattered youngsters he regarded his rise as inevitable and did not think much about anyone else. His head was his weak point. Inevitably Martyn's attitude caught up with him. Five years in the cricketing wilderness followed a reckless stroke played at a crucial moment against South Africa. He returned as an accomplished cricketer and as a better man. Cricket has its ways.

Blewett was unusual in that he had a full-time job. Most of the rest had time on their hands. As a batsman Blewett was either running hot or cold. Most top cricketers learn to hack something out even when their arms feel like legs and vice versa. Blewett had a lovely game but did not score enough bad runs to establish himself. Moreover he used an open blade and was inclined to leave his back leg outside his stumps, a technique that made him more reliant than most on eye and fortune. At the academy he was regarded as a promising player likely to flourish in State cricket but lacking the tightness required in the highest company.

As befits a boy raised in the bush, Harper moved quietly along. Bumping into him in the streets of St Kilda a few years later was to hear a tale of lost confidence and missed opportunities. Laurie said that he wasn't scoring any runs and had lost his place in the State squad. Over a beer he added that he kept losing his wicket in the 30s and 40s. Invited to prove the point, he wrote down the scores of his last twelve innings, nine of which fell within those parameters. Asked to record the means of dismissal in these recent efforts, he realised that he had been caught ten times, nine of them at cover, gully or mid-off. Pausing for a moment to analyse the results, I suggested that he hit his drives on the ground. He seemed to think Moses had appeared in his company. Actually his grandmother could have made the same observation.

More specifically, I advised him to keep his head down at execution and added that furthermore to stop thinking about getting back into the squad and concentrate entirely on the next ball. Laurie returned to club cricket, started constructing hundreds and presently scored stacks of runs for Victoria. Unfortunately a back injury curtailed his career. He worked throughout his time in cricket and has managed the adjustment to civilian life without undue difficulty.

At the academy Warne was a brazen dumpling. He did not look much like a cricketer for the supposedly modern era but, then, neither did Mervyn Hughes or David Boon. From the start, though, he was fascinated with the intricacies and possibilities of spin bowling. Nonetheless it was impossible to tell him apart from other promising youngsters. His cricket was raw and his temperament had not been tested. But Warne kept improving. He just did not stop. He relished the limelight and was fiercely competitive. Warne is full of bluff. His annual discovery of a new ball is proof enough of that. He understands the value of theatre and the rewards that await a man prepared to lead his life in public.

Warne is more fragile than he seems and has suffered from losses of confidence, especially in India where the pitches turn slowly and batsmen are raised on dhal and spin. At one stage he reverted to tossing the ball higher and aiming at off-stump in an attempt to stop Navjot Sidhu and Sachin Tendulkar charging down the pitch and hitting 'sixers'. After another mauling Warne asked how his bowling looked from the boundary edge. By way of reply I said that he was bowling badly and expressed astonishment that a man with 400 Test wickets should abandon the strategy that brought almost all of those wickets. His game was founded on a unique ability to dip the ball into the blind spot around leg stump and then spin it viciously across an opponent, or else let it go straight through. If he kept bowling in this timid style they'd milk him all day.

Warne agreed but added that his captain wanted him to bowl outside off stump to slow the batsmen down. His problem was that the opening bowlers were not taking wickets and the straight boundaries were short. Moreover attacking fields were being set. Only the greatest bowlers can attack top-class batsmen with both ball and field, especially once the innings is under way. Usually it is best to keep trying things with the ball and to set the field as circumstances dictate. Warne needed to push his long-on back as soon as these fellows started to attack and otherwise to continue bowling in his usual way. He had to encourage his opponents to hit across the line. In the next match Warne returned to the tactic that set him apart, concentrating on the broken ground around leg stump and carrying out his plan with the mesmerising accuracy that has been his hallmark. Typically he did not mention that he was restricted by a sore shoulder or that his spinning finger was hurting.

Warne is an unusual mixture of calculation and instinct. To top it off he has a quality hard to define that includes mental domination and the ability to sense and seize a moment. Everyone was excited that a leg-spinner had been found capable of turning the ball a yard. Australia had been relying on finger spin for several years and the spirit had dulled. Fast bowling, wrist-spin and attacking batsmanship are regarded by antipodeans as the cricketing equivalent of prawns and beer. No one was bothered about the more colourful aspects of his character. A leg-spinner had been discovered and all was right with the world.

Of course those five youngsters were not the only students to appear at the academy that year. Most of those attending even the best-run finishing school do not make the grade. The academy sends twelve young men into the world every summer and there are only 100 or so provincial spots to fill once injury and international calls have been taken into account. Moreover players no longer retire at 30 to concentrate on feeding their families. Cricket is their living. Many of the students end up in club cricket or, in the case of those carrying the appropriate passport, playing for an English county.

Nor did Australia's rise depend on the academy. Laurie Sawle and Bob Simpson gathered a committed group of young men together and gave them the encouragement and instruction that was required. No less importantly, time-wasters were dropped. Border was a poor judge of character and found amusement in men who lacked his sense of purpose. Australia was well rid of them and put in their place men like Hughes, Ian Healy and Boon.

Not that Boon impressed in his first series against England, repeatedly playing away from his body and giving slip catches. A year later he scored a century against Richard Hadlee at the 'Gabba, an innings so expertly constructed that I felt obliged to contact him in search of illumination. Boon explained that in his despair he had come across something said by Garry Sobers to the effect that a man was not at the bottom until he was thinking himself there. Boon realised that he had been accepting that he was not good enough when he ought to have been correcting his mistakes. He went into the nets, drew a line a few inches outside off stump, and practised leaving the ball alone. Thereafter he made the bowlers attack the stumps and scored with straight drives and flicks off his pads. Boon became an outstanding batsman and a veritable rock at first wicket down. Among contemporary batsmen, Mark Taylor and Marcus Trescothick have been obliged by failures to return to the nets to recapture the habit of allowing the ball to pass.

Boon and company played their parts in making Australian cricket strong again. After some hard seasons their reward came with a run of victories everywhere except on the Indian sub-continent. Between them officials, selectors, coaches, captains and senior players restored vigour to their country's cricket. Men like Boon, Hughes and Healy, a cricketer plucked from obscurity who survived a difficult initiation to become a champion, were unlikely to tolerate any nonsense from themselves or anyone else. England fell because it could not find competitors of this sort.

The role of the academy has been overstated by outsiders convinced that it has a magic wand capable of turning dust into gold. It was not witchcraft that revived standards in Australian cricket, merely hard thinking and sweat. Australia has been fortunate in its leaders. Three men have been appointed as captain of the Australian Test team in the last 20 years or so: Allan Border, Mark Taylor and Stephen Waugh. Some countries get through that many in a season. Bill O'Reilly dismissed the fuss about captaincy as a lot of hoo-hah and reckoned their job was done once the coin had been tossed and the blokes told to scatter. Bill was right about most things, and is doubtless giving his Creator a hard time about the lbw law and his failure to give wrist-spinners the assistance they manifestly deserve, but he might have underestimated the influence captains can have on the construction and outlook of a team and the course of a match. These three men deserve a chapter of their own.

17

THE GLORY YEARS: BORDER, TAYLOR AND WAUGH

Allan Border took over the Australian team from a captain who burst into tears as he read the statement announcing his resignation. Kim Hughes's emotion reflected his frustration at his inability to control either himself or his men. Hughes had not secured the respect of the senior players, especially those suspicious of his status as the establishment's golden boy during the World Series rebellion. He lacked the strength or stability needed to bind together a fractured outfit. Where the Chappells were tough and loyal, Hughes seemed rash to the point of intemperance. He could bat as few men have ever batted, and he played some of the most inspired innings the game has known. But he could also charge down the pitch on some reckless adventure. At such times the voice inside saying 'Don't be a fool' was reduced to the merest whisper.

Hughes had promised to give up hooking the West Indians because the stroke had proved too dangerous. Far from keeping this resolution to himself, however, he shouted it from the rooftops. Unfortunately a rush of blood to the head cost him his wicket at the 'Gabba. He was broken not so much by the failure as by the humiliation. Border was his vice-captain. Upon hearing of the West Australian's decision to stand down, Border's spirits sank for he was happy where he was and wanted to concentrate on his own cricket. He did not consider himself to be a leader and was not comfortable at press conferences. Not that this last qualification matters all that much. Certain captains have answered questions impressively but been duds in the field.

Border is an honest man and his reluctance to accept the prestigious position can be taken at face value. But he was wrong about his capabilities. Although he had identified his faults correctly, he had forgotten about his strong points. Border's game and character were founded upon an underestimation of his abilities. Knowing nothing else, he believed that life was a struggle and that cricket worked along the same lines. Armed with candles and the sound of the sea, he might perchance have summoned a romantic line, but in any other circumstances he was about as soft as a locust. Survival was all. To that end he eliminated frills and indulgences, regarding them as weaknesses bound sooner or later to catch up with him. Nothing could be taken for granted and no ground could be given to reporters, umpires, bowlers or opponents. Others might chance their arms; Border gritted his teeth and continued batting.

Far from being an unsuitable candidate for promotion, Border was the right man in the right place at the right time. Australia needed someone fierce and bad-tempered, someone who did not give his wicket away and who hated losing. Border's supporters complain that he did not deserve to be called 'Captain Grumpy', yet the nickname was not meant critically. Here was a man who didn't give a toss about appearances, a man with no high notions of his abilities, a man without pretence or politics, a cricketer through and through.

He was a magnificent and practical cricketer. It is no small thing to preside over the transformation of a cricket team, no small thing to get the job done. The figures speak for themselves and under-line the stature of the performer. Border's low opinion of himself was an asset in these hard times. An old Test cricketer once pointed out that the wise batsman is 'a bit better than he thinks he is'. Border played late and straight, and his footwork was quick and precise. He could pull and cut and was just as comfortable, or uncomfortable, against pace and spin. His concentration and courage were unwavering.

Yet he had little regard for these strong foundations. By his estimation he could only put runs on the board whereas others could 'bat'. In some respect this assessment was a limitation because it prevented Border cutting loose. He was inclined to push himself down the order, reasoning that though dictating terms was beyond him, he might be able to organise a recovery. He underestimated simplicity. Reducing the game to its essentials is damnably difficult and Border never really understood that. He was much better than he thought.

Border and his coach, Simpson, restored the sense of purpose in the Australian team. Conservative to a fault, they built a side that was hard to beat. They lasted a long time and, when the time came, they did not want to go. Far from withdrawing in the recommended way, Border growled like a dog sniffing bathwater. He left his post as reluctantly as ever he left his wicket. Border will be remembered for his cutting and cussed bowling, the pinpoint accuracy of his throwing arm and his desperation to win. Modern sport has been overwhelmed by positive thinking and man man-agement. Not the least of Border's contributions was to expose the rot talked by most of these overpaid nincompoops. In the heat of battle he'd kick the ground, curse the umpires and grizzle at his players. It was old-fashioned and superb. The man cared and others cared with him.

Nonetheless, eventually it was time to go. After the leading candidates had been interviewed, Mark Taylor was named as his successor. Taylor was a straightforward fellow from the bush with a dash of imagination and a lot of determination. From a distance he could seem too much of good thing, provoking suspicions that ambition was lurking beneath his benign exterior. Closer inspection confirmed that Taylor was exactly as he seemed. This does not mean that he was a saint. Simply, he was and remains an intelligent bloke with a lot of cricket and bush in him. He wanted to run the team his way, on and off the field. Whereas Border concentrated on the cricket and let Simpson attend to matters of preparation, technique and tactic, Taylor wanted to put his imprint on his side. Accordingly Simpson was replaced by Geoff Marsh, an easy-going bloke who was happy to work within limited parameters.

Taylor's instincts were sound and he acted on them. More importantly, as a captain he was prepared to try anything. During the World Cup semi-final in Calcutta he threw the ball to Stuart Law and asked him to bowl leg-spinners. At the time the Queenslander was a part-time medium-pacer who dabbled with wristies in the nets. After Australia had secured an incredible victory Taylor was asked what had possessed him to take such a risk. He replied that he 'had to try something'. As far as he was concerned it was not a gamble. Australia was down and almost out. There was nothing to lose. Likewise, in 50-over matches he often threw the ball to Michael Bevan, an occasional and hesitant purveyor of chinamen. Here, too, he was prepared to sacrifice runs in pursuit of wickets. It was never for show. In every case Taylor calculated that something different was required and acted upon the thought.

If anything Taylor was too imaginative for the purposes of one-day cricket. Alone among these captains he did not win a World Cup. Perhaps he gave too much away. Brian Close had the same characteristic, always wanting the game to be moving forwards, always preferring the aggressive option.

Taylor was at his best in Test matches. Notwithstanding his reputation as an innovator, he played a hard game, setting attacking fields, trying to crush his opponents, reducing them to the point of despair. From 1988 onwards Australian teams did the basics better than any opponent. Despite all that's been written about daring captaincy and innovations on and off the field, the hallmark of Australian teams from the late 1980s to their current domination of the scene has been their efficiency. The captains have been a case in point with their correct batting techniques, superb catching and adroit throwing.

Taylor also understood the importance of mind games. Whereas Border was a fighter raised upon losing causes, Taylor set out to dominate. On the field he tried to send a message to opponents of 'Abandon hope all who enter here'. It was a form of intimidation. Opposing batsmen felt that the Australians were swarming all over them. There did not seem to be any gaps in the field. Nor was there much of a welcome mat for a new batsman. Apart from the great West Indian sides, no other cricket team of the modern era has been able to create let alone sustain this illusion of a massive and united force bent upon destruction. And all the while this straightforward man was directing operations from his position at slip.

Of course it helped that he had under his command two of the tightest bowlers the game has known, a luxury also enjoyed by Waugh. Whenever Australia was in trouble the ball could be tossed to Glenn McGrath or Shane Warne, or both, and the initiative could usually be recovered. Australia has only ever been pushed back when these bowlers have been mastered. Moreover the Waugh twins were then at the height of their powers and they generally ended up on the winning side in cricket matches.

Border had stopped the rot and it fell to Taylor to lead the renaissance, a task he undertook with characteristic acumen. Throughout, he managed to combine intelligence and simplicity. Border never managed to beat the West Indians. He came within a couple of runs and a brushed glove of taking the series in

Adelaide, but pessimism has a power of its own. In the decider Border scored the only pair of his career. Taylor had not been pounded as badly as his predecessor and thought the West Indies could be beaten. Not for the first time the thought was father to the deed. Under his captaincy Australia returned to the top of the rankings. Spectators enjoyed watching him lead a team, and many tried to predict his next move. Not that Taylor's career was played out on a smooth and even wicket. Along the way he became the first Test captain to be dropped from the one-day side and he led the team during a bitter dispute with the Board.

Separating the jobs of captaining the Test and 50-over sides was merely a reflection of the times. Fears that the authority of the Australian captain had been undermined have proved unfounded. On the contrary, Taylor and Waugh lasted longer and were respected more precisely because they no longer turned out in coloured clothing.

In any case the selectors had little choice but to drop Taylor from the one-day side because he did not bat, run between wickets or field as well as other contenders. They were bound to choose their strongest team in both competitions and acted accordingly. Ian Healy was dropped at the same time as his captain, and replaced by an obscure swashbuckler by the name of Adam Gilchrist. There was an outcry and the decision was condemned on both emotional and cricketing grounds. I supported the selectors, but was swimming against the tide. Gilchrist was barracked during his first appearances for his country, for no fault of his own. Happily the jeers soon turned to cheers. Brave sporting decisions are usually rewarded. A reporter, too, must have the courage of his convictions.

Steve Waugh's captaincy started badly because he tried to be someone else. Most particularly he tried to copy Mark Taylor, and his intuitions and gambles. His predecessor had been successful and had commanded respect, a combination Waugh craved. He lacked the confidence to impose himself on the team, however. In the dressing-room his voice sounded thin and he could not find the right words to express his beliefs. Tactics were not the problem. Nothing can prepare a man for the isolation of leadership and Waugh was unsure how to strike the balance between authority and camaraderie needed by leaders who must both perform and live cheek by jowl with their charges. A quiet man, he felt a need to emerge from his shell, that the team needed him to be someone else. He was wrong, a fact he eventually realised and corrected. Rather than changing, he merely needed to open himself up, to show himself to his players. Lacking the time and inclination to think about such matters, cricketers tend to take a man at face value. Waugh was an introvert whose abilities were respected. No one, not even he, had explored his innermost thoughts.

Waugh's uncertainty in the field could be sensed by his players. In 50-over matches he'd throw the ball to Bevan but cringe as bad balls were bowled and easy runs conceded. 'Act as if ye had faith', the saying goes, 'and faith shall be given to thee'. Waugh's strategies did not work because he did not believe in them. They did not belong to him. He knew he was falling down on the job but could not work out his next step.

Waugh's failings were scrutinised by past players sceptical of his motivations and reluctant to give him the benefit of the doubt. Matters came to a head during a faltering World Cup campaign in England. In the nick of time, with his team facing an embarrassing exit in the early stages, Waugh consulted the most independent members of the squad, blokes who just rolled up their sleeves and got on with the job. They told him that he was not putting his stamp upon the team and that the side was drifting. Waugh had the sense to listen to these well wishers. Moreover, he realised that they were right and acted on their advice. Reasoning that he might as well be hanged on his own account, he decided to be himself.

Thereafter he took the team with him. Along the way he has managed to be both hard-bitten and broad-minded, self-centred and generous, stubborn and imaginative.

He was an unusual leader. Perhaps only those in the dressing-rooms can truly assess his contribution. Waugh defined his beliefs and acted on them. He wanted hungry players, and found them in Matthew Hayden and Justin Langer, cricketers whose careers had stalled. He saw things in them others had missed, not least unrealised ambition, and he had the courage of his convictions. Perhaps he saw a bit of himself in their sharpness, desire, focus and sense of always having to prove themselves in a world that prefers the pleasing.

Waugh also wanted to attack in his own way. Alone among his players, he could remember the thrashings suffered at the hands of the West Indians. Like Bradman in 1948, he yearned to repay the debt with interest. In McGrath, Gillespie and Brett Lee he found a trio capable of making batsmen hop about. He played them at every opportunity, almost regardless of form. He liked to stand at gully chewing gum and remembering when he was the bloke at the wrong end of the coconut shy. Moreover he believed that Australia must always play an attacking game because it suits the national temperament.

Waugh went further. Throughout his career he had been able to focus his entire being upon the matter in hand. But he had also been blessed with the gift of curiosity and an open-mindedness not always found among sportsmen. Whereas many western athletes support conservative parties and the monarchy, Waugh has always spoken up for the Australian Labor party and supported the idea of a homegrown Head of State. He has always been willing to challenge assumptions and limitations. Fashion has never meant much to him, a trait that gradually emerged in his style of leader-ship. Fresh consideration was given to every part of the team's preparation and performance. At times Australia pushed ahead, at other times it returned to the old ways. His team did not spend nearly as long warming up on the morning of a match as its rivals, and often did not undergo a full-scale practice on the day before hostilities were due to begin because the team leaders could not see any point in these activities. Conventions were challenged.

Waugh set out to improve his players by encouraging them to think about their game and their responsibilities. His independence appealed, especially as it was accompanied by a humour not easily detected from the sidelines. Convinced that his players needed to understand their inheritance, Waugh asked them to study the history of Australian cricket. He tried to stretch his charges, challenging them to read about former champions and heroes, inviting them to speak about themselves and their enthusiasms to their team-mates. When on tour players were persuaded to prepare and deliver talks on various topics, the idea being that understanding creates respect. The field was open. Michael Slater talked about Bon Jovi. Everyone spoke in turn about their favourite past players and an aspect of Australian history. It was a risk few would have dared to take. Waugh's players found themselves writing verse, undertaking long train journeys and listening to marathon runners and other guests in the dressing-room. Drinking is not the only way to bring a team together.

Of course proper attention was paid to the basics of the game. Waugh's Australians held their catches, threw down the stumps, bowled a length and played their shots with perpendicular or horizontal bats. Waugh wanted to inculcate the same ruthlessness he had encountered in the West Indians in his early years in Test cricket, when to walk out to bat was to enter a hostile terrain. He set out to build this same forbidding atmosphere, tried to make his team as tough and efficient as a well-drilled pack of forwards. By and large he achieved this goal as the Australians hit the ball hard, bowled aggressively and maintained their intensity from the first ball of a series to the last. Records were broken in both forms of the game. Waugh's team became so dominant that its captain was seldom called upon to rescue the innings, which had long been one of his strongest points. Accordingly his stubbornness became a handicap as he refused to take the risks needed to push the score along. Waugh saw himself as a man not for turning and felt observers should take the rough with the smooth. Critics saw a man scoring at his own pace and more concerned about his own average than the final result.

His last-ditch 100 in Sydney in 2003 saved his career because the selectors were keen to move on. Waugh responded to his predicament by restoring all the shots cut from his repertoire after he was dropped from the Test team. A professional batsman with an active mind learns to play the percentages, dismisses anything else as idleness. But Waugh had forgotten that it is also a batsman's task to get on top of the attack. Alerted to his mortality, his pinned his ears back and cut loose. Although he scored a lot of runs, the respite did not last long as within six months the selectors were back, pushing him towards retirement by offering the olive branch of a dignified exit in Sydney.

Waugh did not want to go because he was scoring runs, besides which there was a score to settle in India, a blot on his record that needed to be erased, and that meant remaining young and active until October 2004. Eventually he accepted that the game was up, and announced his retirement at the start of the 2003/04 home series against India. Like his predecessors, he departed grumpily and his last tour was as exhausting as it was unsatisfying. Worse, the fact that it was his final series unleashed a wave of sentimentality seized upon by the newspapers, eager to sustain the boost to sales caused by Waugh's retirement. Throughout the summer the focus was on the individual. Meanwhile, India batted magnificently and, by squaring the series, retained the Border-Gavaskar Trophy. Waugh's faltering farewell tour reminded all and sundry that cricket is bigger than any individual player.

18

CRICKETING CONTROVERSIES

Cricket corruption reflects both the diversity within the game and the mixture of good and bad that has been man since Adam and Eve. A humble and properly raised Muslim found demons within himself, a desire for riches and a willingness to go to any lengths to obtain them. An apparently upstanding Afrikaaner, a man from a liberal wing of a proud tribe, fell foul of his own greed. It is nothing new.

Over the years I have visited the jewellery shop run by M.K. Gupta, supposedly the main villain in the piece. Actually, he is just a bookmaker among bookmakers. I have interviewed K.K. Paul, the Delhi detective who exposed Cronje and some of his team-mates. I have also spoken to well-informed journalists and well-placed sources, including members of boards, and have always found the same feeling: that the corruption went higher or further than has been or ever will be revealed. Among cricketing bodies, only India, Pakistan and Australia made concerted efforts to confront the issue.

Cricket should be thankful for detectives such as Paul, and investigative reporters such as Malcolm Conn of the *Australian*, together with numerous investigators with sub-continental magazines who brought attention to the rottenness through the game by exposing a few instances of wrongdoing.

A single instance may suffice to indicate the extent of the problem. While in India years ago, I was informed by a senior official from Sri Lanka that a distinguished Sri Lankan cricketer had privately reported an offer made to him in Sharjah. My reason for not naming the player concerned is simple. Sometimes innocent men are condemned by association. He was approached by a former captain of Pakistan and left alone in his hotel room with a man who promptly offered him US$250 000 as a 'signing-on' fee, with an understanding that he would provide future assistance in the matter of pitch conditions and other apparently minor issues. Upon the offer being summarily rejected, it was doubled. When this offer, too, was angrily received, the gangster produced a mobile phone and invited the player to call one past and one present international captain who could vouch for him. Shocked, the Sri Lankan threw the man out and told him never to return.

Can anyone suppose that he was the first player from his country to be so targeted? Can anyone suppose that any country was not involved? After all, two Australians were identified. In some countries the truth was smelt out, in others it was buried, while others lacked the reporters and other resources required to expose the culprits. Some men escaped simply because cricket was not prepared to bring them down.

It was a colleague on the *SMH* who broke the story about match fixing. Phil Wilkins, an old trooper, was invited out to coffee by an employee of the Australian Cricket Board, who told him that he had a big story for him. 'Not drugs?' Wilko asked anxiously. 'Bigger than that, mate,' came the reply. Our paper ran the story and Wilko called to get my reaction. 'Phil, it's going to be bigger than Bodyline,' was my response. Debate raged over naming Salim Malik as the man responsible for trying to persuade the two Australians to throw a Test. The *SMH* did not think it had sufficient evidence to take the risk. Patrick Smithers, sports editor at the *SMH*'s sister paper, the Melbourne *Age*, was keen to go the whole hog. Accordingly, a senior Australian player was contacted and informed that the paper intended to name Malik. He was asked whether it was safe to do so. 'Go ahead, mate,' he replied, 'it'll be right.' The next morning Malik was outed and the investigation proper began.

I first met Hansie Cronje in the study of Mnr Volsteedt, his old headmaster at Grey College. Rumours had been flying about events during Pakistan's tour of that country, with suggestions that matches had been thrown and so forth. Indeed Basat Ali and Rashid Latif had said as much publicly only to find themselves in hot water. Cronje said that it was all true but did not add that he intended to join in. This was in 1994. He seemed too upright, too righteous, too massive to indulge in such activities. In those days much less was known about his hunger for money. He was a complicated man whose father, a splendid fellow, had not advanced as far as he might within the academic world because he refused to join the right-wing Afrikaaner brotherhoods whose blessing was required. Cronje was in many respects a typical leader of his people, strong, remote, unyielding. Afrikaaners are a hierarchical lot, and masters, pastors, prefects and fathers are put on a pedestal, an outlook that helps to maintain traditional ways as well as hold families and groups together.

When Cronje was first accused of taking money from bookmakers, there was an outcry in his homeland and elsewhere. Of course, racist undertones were found in the accusation; the pure white man was being maligned by an incompetent Indian. Most observers assumed it was a lot of nonsense, an opinion eagerly confirmed by South African reporters convinced that their man was squeaky clean. Rather than seek information from South

African sources sympathetic to the local hero, I called a well-placed friend in Chennai to ask for his assessment of the man at the centre of the storm, Detective Paul. 'Ruthless, cold and efficient,' was the response, not at all the picture painted in the press. And this was the man who had put his reputation, his career, on the line? 'Not an Inspector Clouseau, then?' I ventured. 'Not at all. He believes only in facts. Cronje is gone. Count on it.' So I wrote my story that way.

I met Paul after everything had blown over. He said that Cronje had been caught because he had unknowingly accepted a free mobile phone from a 'businessman'. Detectives had been taping this gangster's calls for some time, and were surprised by the sudden, but frequent, references to cricket. Paul knew something about the game, enough to decide that further investigations were warranted. And so Pandora's box was forced open.

Later would come the claims that Cronje made a lot of money, millions of American dollars, and had 72 accounts in the Cayman Islands, but this was after he was dead and the points were not proven. Nonetheless it is clear that Cronje was a leader who betrayed his trust. Not that his South African colleagues can be absolved from blame, especially the senior men. No one who has spent any time in a cricket dressing-room can believe that, at the very least, the suspicions of the senior men were not aroused. But the King Commission fulfilled its role of sweeping everything under the carpet and South African cricket lived to fight another day.

Of course this cancer of corruption was far from the only controversy to affect the game during these turbulent years. Always in the forefront of cricketing change, Australia experienced a struggle for power between the players and the Board which dominated the back and front pages of the newspapers and would, for a time, threaten the well-being of the game.

A strong tide was running against the players during the contractual dispute that broke out towards the end of the 1990s. Upon returning from a coaching trip to Africa I discovered that players and the Board had fallen into one of those disputes over pay and power that break out now and then in most enterprises. As far as the newspapers and cricket followers were concerned, the players were being greedy. Front-page stories were written about the generous contractual terms enjoyed by the top players, pointing out that men such as Waugh and Warne, the leaders of the uprising in the Australian team, were especially well rewarded. Every attempt was made to paint the players in the worst possible light.

But the players' case was stronger than it seemed and the suggestion that the senior players were merely lining their pockets did not survive disinterested examination. After reading the papers and listening to the debate, and to the surprise of most of my colleagues, I sided with the players. No one reading the early chapters of this book will be surprised by that decision. Mungo McCallum used to say, 'When in doubt, side with the workers!' Mungo became a friend while covering a Test series for the *Australian Financial Review*. He was an entertaining companion. One evening he spent a considerable time trying to open the back door of a car that was not so well endowed.

In my mind, the rights and wrongs of the dispute were clear cut. Through their association, the players were demanding a larger share of the revenues generated by the game. They also wanted the monies to be more evenly distributed so that State players could make a proper living from their skill. They were seeking about 23 per cent of revenues, an amount in line with other sports in the country. Some sympathisers baulked at the idea of paying a living wage to Shield players, arguing that full-time Australian cricket had been built upon the democratic notion that every player in the country was only ten innings away from a spot in the Test team. Professionalism might breed exclusive squads, conservative selection and longer careers. Previous generations had supposedly been working alongside their cricket, an approach that produced broader characters and a more attacking game, because players were trying to win and not as concerned with their mortgages as their English counterparts.

But this was old hat. Despite playing for years in front of huge crowds, some past players were struggling to pay their bills. Moreover, cricket was not living in isolation. Rather, it was competing with other sports, especially in Melbourne whose main footballing code offered fame and fortune to young athletes. Cricket had to adapt to the times. The players were right.

Patronising remarks about the players' capabilities and revelations about their current pay levels reinforced hostility towards the sport's administrators. Newspapers argued that the cricketers were being unduly influenced by opportunistic advisers, including a recently departed chief executive of the Board and an entrepreneur from England with a silver tongue. Australia's senior cricketers were portrayed as naïve sportsmen being led a merry dance by dubious types. This was a misconception. Realising their weak points, the players sought advice and information but remained in charge of their campaign. The Board objected strongly to the association's choices of hired hands, but that was none of their concern.

Scepticism about the motivations of the senior men was also unfounded. By taking such a prominent position in this bitter matter, Waugh and Warne were risking their reputations for little pecuniary reward. They might easily lose lucrative sponsorship deals. A strike was mooted, a manoeuvre bound to harden opinions against them. Broadening the base of the professional game was bound to provoke opposition, but the players thought their case was just and the battle worth fighting.

Aghast at the Board's conduct and dismayed at its domination of the headlines. I advocated the sacking of its chairman and chief executive. Of course this was nothing personal, it was just part of the rough and tumble. The Board could not expect to have things all its own way. Since the players' contracts had been leaked, it seemed only fair to ask for details of the contracts of all employees of the Board, especially its senior officers. None was forthcoming. Still, it was important that the point was made, and the ensuing silence was amusing.

Mark Taylor found himself in the midst of the warring parties. Although his sympathies lay with the players, he did not enjoy conflict and thought strike action should be avoided at all costs. His team regarded it merely as a last resort. Waugh and Warne remained resolute and both sides held their nerve until outside forces brought about a compromise.

Nowadays less is written about the selfishness of the Players' Association. A relationship has been formed between players and employers whereby issues are discussed and contractual matters settled before a season begins. The players had to fight for this recognition. They wanted their voices to be heard and a fair share of the revenues to which they were entitled. It remains galling that sportsmen are not treated with more respect.

After standing alone in defending the selectors over their separate captains and teams and the players in their stoush with the board, it came as a relief to find myself thinking along the same lines as colleagues over the 'Can't throw, can't bowl' affair. From the start, I had the singular advantage of not hearing the voice on the tape, a virginity that remains intact. When the rumpus began my mind was open. Not that I grasped the seriousness of the affair. My Devon players suffered worse abuse every day. At stumps I'd buy a drink for all those insulted on the field, and usually ended up sending for a jug. Competitive cricket is not a tea-party. Once I did try to be more circumspect, whereupon my senior players wondered what was wrong with me. They said they preferred all the cursing because it made them play better.

The newspapers viewed the matter differently, with the Murdoch press convinced that Warne was the 'culprit' and the Fairfax men arguing that the case was unproven. Presently the search for facts began. An overseas journalist said he'd been told by the television producer that the words had been uttered by a cameraman. Ian Chappell said that men who had never lied to him had told him that it was not Warne. In the press box, the tension between the camps was palpable and fisticuffs broke out between senior writers after one objected to being called a goose. Tim Lane and I argued so furiously over breakfast that my amiable, respected and relentless colleague stormed out. I challenged opponents to provide some evidence or, at least as a starting point, test the voice on the tape. This always happens in court cases, anyhow in those involving Mr Perry Mason. An expert concluded that the voice did not belong to Warne.

Of course, it was all stuff and nonsense. In 25 years of waffling about the game, I cannot recall a story that so far exceeded its natural proportions. The only thing that set this episode apart from other controversies at the time was that money did not seem to play a part.

Sledging was an altogether more serious matter because it affected other countries and revealed a need for a code which could be accepted by nations with different outlooks. No longer can any country regard its own approach as the last word. Even within countries, the approach can change.

Sri Lankan cricket was once the preserve of blue-bloods raised in the sporting tradition. Even now, as much coverage is given to long-standing matches between old schools as to Test matches. Moreover, the crowds are altogether larger. Boys from these schools behave impeccably. One captain sent his batsmen out in semi-darkness and drizzle to give his opponents a chance to win, and was celebrated for it. Another offered his opponents an extra 15 minutes in which to take the last wicket, yet another bowled

23 overs in the last hour of a run chase. Valour and manners were always to the forefront. Now the game has spread and its administration has fallen into the hands of 'businessmen' raised in a very different tradition and, understandably, regarded with the utmost suspicion by the old guard.

In part, the various reactions to sledging reflect such diversity. Hindus are raised to address their elders as 'Sir', a respectful practice maintained in adult life. Raj Singh Dungapur, a senior figure in his own right, addresses his friend Mr Salve, once a member of Mrs Gandhi's government, in this way. When in India, I call my elders and superiors 'Sir'. My sub-continental pupils call me 'Sir' throughout their lives. Buddhists are likewise polite towards their seniors. Until recently, Sri Lankan cricketers called umpires 'Sir'.

In contrast, Australians are an egalitarian lot and quite capable of calling their most important citizen 'mate'. They learn their cricket in backyards and in clubs, academies full of teasing and curses. As far as they are concerned, banter is part of the game. Indeed, they cannot understand the objections raised by other teams, and were aghast when Arjuna Ranataunga refused to shake hands with them after an especially bad-tempered match. Australian sportsmen regard the field as a battleground, a place where almost anything goes. Only once the field has been abandoned will civilities resume, with all and sundry laughing about this incident or that. By and large, the insults that fly thick and fast are not meant personally.

Australian sportsmen are inclined to think the rest of the world should adopt their customs and it has taken them a long time to step back from this position. Not until McGrath lost his temper with Ramnaresh Sarwan in Antigua did the Australians accept that change was necessary. Even then, it took an overwhelming backlash from supporters back home and the words of the secretary responsible for answering the phone back at head-quarters (who said that she hated going to work because of the abuse she received from callers whose true target was the players) to make them adopt a Code of Conduct.

Despite the adverse public reaction to sledging, the Australian players, even Adam Gilchrist, were startled with the furore when the wicket-keeper left the crease of his own accord during the World Cup semi-final in Africa. No article of mine has provoked more reaction than a comment piece written at the request of my employers about this apparently unimportant incident. Here was proof that a better game was trying to escape from the steward-ship of current players. But, then, a better self is always trying to find its way to the surface—in every country, every religion and every man.

19

DEVON DAYS

Having retired from the professional game after eighteen topsy-turvy years with Somerset, playing cricket again was the last thing on my mind. Then the sun started to shine and I made the mistake of watching Somerset's Second XI play a friendly against Devon. Going to the ground was part of my routine because it contained a car park and just about the only people in town still talking to me. There was no point putting down roots anywhere else because my future lay overseas.

Before long the secretary of Devon, a crafty fellow called Geoff Evans, asked whether I fancied a game. Doubtless a few flattering remarks were thrown in, a tactic that generally works. The Devonians seemed to be a jolly lot and I had been a cricketer all my life. Obviously playing again was a risk because an ageing player can make a fool of himself or, worse, become bad tempered. On the other hand I enjoyed the camaraderie and challenge of the game and was not especially worried about my reputation. Adopting a characteristic strategy of driving people away to see if they came back, I told Geoff that things changed whenever I became involved, sometimes for the better, sometimes for the worse, and advised him not to repeat the enquiry as there was a danger I might say 'Yes'.

A few days later Nick Folland, captain of the minor county, rang to say that he'd really like me to play and that his team felt the same. Other officials put out a welcome mat. Their enthusiasm was obvious. Nick said that he had a strong team but needed to add a competitive edge. I told him that with me it was all or nothing and added that I intended to be a different cricketer; that I wanted to work at my bowling and to bat down the order. Also I made it plain that I did not want to be paid for playing as then I'd bat like a dead fish.

So began a fruitful experience that prolonged by a decade my time in the northern hemisphere. My first match was against Wiltshire at Torquay. Nervous as a kitten, I ran myself out and my first two deliveries did not bounce. Nonetheless it was great fun and the dressing-room was full of laughter. The players teased each other and seemed to be an altogether jovial lot. From that moment I realised that my task was to harden the team without spoiling the atmosphere.

Things improved as the season went along and I managed to hit a few sixes and take a few wickets with fastish off-cutters. Devon reached the finals of both competitions and won the cup at Lord's but I had slipped over on a wet outfield in deepest Berkshire and could not play. As usual I was playing in any old kit and wearing ripple soles. Anyhow my ankle cracked and I hobbled from the field to the shouts of comrades impatient for the ruddy ball to be thrown in. A midwife in the audience took a look at the ankle and pronounced it to be a bump. Unfortunately X-rays painted a gloomier picture and the offending limb was put into plaster for the rest of the summer.

Towards the end of the campaign Folland mentioned that he had decided to have a crack at the professional game. Doubtless he had watched me bat and thought he could manage just as well. Devonians were inclined to be intimidated by county cricket. A shy, unambitious lot, they had lacked the confidence needed to push themselves to their limits. Devon asked me to take over as captain. After all the controversies at Somerset I was reluctant to accept. Most particularly I did not want anyone to think I was trying to prove a point. Accordingly I suggested various alternatives, including Donners, our 'fast' bowler, Gaypers, our swashbuckling opener, or Pughy, our belligerent middle-order man. Geoff and his committee countered by pointing out that if Donohue was made captain they'd never get him to bowl, adding that Gaywood was mad as a hatter and Pugh was bound to thump someone. All of these observations were incontrovertible. Plainly it was a matter of accepting responsibility. So I found myself captain of Devon CCC, a position I would occupy for the next ten years, during which time the county dominated the competitions.

Devon had some fine cricketers. Tony Allin was our left-arm spinner. A farmer from the remote northern parts of the county, he had tried his luck with Glamorgan, topping the averages before retreating to the more relaxed atmosphere of the family farm. Not that life among cows was always easy. The first time I invited him to play he replied, 'Can't cos one o' they blessed cows has kicked I.'

Nick Folland was a superb batsman and Gaywood was a glorious striker of the ball. Both had joined counties at an early age only to feel out of place. As apprentices they had pushed and prodded, now they tore into the bowling. Folland repeatedly topped the national averages and his friend repeatedly won Cup and Championship finals with blazing hundreds scored before lunch. Both were teachers whose wives had some reservations about the game. Garreth Townsend was also a gifted player capable of lashing sixes over point or rebuilding an innings depending on the circumstances. Chris Read kept wicket, a shrimp of a lad chosen after he had taken a blinding catch off Malcolm Marshall in a charity match. Orlando le Fleming also played as a schoolboy and promptly hit a six over extra cover in his first match.

After a few years he went off to concentrate on his jazz and has become a brilliant musician. Mark Woodman was a deaf medium-pacer who used to look elsewhere whenever he blundered so that, short of marching across the field, I could not rollick him to my satisfaction. A lovely man, he used to use his hands to indicate his intentions between the wickets and never seemed quite as hard of hearing or silent when he sensed a snick off his bowling.

Donohue and I did most of the bowling. Donners was a police-man with a fine action and a strong competitive streak. He played so much cricket that he started and finished his career with the county still pounding the beat. All of these fellows became close friends and helped put the team back together when the furies were upon me. They were also strong, honest and loyal men, and the team was happy and close knit. Many adventures arose on and off the field, and choosing the team was never without its compli-cations, but the county was well run and the players were wholehearted. Many took annual leave to represent their county.

After a quiet season in 1993, Devon did the double in 1994. Previously the county had won the title once. Our strategy was to select bowlers capable of swinging or spinning the ball and batsmen capable of pushing the score along. Really it is only common sense. Obviously I had learnt a lot from Australian cricket. We played an aggressive game, taking risks, setting generous declarations, always on the attack. Of course Devon was a strong team and could afford to gamble. Perhaps, too, our strategies were craftier than they seemed because rather less gen-erosity was shown to serious rivals let alone supposed enemies.

Over the next four years the team won more matches than anyone else and lost more than most. As Sammy Woods once said, 'drawers are only useful for bathing in'. Although we were a popular side, at first anyhow, some feuds did arise and could be pursued because minor counties play their cricket far from the madding crowd. A couple of the matches were downright unpleasant but most were enjoyable. Good relations with other teams were important. Once Devon needed to secure full bonus points to take the division and our opponents kept batting till they were all out because the other challengers had upset them in a previous match by running through the crease. By and large our matches were open because our men did not learn their cricket in the hard-nosed leagues to be found in Birmingham and the North. Every Saturday night the players would gather in the bar to wait for Gaywood, a born and bred Devonian who drove down from Yorkshire for every match. The players liked their beer but were also interested in the colour of the trousers worn by the free-thinking left-hander.

Devon won the championship again in 1995 and repeated the feat in 1996. Winning things is not easy. Not once did the team romp to victory. Usually we started slowly and came with a late charge as the pitches dried out. No team in the history of Minor County cricket had won the title four times in a row, not even S.F. Barnes' Staffordshire side. After all sorts of adventures and amidst wild celebrations, Devon overcame Wayne Larkins' Suffolk side to take the spoils again in 1997. Soon afterwards the side began to break up, with the old hands retiring to the bosom of their families. Happy to relate, Devon has remained strong and nowadays I follow its fortunes from Africa, which is not to say that the secretary has completely given up hope of a comeback! Actually, I intend to wait until I am qualified for the over-50s, an appearance eagerly awaited by former colleagues convinced that numerous heart-attacks will be the inevitable result. Lots of stories are told about my time as captain and I regret to report that all of them are true, including the tale about my stopping a match in the middle of an over to tell all the players on the leg side to swap with the blokes on the off side. The provocation had been considerable. Fortunately the boys appreciated my overall effort and laughed a lot, though not always when I was looking. Along the way I managed to hit a lot of straight sixes and also bowled 47 overs in a day in Reading.

Besides the championship, the team also reached the Amateur Cup Final, generally played at Lord's, six times in twelve years, taking the trophy on three occasions. Devon also pushed the first-class counties hard in the Nat West Cup, nearly beating Yorkshire and Leicestershire, the latter in an unpleasant contest.

Determined to confirm my commitment to cricket in the county, I also turned out regularly for Budleigh Salterton CC, a small coastal club whose ground spent its winters under water and whose players had a reputation for enjoying themselves after stumps had been drawn. Our team included a 'pace' bowler who once demolished an entire chicken just before play began. Judging by the regularity with which the position changed hands, captaining the team was a tricky operation requiring tact, patience and a thick skin. Eventually the crown of thorns fell upon the head of my chum Norm, who was barking only on the field of play and whose willingness to produce Chinese shrubs for my garden added to his charms. I turned out most Saturdays, taking wickets on pitches suffering from silt and once securing the batting prize.

Budleigh was never dull and became part of my life in England. Here, too, I was not at all bothered about getting hit around by a rough-and-ready carpenter, or losing my wicket to one of those infuriating old fellows whose deliveries never quite arrive. After all, it is only a game. We argued furiously on the field and had a lot of fun off it. Devon and Budleigh would both offer staunch support when it was needed. In any case, the fact that I was able to play for one first-class county for eighteen years, a minor county for eleven seasons and a club about twice a week for countless summers tells a story of its own. Not that my critics understood. People only see what they want to see. Towards the end of Devon's unprecedented run of success I sat anonymously in a noodle bar in Perth and overheard three members of the Barmy Army talking about the worst experiences suffered by friends. One said he knew someone who had played drums for Gary Glitter, another announced that a pal of his had put wallpaper up for Elton John and the third proclaimed that he knew someone who had played cricket under my captaincy. My detractors had done a pretty good job.

Captaining Devon prolonged my stay in England by several years. At the end of each season I assessed the situation and decided to continue. A man only lives once and it was going well. There did not seem to be any point moving house, though, as it might end at any moment. Nevertheless this unexpected turn of events required changes or else it could not be sustained. Keen to bring my overseas life to England, I started to allow young cricketers from Africa, India and Australia to spend the northern summer in my house.

Detesting the craven culture in England, I had rejected all invitations to coach at English schools or take promising English cricketers under my wing. I created a little Africa of my own in Taunton, and for the following nine summers a stream of promising cricketers joined my household, two or three every year, sometimes more, an experiment that, taken as a whole, was extremely successful.

20

AFRICA

Throughout the 1990s I was trying to find a way of combining my lives in Australia and Africa. Since their cricket seasons coincided it was not a straightforward proposition. I did know that I wanted Africa somewhere in my life, and the thought struck that a man only lives once. Accordingly I started visiting the continent in the periods between the northern and southern summers, taking a look around with a view to putting down roots once my cricketing days were over. Eventually I bought a patch of land and built a house.

I had been a member of anti-apartheid groups for many years. Martin Luther-King and Mahatma Gandhi were particular and obvious heroes of mine, and the idea of judging a man according to the content of his character rather than the colour of his skin appealed. It's not a bad starting point for work within a game that embraces Africa, Asia, Europe and the antipodes as well as numerous religions. As a callow youth I imagined confronting racism through cricket and appearing on the 'Parkinson' show. In the event my career has not been so brilliant but the interest remains, alongside a determination to contribute something.

The opportunity to visit South Africa did not arise until the early 1990s. Till then distaste for the system had discouraged adventures in that direction. Then news arrived that players and reporters had been invited to attend South African cricket's centenary celebrations. Although Ali Bacher and I had never spoken he had read my articles, and assumed that any invitation would end up in the wastepaper basket. My view was different. I had become a journalist, and they are supposed to take a look around. Moreover things were clearly changing, as confirmed by various sources. I had long been a supporter of the ANC and at Somerset had bequeathed my compulsory life insurance to them, although this had been more by way of provoking Jimmy Cook. Provided it was understood that I was free to move around independently there seemed no reason to stay away. The *Sunday Times* was unwilling to pay my airfare so the South Africans footed the bill, an arrangement that ended my friendship with Dudley Doust, who argued that my objectivity must have been compromised.

After arriving in Johannesburg, I drove down to the Orange Free State to meet a Mr Van Riet, a longstanding member of the Liberal Party in its various guises. A sprightly old man, he had been an ally of Alan Paton and Helen Suzman and remained defiantly optimistic. Next I contacted the Watson brothers, whose decision to leave mainstream rugby, at which they excelled, and join black clubs had turned them into public enemies. The clothes shop they ran in a township had been burnt down and the authorities were claiming that it had been an inside job. Of course we were followed as we drove around Alexandra and Soweto, stopping now and then for a chat with the locals. Upon returning to Australia I wrote about the brothers. The wife of a famous Australian playwright had written previously about their plight in a doomed and obscure publication. Imagining that she'd be delighted by the free publicity provided by my contributions I rang her, only to be received frostily and accused of stealing her story. God bless the liberals.

I attended a meeting of Black Sash and even managed to watch some cricket. Dr Bacher occasionally appeared with his assistant, a man regarded as a plant by the more paranoid visitors. Bacher struck me as an unusual mixture of Machiavelli and morality, in which combination the Italian philosopher seemed to play the greater part.

Having protested about the past, it seemed incumbent upon me to try to make the future work. Accordingly, when Australia undertook its first tour of the country since the freeing of Nelson Mandela and the election of a democratic government, I contacted Mnr Volsteedt, headmaster of Grey College in Bloemfontein, a strong cricketing school set in the Afrikaaner heartland. I had been told not to go near such a flat, old-fashioned place, but to stay in Cape Town which was 'full of Englishmen'. I didn't see the point in travelling so far only to be surrounded by Englishmen, so I ventured into the Free State and have never for a moment regretted the decision.

Grey College turned out to be a proud school with strong traditions and a liberal inclination—I am using 'liberal' here to indicate adherence to a great philosophy, not contemporary indulgence. No sooner had I driven through the gates than I saw hundreds of boys running, practising rugby and cricket, and swimming. Of course these are the routine activities of any boarding school after the day's lessons have been completed but there was an intensity about the youths here that was missing elsewhere. Moreover the youngsters were respectful and committed.

Most unexpectedly, I had happened on a school that thought along the same lines, an establishment founded in a rigorous form of liberalism, and in the tribal ways of respect and hard work as part of the process of turning the youth into a man. Accordingly, I started coaching, rising with the sun to go into the nets with the boarders and staying till dusk to assist the day boys and between times helping the PE masters. Of course the discipline was tough, but there was a sense of belonging that shone through. At times I was able to help the less gifted children by encouraging self-worth; more often I was throwing cricket balls at young cricketers, including Boeta Dippenaar, a delightful boy who was either batting or thinking about cricket bats. Often I'd rise even earlier to go for a run and sometimes a group of boarders would come along, usually as a way of getting to know this mad *rooineck* who lived on tea and cricket.

Grey College became part of my life, and every autumn and spring I'd break my journey with a week or so coaching and teaching. Of course I was a hard taskmaster whose methods were intended to deter timewasters, not that there were many of those. Once I coached the head boy for an hour in a futile attempt to make him drive the ball on the ground. Finally I expostulated, 'Hoski, if you hit another ball in the air so help me I'll wallop you with this bat!' He did not lift another drive and I said, 'You see Hoski, even with head boys it works!' He laughed and scored some runs.

Every September Grey players travelled to Pietermaritzburg to take part in a cricket festival. When the time came to build a house in Africa I did so in this university city, because the winters in Kwa Zulu Natal were glorious and in the summers I'd be in Australia. Moreover I had friends and former students in the area so it was not a leap in the dark. Nonetheless a part of me remains in Bloemfontein.

After a few years visiting South Africa the opportunity arose for me to tour Zimbabwe. I had previously played cricket in Sudan, scoring 96 not out before breakfast and playing squash with a remarkable man who had refused to let the debilitations caused by thalidomide inhibit his sporting life. Zimbabwe proved to be a wonderful country with an increasingly rotten government. Along the way I met opposition leaders and a splendid young man whose father was in the Cabinet and who would sometimes stay with me in Sydney. Coaching took me all around the country, to State and private schools, most of them outstanding in their manners, conduct and effort. I visited Lomadgundi, a co-educational school for the children of white farmers where boys were nonetheless obliged to rise at dawn every winter morning and to complete a long cross-country run. Sean Ervine was a pupil there, and I met his family and became friendly with them. Tatenda Taibu and Stuart Matsikenyeri attended Churchill College in Harare, where most of the promising black players were sent on cricketing scholarships. As boys they had practised on a field in their teeming suburb until the local council, in its infinite wisdom, had planted trees on their version of Lord's, whereupon the boys removed a tree a night in the hope that no one would notice, a strategy that provoked umpteen hidings but a flat cricket ground!

I was invited to Falcon and Milton colleges in Bulawayo and considered buying a house there, because I liked the Zimbab-weans so much. I also visited Prince Edward's, alma mater of Graeme Hick, the current England coach and countless other fine sportsmen, and St John's, and I always found the same thing: rising at 5.30 at the boarding schools and keeping going until the glorious African dusk brought its relief.

Of course, the Flowers were around, the father coaching in the townships and the schools, Andy trying to bring profession-alism to his country's cricket, the younger brother seeking those two handmaidens: maturity and fulfilment. Andy would later realise that the rich whites of Zimbabwe had not done enough to assist their fellow citizens. For the time being, he was living in the cocoon inhabited by most sportsmen. Zimbabwean cricket was a family affair, one in which the Streaks were also heavily involved, a wonderful family whose loyalty to their country has been misunderstood and misrepresented by malign elements within and without. Sometimes those who stay behind are also heroes.

In their different ways, Andy Flower and Heath Streak both showed immense courage in fighting for causes they believed were right. While respecting Flower, I disliked the way the white world fawned over him while treating Streak as either a coward or a fool. Doubtless influenced by my happy experiences there, I argued against boycotting a country whose leadership had turned nasty after an attempt to extend presidential powers was defeated in a referendum.

My most rewarding moment in Zimbabwe came during the first day of the Test in Harare when a group of boys played their marimbas in the lunch break. At the end of their concert one of their number, the youngest and least imposing, asked if I had a telephone. Informed that such a device could be tracked down in the press box he provided a number and requested that I call and pass on the message that 'the Captain would like the bus to come now'. The child introduced himself as 'Captain Psychology', and seemed surprised by my raised eyebrow.

A fortnight or so later I arrived at the address given by the captain and discovered it was an orphanage. In the ensuing five years the Captain, his brothers Immigration and Integrity, and their friend Pride, have become an important part of my life. Not long after I first met them I offered to buy them a present and was taken aback to hear that above all else they wanted exam papers. That afternoon we caught a bus to the university to buy some books of questions and answers. Afterwards we sat in silence in a nearby park as the boys devoured their new possessions, an experience that counts among the most humbling of my life. Captain has a fine way with words and responded to the news of the disappearance of my mobile phone by saying that such things are 'inclined to develop legs'.

Captain is now reading Law at Pietermaritzburg University, the first boy from St Joseph's Orphanage to take this step. Hopes are high that his brothers will follow in his footsteps. Pride thinks mostly about football but is a splendid fellow with an individual-istic approach to spelling. These fellows have had to fight every inch of the way—at times it has been difficult to keep food upon their plates—but they have never lost heart and keep in almost daily contact through the belatedly discovered magic of email.

21

TRIAL AND
TRIBULATION

S taying in England to write for the papers and play for Devon proved to be the right decision. My households were happy, work was going well and my adopted county reigned supreme. There was no rush to leave. Of course, Taunton remained a hostile home town and the county club did not exactly lay out the welcome mat but these were minor matters beside the laughter in my home and the enjoyment obtained from playing cricket for club and new county.

In order to sustain my life in England, and reluctant to coach born and bred locals, I started filling an otherwise empty house with school-leavers from Africa and Australia, mostly cricketers committed to improving their game. Ant and Shome came in that first year, Blisters and Riggers in the second, Crocks and a surfer in the third, Justin, Jon, Michael, Siya, Waleed, Garreth, Glenn, David, Garret, Heinrich, Aaron, Peter, Carlo, Bruno and Omari Banks in subsequent seasons. Mostly they came in twos and threes, though five of them appeared in 2001. Almost all of these fellows remain in regular contact, and some of them live in my various houses around the world. Also, I had come to an arrangement with Dr Bacher to bring over four or five young black cricketers on scholarships, my task being to provide clubs in Devon prepared to act as their hosts.

Until the late 1990s everything went along well. Later attempts were made to pretend otherwise but the unstinting support shown to me by former students and their families tells the true story. Money was thrown around by newspapers; journalists, local detectives and Interpol took my life apart over a period of three years. Bitter and longstanding enemies, including four former Somerset players, did their utmost to pour oil upon the fires but, by and large, my life survived their scrutiny.

Not that I was blameless for the trauma that began in 1999. Perhaps it is coincidence that around this time a young man I knew committed suicide by attaching a hosepipe to the exhaust in his car and gassing himself at 3 o'clock in the morning. Perhaps not. His mother had asked me to assist him and we had spoken a few times on the phone and once at my house but then I had gone away, promising to get back in touch upon my return. By then he was dead. After showing promise with his studies at school he had encountered complications—something about a girl—and academic difficulties and had become a depressive. Upon hearing he was gone I made a vow never again to go halfway. It was a hard time.

Before 1999 I had always known my students and their families before they came to stay. The three young South Africans who arrived that spring were unknown quantities. K's grandfather had served as mayor of Salisbury in Rhodesia and his only regret was that he had not polished off Mugabe when the opportunity arose. K's uncle, a senior policeman in Wales, brought him to Taunton. Another boy, R, came to stay and was soon joined by some of his relatives. Of course, both young men were in regular contact with their friends and families, and were emailing home almost every day.

K arrived first. I was hard with him to begin with, because he was unfit and had a reputation as a rough diamond, but he settled down well. Like previous visitors, he was playing for a club run by Botham's closest friend in town. On his first morning, we went for a run in the snow. He was unfit and fell so far behind that I had to jump in the car and retrace our route to find him. When I did, we laughed about the fact that I would now not have to tell his parents that he had frozen to death in a ditch on his first day. When we go home I gave him a few whacks with a stick from a bunch that he had brought home before we had breakfast and went to the ground to practise. It was over in a few seconds. After that we went running at dawn every day, once he had woken me with a mug of tea.

He had arrived unfit, overweight and unhappy but thereafter K improved, lost weight and seemed happy enough. Fairness demanded that the same process be followed for R. Unfortunately, he was spoilt and unable to accept correction, or so it would emerge.

Soon an Australian lad turned up, a fine fellow. Confident of his character and abilities I sent him down to my club in Devon and he divided his time between Budleigh and Taunton. H, another African, was also staying in the house and proved to be a likeable fellow. He would have become a fine man and a handy cricketer.

One weekend R's relations came to stay—a hysterical girl with a likeable boyfriend. That night they argued loudly, long into the night. It never occurred to me that my treatment of their cousin was the topic of conversation. The next day I went off to play a match, returning to a quiet household. Finding no one home I left the lights on and went to bed. Suddenly, at 3.00 a.m., the thought struck me like a thunderbolt that the bedrooms were not tidier than usual, they were empty. I was shocked, as the possibility of them leaving had not occurred to me. R had been encouraged to do so and had chosen not to.

The youngsters had left and there was trouble brewing. The next morning I bumped into R, who seemed to find the entire episode hilarious. He wanted to return but not right away. For the time being he was staying with Botham's second-closest friend in town.

Eventually those involved, or rather those around them, took their story to Botham's newspaper. They met Botham and Lander, his journalist, when Somerset played Gloucestershire in a Cup Final at Lord's. As soon as I found out Botham was involved I knew that any chance of the matter being dealt with quietly had gone. Journalists confirmed that he was gleeful.

A few days later, I flew to Sri Lanka to cover a Test series. A stringer for the newspaper tracked me down to a hotel in Kandy. As ever, I made no comment but alerted colleagues to the situation as they might be obliged to follow it up. That Sunday I rang Peter Robinson in Taunton and he confirmed that the story had been in the paper and that two nineteen-year-olds had made a complaint, but that the episode had been overshadowed by the uncovering of an 81-year-old female spy.

Nothing happened for the next few months. Of course I informed my employers about the developments. Not wanting to embarrass the county I had resigned as captain of Devon, a move regarded by officials as unnecessary. Anticipating a long and painful struggle, I had bought a ramshackle house in Exmouth, a place with a large and beautiful garden.

Throughout the Australian summer I debated whether or not to return to England. On the one hand my family knew nothing of the case and were entitled to their peace and quiet. On the other hand I had never run away from anything or anyone, least of all youngsters who had run up huge phone bills by calling sex lines and taken a radio with them when they left my house.

In April 2000 three detectives arrived at my new house, arrested me for assault and took me to the local station where my belongings, including my belt and shoelaces, were confiscated, a debasing experience and intentionally so. I should have been warned when an answer I had given was recorded as 'Yeah'. I never say 'Yeah', only 'Yes'. However, it seemed a minor matter and I let it pass. It was a mistake.

I did not have a solicitor and answered every question put to me. None of the answers was ever contradicted. The story was leaked to the local papers and splashed across the front pages, but there the matter rested. Accordingly I was able to continue writing. Of course I kept playing cricket for my club and I coached the young cricketers staying that summer.

Meanwhile the complainants were back in Taunton, and surrounded by ill-wishers. K returned for a week and then flew back to Johannesburg. A mutual friend said that he had been shocked by the bitterness of the campaign against me. Another reported that he was missing his girlfriend. R and his family had settled in Taunton, and this unpleasant young man was coaching alongside a Somerset player. H, a likeable fellow, had also returned and, after a year of trying, they finally persuaded him to make a complaint. Throughout, enormous pressure was put on past guests, and one reported that a former Somerset player had urged him to help the prosecution. He bumped into me on Bondi Beach and apologised because his name had been bandied about.

At the end of the summer, my police bail was extended and I was able to return to Australia. Most of my friends and even former students were unaware of the situation. A senior lawyer rang to say that as far as he could tell, no offences had been committed: consent to physical punishment was clearly present, besides which, no one had seen any sign of distress, physical or otherwise, on any of the complainants despite the fact that they were leading very public sporting lives.

In May 2001 I returned to England once more and reported to Taunton police station. By now the investigation had been going on for twenty months. Acting on legal advice I had not contacted former students. From friends I discovered that Interpol had been interviewing past visitors. I also learned that some had been offered money by newspapers. Peter Anderson, the Somerset chief executive, rang to say that he had some helpful information and wanted to speak to my solicitors, but they regarded him as hostile and did not return the call. I disliked him and avoided him whenever possible. Conrad Sutcliffe, a journalist based in Devon, said that he was being badgered by stringers for national newspapers. He was happy to be able to tell them that he had known me for ten years and had nothing to report.

The police outlined their investigation. Interpol's interviews had been unproductive. Most former students had refused to answer questions. In hindsight this was a mistake because it forced the detectives to rely upon the false picture of life in my house painted by hostile elements. I had wanted the investigation to be wide-ranging, because I knew they'd find all the bad things in a week and I wanted them to leave Taunton and its influences. They did not do so.

From the start of that interview in 2001 it was clear that a serious charge was going to be laid. Incredibly the detectives had not spoken to the key witness, the Australian who had also stayed that summer and who understood neither the case nor the motivations of the complainants. He and his parents were bewildered that the police had not spoken to them. I was appalled. The detectives said they had not been able to track them down, but I did not believe them. Budleigh had provided the requisite phone numbers and he had been playing cricket in Devon throughout that summer of 2001.

I wondered if the detectives realised that I had letters of thanks from the parents of some of those mentioned, or that another had been expelled from school for stealing. Fortunately I had coached only youngsters with strong overseas connections. My house was an alternative to the feebleness of the prevailing youth culture.

Youngsters could like it or leave it. Those that fought it out felt their lives improving. Those who left early regretted it, and said so in writing. It was an opportunity not to be thrown away.

After being questioned I spent hours in a cell waiting for the charges to be made. Eventually charges were laid, and a restriction imposed that no male under 21 years of age could live in my house. The charges did not bother me because I knew they were untrue. I had not read the complaints. Now and then I did try to read them but always felt ill after a few paragraphs. No mention was made of the neighbours who came around, the nights in pubs and clubs, the golf, the movies, the constant contact with their homes, the cricket matches and the laughter. Isolated incidents were blown up out of all proportion.

Inevitably the charges made headlines in the papers, and reached both Australia and my parents, who were as usual spending the summer in a house we had bought in France. My employers felt obliged to suspend my contract and only *The Cricketer* allowed me to keep writing. After a few months of that Ashes summer, the *Sun-Herald* in Sydney invited me to resume work. The rest followed once the more serious charges were dropped. My family was worried but I tried to keep them out of it.

By now Charles Bott, a friend from my student days, had become a tower of strength, as had friends and colleagues in Devon, Africa and Australia. Following Charles's advice I had employed a lawyer in London on the grounds that he might be better placed to stand up to the police, whose hostility had taken me by surprise. Interminable delays followed and summer started to turn to autumn. Statements were belatedly collected from past students and were still pouring in as the case closed.

Otherwise, life did not change all that much. Devon had asked me to start playing again and I had agreed. Ironically the players met after a match in Taunton attended by two of my more unpleasant adversaries, whose conduct shocked Folland, normally the most affable of men. He rang that night to invite me to play again with the unanimous support of players and officials, and also to warn me to expect the worst as former Somerset players involved in the case were behaving in a knowing and sinister way.

Soon Folland stepped down as captain because he had been appointed as headmaster of a junior school. Accordingly, I found myself suspended from work, playing for my club, captaining a minor county that had another brilliant season, living in a house full of young cricketers and wondering if I was about to go to prison.

Eventually my lawyers suggested a deal whereby I would plead guilty to the lowest form of assault. This was a risky move, because the sentence could not be predicted. But I was tired and wanted to see my orphans in Zimbabwe. Moreover my employers had confirmed that my career would not be ended by a conviction on minor charges. Despite the urgings of friends, convinced that these witnesses would not turn up and, anyhow, had been fortunate to meet a coach willing to spend several hours a day working with them for nothing, I decided to accept the deal. The time had come to get on with my life.

Accordingly I agreed to plead to the lesser charges and the case was set for October 2001. Folland and Rear-Admiral Roger Moylan-Jones offered to appear as character witnesses. Strong statements of support came from many players, past students, families in Australia and India, and my club and new county. Charles said he had never seen such an impressive collection and added kind words of his own.

Even so, the hour in court counts among the most unpleasant of my life. I had not grasped that pleading guilty meant accepting everything in the statements made by the complainants, not just the parts relevant to the supposed 'assault'. As part of the deal, we had to pretend that consent was absent. Of course it was nonsense.

African schools are far more robust than their English counter-parts. At schools and even among first year students, chastisement is part of the programme. Moreover, this approach has the over-whelming support of educators and pupils alike. These schools are not oppressive or violent; rather, they are demanding and committed.

The judge was not impressed by the feeble mitigation put forward by my barrister, who did not confront the illusions of isolation and exploitation created by my enemies. I was sentenced to three months in prison, suspended for two years. Folland was dumbfounded as he listened to the judgment. I did not care any more, wanted the thing to end and life to resume. Andy Proctor, a former marine, a friend and a colleague at Budleigh and Devon, drove me to Heathrow Airport. At least, and at last, it was over. After 28 months of investigation, after reporters from three news-papers, Interpol and opponents had been let loose on me, I could resume my life.

The next day I was coaching at a school in Harare and that night took my orphans out for supper. It was good to see them again. They were the ones who had been having a hard time.

As a private person, it was the intrusion I hated most of all. But I cannot waste time on accusers who have never produced a player or a young man worth tuppence, and who never will. I stand by my overall record with young people.

Long before the conclusion of the case, I had decided to return to England for one more summer, and to continue as captain of Devon. By the end of the summer of 2002, another triumphant one for Devon, the time had come to say farewell to my friends in the county and to England at large. It had taken me too long to follow my instincts and to put down roots in the places where I belonged and was appreciated.

22

THE
AUSTRALIAN WAY

Australian cricket has been strong for 125 years. Now and then it has fallen back a little, most notably during the early 1980s, when unsanctioned trips to South Africa weakened the game, a lapse that allowed England to secure victories that promoted complacency. The weakness of English cricket in that period has been exposed by Syd Berry in a crucial re-examination of a past on which numerous reputations rest.

Otherwise, Australian cricket has been the proud product of a nation whose peoples were in search of a binding force and a means of identification. Cricket is the national game and its heroes have reached into the homes of farmers and publicans, young and old, rich and poor. Whereas cricket elsewhere has belonged to the blue-bloods, in Australia it is played and followed by the red-bloods.

In many respects Ricky Ponting is a typical Australian cricketer. Born in an unfancied part of an unpretentious city on an island even Australians sometimes forget to include on their maps, he did not think much of school and enjoys beer, golf, gambling and camaraderie. After some early misadventures, he has matured into a responsible leader. No one worried about his youthful escapades, most people saying, 'Sounds like the boy has some spirit'.

Australian cricket might remain frustratingly Anglo-Saxon in some ways, but it does not exclude anyone and its heroes are down-to-earth characters. Beer is drunk at the matches, and working-men's clothes are worn. Every urban club fields five or six teams on a Saturday afternoon and the players practise together twice a week. A man who scores runs or take wickets rises through the ranks. A fellow in a bad patch falls back. There is nothing complicated about it. At practices, players bat in order of arrival and never mind that a first-grader must wait his turn. Crucially, the culture is strong.

Even the sixth team plays competitively, with short-legs and team talks and so forth. Most players want to improve and believe they can. Every player sees himself as part of Australian cricket, as a part of the system that has produced so many great players. A batsman knows that he can rise to the very top, provided he keeps scoring runs. The path is clear.

Accordingly, Australian cricket operates as a united and mighty force. The Australians often play with a single mind and a single voice, and to outsiders that voice can sound abrasive. Aggression has always been the Australian way, in cricket and much else. Other countries wait for mistakes to be made, Australians are always on the attack.

Australian cricket has another neglected quality, a sense of service unmatched by any rival. Past players are prepared to play any role given to them to help to drive the game along. Geoff Lawson regularly attends practices at his club, and moves around the grounds on weekends supporting the players in his charge. Brian Booth, a gentleman, coaches St George's Under-16 side. Richie Benaud bumped into a student of mine buying a newspaper one Sunday morning and, upon hearing his name said, 'Well bowled last week.' He had taken 3/44 in a club match. Kerry O'Keeffe has assisted many young spinners and umpires his son's club games. A few years ago, Dennis Lillee finished his post-hangover exercises and spotted me coaching a youngster. He strode across, said 'G'day', asked if he could join in, picked up a ball resembling a haggis and spent an hour bowling perfectly pitched leg-cutters and deliberate half-volleys to a lad he had never met and was never to meet again.

Allan Border sums it up as well as anyone. India has long been intoxicated with the game. Indian stars, the great Vishy apart, are inclined to join the parade whenever they appear at a ground. During Australia's brief visit to the sub-continent in 2003, and wanting to make himself useful, Border put on a pair of doubtful shorts and went out to hit some catches to the players. No one took any notice of him; never mind that he had scored more runs in Test cricket than anyone else, and never mind that the trophy at stake in the Test series between Australia and India is in part named after him.

Ian Chappell also reflects the character of the game and its players in Australia. Unapologetic, opinionated, relentless and stubborn, Chappell can seem limited by his aggressive masculinity. He drinks, swears, tells jokes and runs with the bulls, and has never pretended otherwise. But Chappell is not so easily defined. He has condemned his Federal government's treatment of refugees, arguing that anyone prepared to endure such hardships to become an Australian must have something to offer to their country of choice. He has spoken out in favour of an Australian head of state, rather than one appointed from England. Also, he has treated his new profession with respect, working hard at it and becoming a cricket writer rather than merely a past player with opinions. Chappell and his team of the 1970s retain a strong hold on Australian cricket and promote both the deeds of its mentors and those of its favoured sons. It is part of Steve Waugh's attraction that he refuses to join this or any other group.

Australian cricket has two other distinguishing marks. Test cricket is not regarded as a private world understood only by past players. Neither of the last two chairmen of selectors had particularly brilliant careers, nor did John Buchanan or Bennett King, his fellow Queenslander now working at the academy. Positions are awarded on merit and with more notice taken of current performances rather than past achievements.

Not that past players are neglected, for the suggestion that they have nothing to offer is as arrogant as the notion that they alone grasp the requirements of the game. Dennis Lillee serves as a fast bowling coach, Rod Marsh took over the academy, Andrew Hilditch and David Boon serve as selectors.

Australia's other strength is that it does not take any notice of its youth teams. Whereas England's Under-19 matches are covered on television and the Indian boys are feted upon returning from Pakistan after winning a minor tournament, the Australians routinely ignore the performances of their boys. Winning an Under-19 World Cup might be awarded a few paragraphs on an inside page, otherwise Australian youngsters must prove themselves among men. The contrast with America, with its spitting children playing Little League on television before large crowds and doting parents, could not be greater. Anything that makes talented teenagers feel important is a betrayal of them.

Australia has its faults, but better than most it takes Everyman on his merits. The way the game is played and life is lived reflects a past that cannot be avoided but, anyhow, is a source of strength, and a climate and country that can be harsh but also provides warmth, succour and a thousand opportunities.

23

THE POWER OF
THE PEN

L eaving England gave me the opportunity to concentrate
upon working in the countries that had become the home
of cricket and cricket writing: India and Australia. India's
power had come from its devotion to the game, its enormous population from which to draw players and the money provided by its
television networks. Australia fielded the strongest team, many of
the most exciting players and the most effective administrators.

Cricket must survive in a world in which the proud peoples of
the Punjab and Kashmir fight for their own freedoms, in which the
seven sisters north-east of Bangladesh try to establish their identi-
ties and importance. It inhabits a world in which the Tamils seek
a homeland; in which the black tribes of Africa have demanded the
democracy enjoyed by whites elsewhere; in which several sometimes hostile islands and a country in South America must
somehow forget about their differences and join forces to form a
team. Frank Worrell, the greatest man of the game and a sometime
alcoholic, yearned, along with many others, for a West Indies
Federation, but the past is not so easily buried.

Cricket must survive in a world in which one country is ruled
by a military dictator and another by a despot, in which Muslims

and Hindus pursue their ancient rivalries, in which a country once regarded as a dumping-ground for undesirables seeks to rise from these unpromising beginnings to surpass its disdainful patrons, in which that same country sometimes forgets about its own struggling peoples, the original inhabitants too often viewed through tabloid cliché.

Cricket is no longer a simple game promoted by a single race. Rather, it reflects the forces of good and evil at loose upon the planet. The world is not an easy place. Nor is it merely a battleground between black and white or communism and capitalism. These were minor skirmishes. Nor is it even a struggle between faiths, among which Islam and Christianity have been the most ruthless. No, the true battle is between faith and progress, between the unchanging nature of man and the discoveries of each age. Christianity sensed the threat posed to it by Darwinism and tried to suppress it. Eventually it realised it must find a way of living with the new creed. Islam is scared of the contemporary seducing its children. But attempts to resist the moment are doomed. Unfortunately, the collapse of liberalism means that there is no middle ground, no philosophy that advocates the eternal without rejecting the present. But mankind has not changed, and eventually both parties will be forced by their younger adherents to find a way forward. In the meantime, western youth flounders while their counterparts raised in religion become the ever angrier tools of alarmed elders.

Unavoidably, cricket both lives within and reflects this reality. It is also fighting a battle on another front, against an illusionary past created by romantic writers. Until modern biographers started taking a closer look at the players of the past, cricket might well have been a noble game played by sporting heroes and blemished only by Bodyline. Harold Larwood and Douglas Jardine are among my favourite English cricketers, precisely because they challenged this codswallop. Now past champions such as C.B. Fry,

Ranji, Wally Hammond, Percy Chapman and many others have been studied as men and not as figureheads, so that the past can be seen in a different light. Nor have they necessarily been diminished by the discovery of their failings. One day, even 'the Don' may be reduced to mere humanity. Again and again, one comes back to Graham Greene's remark that, 'Man is not black and white. More black and grey really.'

Unfortunately, the abandonment of romanticism has not led to a sympathetic appreciation of the men who play cricket, but to a mean-spiritedness and voyeurism that has turned newspapers—English ones anyhow—into a latterday peepshow. Now and then understanding articles are written about Frank Bruno and other sportsmen who have fallen on hard times. But the truth is that Bruno is not an exception, because players fight these sorts of battles every day. Books have been written about cricket suicides, but such tragedies are still happening and will continue to happen. The sooner this vulnerability is faced the better.

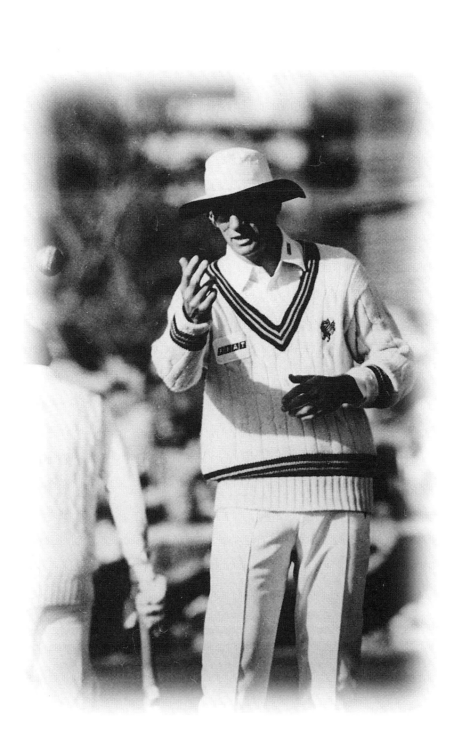

24

TWO GREAT
BATSMEN

Ihave been privileged to play with, watch and write about many wonderful cricketers and characters over the past years. Notwithstanding the contributions of many other gifted competitors to the world game, two contrasting batsmen have been the dominant figures of the last twenty years: Lara of the West Indies and Tendulkar of India.

Considering his undoubted genius, it took Brian Lara a long time to force his way into the West Indies team. Something had held him back, a perception of immaturity, perhaps even a certain jealousy. Eventually he could not be ignored, but by then he found, to his dismay, that a decline had set in, a deterioration he was supposed to reverse. Nothing had prepared him for this challenge. Lara had imagined himself following in the footsteps of the mighty cricketers who had dominated the game, and doing so with a style and pride that could be sensed far beyond the boundary's edge.

Seeking unity, he found only disarray. Anticipating power, he encountered only pretence, and the more West Indian cricket languished the more it looked towards the youthful Trinidadian as its saviour. But Lara was poorly cast as Atlas. He lacked the stamina and the intent to maintain a standard for longer periods. Rather, he summoned his powers for mighty efforts now and then, and afterwards retreated into his tent. Inevitably, his faults came ever sharper into focus as the team went from bad to worse, despite the fact that the true fault must lie with the complacency of the past and the feebleness of colleagues prepared to take more than they gave.

Accordingly, Lara waxed and waned, playing brilliantly in some series, moping around in others. At times he was scintillating, always he was sporting. On other occasions he seemed happier away from the game and especially from the rigours of touring. He did not seem to enjoy the camaraderie of the dressing-rooms, preferring a lighter life among friends. By the time the Australians arrived in 1999, he had broken batting records in Test and first-class cricket yet seen his reputation fall so low that many regarded him as a liability.

Seldom in the history of the game can any batsman have put together a series of innings as varied and inspired as did Lara that northern spring. Fighting to maintain his captaincy, he saw his team skittled in the first Test and thereafter put his head down to such effect that his team almost took the spoils. Jimmy Adams was his main accomplice. Over the years, West Indian cricket has produced most of cricket's finest men. Doubtless it helped that many were raised in religion and taught to respect learning. Hardship was their nursemaid and the need to overcome prejudice their driving force. Hereabouts, though, the most impressive of the West Indians were not always to be found in the ranks of the leading players. Adams, Ian Bishop and Roger Harper could not correct the problem.

Lara crafted a diligent, controlled double-century after the Australians had batted carelessly in Jamaica. At Bridgetown he dominated his team's chase on an epic fifth day played in front of an ever-growing, ever noisier crowd, and struck another flashing off-drive to take the West Indies to victory with a single wicket to spare. Earlier, Courtney Walsh had somehow survived the deadliest of yorkers, sent down by Jason Gillespie. Accordingly, Lara and his team arrived in Antigua 2/1 ahead in the series. Exhausted, Lara contributed a stirring 100 in the first innings at St John's, but his colleagues could not respond and the match was lost. Throughout, the twinkling left-hander demolished the visiting leg-spinners. Refusing to allow them to settle, he repeatedly stepped down the pitch to thrash the ball over the ropes.

Lara's assault brought to mind a story told by Maurice Foster about Frank Worrell. The great and dignified West Indian was playing in a club match against Roy Gilchrist, amongst the most feared of all fast bowlers. By now Worrell was past his peak and, batting down the order, was reading a book in the dressing-room when he heard a commotion. Asking for an explanation, he was told, 'Gilchrist killin' everyone.' Worrell put on his yellowing pads and sunhat, walked out to the crease, scored 84 runs in 75 minutes and returned to say, 'You see, boys? Mr Gilchrist can be hit.'

By all accounts Lara batted just as well in Sri Lanka, contributing most of his team's runs in a performance that ought not to be forgotten. In his early days, Lara made his name and played many wonderful innings, but he was immature and unable to accept either the situation or his responsibilities. Had he not returned to the world stage he would have been dismissed as an inglorious failure, and never mind the evidence of the history books. But this second coming has been another matter, a revelation of a sportsman of substance. Lara's batting has always been a delight to watch. Now it is also satisfying, as a gifted sportsman reaches within himself for the inspiration needed to turn a team around. Moreover, Lara has become a craftsman, so that his sense of adventure and desire to dominate are supported by a tighter technique founded upon a shortened backlift and a straighter bat.

Always a cricketing genius, Lara has become a great batsman, an altogether stiffer task. Genius can be expressed in a sublime moment. Greatness requires repetition. Despite their differences,

Lara and Tendulkar have some things in common, including an acute ability to read the game. No one in the last 25 years has judged a single as well as these players. No one has judged the ball as quickly, or paced a chase as well, or sensed the exact location of each fieldsman. In part their greatness has been a triumph of the mind, in part it is due to intuition.

Sachin Tendulkar is, without doubt, the best batsman I have watched or played alongside, but he has always kept his feet firmly on the ground. He comes from a professional family and might have become a lawyer had not cricket claimed him. Not that he was a dedicated student, because he could not wait to return to the fields to play some cricket. Rather, he was fortunate to be raised in a close family in which learning was respected and sporting prowess kept in its place. Happily, Tendulkar's father had the wisdom to encourage his son to play cricket, and even advised him to pursue the game, pointing out that 'there are thousands of lawyers and only a few truly gifted batsmen'.

From the start, Tendulkar was devoted to the game. In his early days he'd join hundreds of boys for coaching at the famous nursery in Shivaji Park, where the fundamentals were drilled into generations of boys, including Manjrekar, Wadekar, Gavaskar and Vino Kambli. Shivaji was, and remains, typically Indian. Those arriving early for practice might find a light mist hanging over a park about half the size of a proper cricket field. They'd see old-timers taking their morning constitutional around the park and would be advised to take off their shoes and join them as walking barefoot in the dew was deemed good for the soul. Sometimes the RSS, the militant wing of the governing Hindu fundamentalist party, would be completing its drills. In summer the earth was hot, baked red and full of pebbles, but after the monsoon it was lush and fresh.

Achrekar and Das Shivalkar were the presiding coaches. Achrekar instilled the finer points in a select group of older boys, and is remembered as Tendulkar's first coach. Shivalkar has been almost forgotten but did most of the early work, coaching the boys until they reached the age of ten, whereupon the best were passed on to his elder. Shivalkar was a character. He'd turn up in his slippers and a long shirt, and sometimes his students swore there was a whiff of alcohol on his breath. As David Innis recalls, however, he could 'bowl a wicked off-cutter and ran a hard school'. As the only 'Christian' in the group, Innis was often made captain. He was also more willing than his shy Indian friends to change and shower in the rudimentary 'pavilion' that is Shivaji's only building. It was a rough construction, hidden in a corner of the field, where for a small fee the boys could deposit their kits and school clothes until after practice. Then they could head for the little stall which sold sweet tea, puffed rice and buttered buns. Those with deeper pockets could buy omelettes spiced with peppers cunningly hidden in their folds.

Practice started at 6.00 a.m., as Shivalkar split the boys into pairs. Soon matches began and everyone was given a chance to bat. According to Innis, the rules were simple: 'Whether you hit the ball or not you had to run. If you didn't, you were out.' Tendulkar was in his group, and swiftly learnt to find the gaps. About twenty games would be played at the same time, and a lad fielding at third man had to keep his eyes open, because he would also be leg-slip in another game. Fieldsmen kept their ears open for calls of 'Look!', an abbreviation of 'Look out!', whereupon everyone in the area covered their heads.

Tendulkar's dedication was legendary even then. Innis recalls arriving early one morning and chatting to his coach when a small, curly-haired child arrived complaining that the 'maalis' would not put up the nets until 6.00, and could Sir Shrivalkar please tell them to put them up now, or authorise him to erect them himself? A few years later, Tendulkar travelled through the night with a youth team, arrived at 3.00 a.m. and practised in the corridors until dawn. He woke his coach up at 5.30 a.m. and said that he was ready to go to the ground now, as he was not happy with his batting. In those days, his captains and coaches used to send him to third man, because he was full of suggestions and this was the only way to keep him quiet. Sourav Ganguly had the same strategy, although his reasons may be different.

Shivalkar coached Tendulkar and Vinod Kambli and wondered which might rise furthest. Kambli used to hop onto a lorry bringing fruit and vegetables to the market. Shivalkar worried about the precocious left-hander because he came from a lower caste and might not be given the chances he deserved. Even if he was, would he be able to take success in his stride?

Shivaji Park was Tendulkar's academy. As informal matches in streets and parks produced so many West Indian cricketers, so these early mornings in Bombay were a testing ground for many of India's aspiring cricketers. Innis recalls Shrivalkar fondly as a man who 'loved the game, instilled an aggressive attitude in his charges, brooked no nonsense and gave of himself willingly'. Tendulkar was lucky to meet such a man in his formative years. Shrivalkar and Achrekar were lucky to have such a committed student. Doubtless it was a reward for all those misty early starts.

Sachin Tendulkar has given many fine performances, but his innings in Sydney in 2003 must count among the finest in his career. Arriving at the crease after the Indian openers had given the visitors another solid start, the man from Mumbai built a wall around his wicket with a conviction that must have impressed the home captain. Batting with the utmost discipline and to a clear plan, Tendulkar collected runs carefully, denying the bowlers hope and putting his team in a powerful position. Over the years he has played by instinct, attacking the bowling with a gusto that filled stands and scared bowlers. Now he has decided to play within himself, the better to sustain his innings and serve his team.

Several breakthroughs were made in the course of this compelling effort. Never again can Indian supporters claim that Tendulkar does not score runs when his country needs them. Of course, such a claim was nonsense, anyhow. Great players are remembered for their failures, ordinary men for their triumphs. An objective scrutiny of the facts reveals that Tendulkar has contributed hundreds in most of India's victories in Test cricket.

Nor can it be said again that Tendulkar does not play long innings. Previously, he had been inclined to lose his wicket soon after reaching three figures. This time, he took a fresh guard upon reaching his 100 and simply continued gathering runs. Not until India was powerfully placed did he change tempo, whereupon the old Sachin emerged and began to flog an exhausted Australian attack.

During the course of this magnificent effort, Tendulkar did not score a single boundary between bowler and point. Only towards the end did he even attempt shots in this direction. Nor did he pull or hook the faster bowlers until quick runs were needed. In other words, he played the game on his terms, whereupon the beauty and mastery of his defence was revealed.

A new Tendulkar was launched in Sydney. The younger version first drew attention to itself with an audacious attack on a flummoxed Australian attack that included a portly novice by the name of Warne. No regrets should be held about Tendulkar acknowledging the passing of time and becoming a robust, rather than a dazzling, batsman. He must be allowed to grow. Watching him bat may not be as exciting, but it will be enormously satisfying. Those who love cricket will be given the opportunity of watching a master craftsman at work. Tendulkar is going to score an awful lot of runs. He will score more double centuries in the next five years than in the previous decade. Like Brian Lara, he has turned a corner and realised that brilliance must, sooner or later, be replaced with method.

Watching Tendulkar bat counts among the many wonderful things in my life. It was a privilege to play for Somerset in its most exciting years. It was a privilege to captain Devon in its years of success. It has been a privilege to write and talk about cricket, and a stroke of luck to be paid for doing so. Most of all, it has been a privilege to be surrounded by so many friends, former students and the orphans who have come into my life—Psychology, Miggy, Integrity and Pride in Harare, and the magnificent Malabika in the SOS Village at Kolkata, a girl dumped on the streets on her first days of life who blossomed with love and grew with opportunity to become head girl at her school and is now training to be a teacher.

Mistakes have been made, and one or two people have been hurt, but I like to think the good has outweighed the bad. Life has been fine. Indeed, it has improved with every passing decade. Nowadays I have houses and households in Sydney and Pieter-maritzburg and divide my time between them. My views have not changed. I was always uncomfortable in England. Doubtless it was partly my fault, but the hostility was deeply felt and long-standing and reaches beyond particular institutions and into a way of life. I came to realise that I believed in many things incompatible with the country of my birth, most particularly a blend of egalitarianism and authority not easily put into words. Eventually I realised that Africa could not be recreated in England.

Happily my career has also flourished, especially in Australia and India. Every overseas trip is enjoyable, because it means seeing old friends, making new ones and meeting respected fellow cricket writers, among whom the Australians and the Indians stand out. John Woodcock has been the best of Englishmen, while David Hopps is the most worldly of the current mob. Unfortunately, the reputation of English cricket writing has not survived its failures in the most important subjects of the period: corruption, throwing and Zimbabwe. There was even reluctance to condemn the practice of bowling two feet outside the leg stump to Sachin Tendulkar.

With a bit of luck I will continue writing about the game and broadcasting for the ABC for another twenty years. After all, every year brings a fresh batch of cricketers, and more controversies. Of course, the great players will continue to impress, and the battlers continue to inspire. Alas, the dismayed will continue to take their lives for it is all more fragile than it appears. All a man can do is find a niche for himself and then make the best of it. There is still a lot to be done.

EPILOGUE

When I was looking back through some old papers, I found this character assessment written by my father. Perhaps it will enlighten or amuse.

In orthodox spheres, Peter might be regarded as odd, whereas he is merely obscure and oblique. He is an unconventional loner, with an independent outlook on life, an irreverent sense of humour and sometimes a withering tongue. His prickly response to challenge is promoted by a personality that is tough and austere and responsive neither to bribes nor threats. Since he does not seek reward or bother to avoid punishment the normal pressures of life do not affect him. Accordingly he can strike as hard and often as he wants without fear since he is beyond the range of normal weaponry. Fortunately he is generally kind and tolerant and uses his advantages only under severe provocation. His toughness on himself can, though, make him harsh in his judgement of others, especially the self-indulgent.

His kindness extends to old people, children and even animals. Sometimes people mistake this gentleness for weakness and try to take advantage whereupon they'd discover their mistake when he struck back with stinging finality. Few people returned for a second helping and fewer were given a second chance. He has a sharp mind and would have made a fine barrister. Instead he chose cricket and fought for his place in a world that did not suit him nearly as well.

INDEX